Spies Among Us

How to Stop the Spies, Terrorists, Hackers, and Criminals You Don't Even Know You Encounter Every Day

Spies Among Us

HOW TO STOP THE SPIES, TERRORISTS, HACKERS, AND CRIMINALS YOU DON'T EVEN KNOW YOU ENCOUNTER EVERY DAY

Ira Winkler

Wiley Publishing, Inc.

Vice President & Executive Group Publisher: Richard Swadley
Vice President and Publisher: Joseph B. Wikert
Executive Acquisitions Editor: Carol Long
Development Editor: Kenyon Brown
Editorial Manager: Kathryn Malm Bourgoine
Production Editor: Angela Smith
Project Coordinator: Erin Smith
Copy Editor: Susan Christophersen
Text Design & Composition: Wiley Composition Services

Published by
Wiley Publishing, Inc.
10475 Crosspoint Boulevard
Indianapolis, IN 46256
www.wiley.com

Copyright © 2005 by Ira Winkler

Published by Wiley Publishing, Inc., Indianapolis, Indiana

Published simultaneously in Canada

ISBN: 0-7645-8468-5

Library of Congress Cataloging-in-Publication Data:

Winker, Ira.
 Spies among us : how to stop the spies, terrorists, hackers, and criminals you don't even know you encounter every day/ Ira Winkler.
  p. cm.
 Includes index.
 ISBN 0-7645-8468-5 (cloth)
 1. Espionage. 2. Business intelligence. 3. Computer crimes--Prevention. 4. Terrorism--Prevention. I. Title.
 UB250.W55 2005
 658.4'72--dc22   2004028735

Manufactured in the United States of America

10 9 8 7 6 5 4 3 2 1

*To the Silent Ninja, Jazz, WWW, and the
Big Bad Wolf, who make it difficult to
want to sit down and write a book.*

Contents

Contents

Acknowledgments

There are many people I should thank. Most of what is in this book is due to my combined experiences of the last 20 years. All the people I have met in those years have helped me. Ironically, some of the most useful knowledge I have gathered came from the people who are the walking horror stories. It is a lot easier to learn what not to do when it stares you in the face.

The groups of people who deserve special mention (for doing things right) include, but are not limited to, the security awareness division at NSA for giving me an incredibly good base of knowledge, whether or not I wanted it; the Information Systems department at the University of Maryland, Baltimore County, especially Tony Norcio and Jack Stott, who taught me that computers are only tools that support business; and also the many security managers I have met and worked with during the last two decades. I sincerely hope this book helps them to do their jobs.

I have to thank all the people who kept bothering me to write another book. I must also thank Carol Long, the acquisitions editor, for thinking more highly of the book than even myself. Kenyon Brown was also invaluable for giving me suggestions that I didn't want to hear.

I also appreciate the time the following people worked into their schedules to meet with me: General Kenneth Minihan, James Woolsey, Larry Hale, Christopher Painter, John Nolan, Colonel Stanislav Lunev, and Ron Dick. There are also many other people I should mention, but either forgot because I am rushed to get this in (it is still appreciated and sorry about that), or left out because they prefer not to be mentioned for a variety of reasons.

Last, I'd like to especially thank the agents who didn't want to represent the book, allowing me to keep all my royalties.

About the Author

Ira Winkler, CISSP, CISM, is one of the most noted people in the security field. CNN and other news sources named him as a Modern Day James Bond. The *San Francisco Chronicle* called him an Internet Sage. He was also named to the Information Systems Security Association Hall of Fame and has been featured in many major news sources including *USA Today*, *Forbes*, and the *Wall Street Journal*, as well as on TV around the world. Ira began his career at the super-secret National Security Agency and moved on to support other intelligence agencies throughout the United States and the world. He went on to help the commercial world through performing espionage simulations and penetration tests, as well as investigating crimes against that world. He created a reputation for consistently "stealing" billions of dollars from some of the world's largest companies and then helping his clients to protect against their thefts. Ira resides in the Washington, D.C., area. Ira can be reached via http://www.irawinkler.com.

Introduction

It's Not Terrorism. Don't Worry!?!

All of a sudden, TV stations interrupted normal programming with breaking news that there was a power outage in New York City. As the news reports went on, they told how the blackout wasn't limited to New York City but included many other states and parts of Canada. TV viewers saw tens of thousands of people waiting for ferries to New Jersey. They saw millions of New Yorkers walking home over the Brooklyn Bridge. Newscasts around the country focused on how New Yorkers were dealing with their tragedy.

Periodically, you heard that there were 40,000,000 other people who were also affected. Then the newscasters speculated that the massive blackout could be terrorism. TV stations brought in terrorism experts to discuss the possibilities and the potential goals of the terrorists. The proclaimed experts went on to discuss how there were protection mechanisms in place that should have prevented the domino effect of an outage in the Midwest from spreading all the way to the Northeast. Of course, there had to be a malicious party involved in causing such widespread damage.

Then the news reports interrupted themselves for a news conference from members of the Department of Homeland Security. With great confidence, they stated that the blackout was not terrorist related and that there was nothing to worry about. Everyone breathed a great sigh of relief, except, of course, for the news directors who now had to figure out how to fill in an unknown number of hours of watching people cross a bridge.

This situation honestly baffled me. Why is it better that fail-safe mechanisms throughout the power grid failed on their own? People were expecting riots in poorer neighborhoods. Is that okay, too, as long as the blackout wasn't caused by a terrorist? Either way, the economy lost billions of dollars. Is that okay?

To me it is worse that a blackout can happen without someone purposefully causing it. If terrorists were involved, I would believe that the terrorists planned their attack for months. They would have studied the strengths and weaknesses of the power grid and would have likely known the grid better than most of the people working at the power companies. The fact that terrorists would have had some success at taking down a portion of the U.S. power grid would not have been a surprise. There is no such thing as perfect security, especially with something as massive and complex as the U.S. power grid.

However, the fact that 50,000,000 people can be thrown into darkness for days for no reason whatsoever is frightening to me. After all, there have been several major power grid crashes in recent years that most people have forgotten. Power companies have supposedly learned from those experiences and put fail-safe mechanisms in place to contain power outages. This incident was more massive than the previous incidents with regard to the number of people thrust into darkness. What does this say about our preparations?

Although the immediate effects of the power grid crash involved the lights going out, there were much more critical results. At a basic level, most businesses shut down due to their reliance on computers. The combined loss was billions of dollars. Many hourly workers, who live paycheck to paycheck, lost critical income. Food went bad in restaurants and homes. Air travel was crippled, costing hundreds of millions of dollars more.

From a more life-threatening perspective, traffic light failures caused the delay of ambulances in reaching patients. People requiring life support at home were sent to hospitals where the backup generators could provide electricity for longer periods of time. The power grid crash amounted to much more than the loss of lights. Again, is it okay that all this was not the result of terrorism?

Power grid problems are not unique to the United States. Shortly after the August 2003 outage, a major portion of the Italian power grid crashed. Again, no terrorism was involved, so again it was okay. The fact of the matter is that the power grids of the world regularly suffer outages of varying degrees.

Some of those outages relate to technology failures. More frequently, they result from natural disasters. For example, Hurricane Isabel went through the East Coast of the United States within one month of the blackout. Millions more people lost electricity for much longer periods of time. Physical damage cost billions of dollars. It was not just a matter of the losses that occurred as a result of the loss of power, but the requirement for rebuilding large portions of the infrastructure itself.

Windstorms, trucks crashing into telephone poles, and other accidents and natural disasters knock out power on a regular basis. Why do people care about a common incident more if it is the result of a malicious person, when it is otherwise considered a nuisance that people reluctantly accept?

Now consider the fact that even if the power outage was the result of terrorism, it wasn't a good terrorist attack. Within a couple of weeks of the incident, life was back to normal. People in the heart of the affected area barely remember the incident. Many even have good feelings about how people came together during a time of hardship. Aside from the general inconvenience, there was no real threat of a loss of life for the average person. I was even considering not using the incident as an example because readers may consider it ancient history. However, that possibility makes the event even more ironic.

Terrorists by definition want to create terror that makes people change the way they behave. Attacking computers just proves that computers are unstable, which people already know. Although under certain extreme conditions, if the stars align, the possibility of loss of life resulting from a computer attack does exist, the reality is that computer outages are accepted as a fact of life. Intentionally causing such an outage may initially cause concern among the general public and cost the economy billions of dollars, but it will not substantially change the way people behave.

On the other hand, any attack that specifically targets individuals with even a minute possibility of death can change the way people behave. Consider what happened soon after September 11, 2001. A week after the attacks, I received a call from CNN asking me to come in and comment about a new computer virus that was possibly terrorist related. I asked the reporter to briefly describe it to me, and I said it sounded like the well-known Code Red virus. They told me that it was called Nimda and that it was a little different from Code Red and, more important, terrorist related. An hour later, I received another call telling me not to come in. The reporter said that the FBI just declared that Nimda was not terrorist related and that CNN wasn't going to spend time covering the story.

At that point, I reminded the reporter that Nimda was nearly identical to Code Red and was therefore likely to cost the world's economy billions of dollars. He readily agreed that he thought the story was important but dejectedly stated that unless a story was terrorist related, it was not going to be covered. Nimda did go on to cause nearly one billion dollars' worth of damage around the world.

At almost the same time, the anthrax incidents occurred. In these widely reported incidents, one or more people sent anthrax-laden envelopes through the U.S. mail. People were terrified to go to their mailboxes. Five people died over a 10-week period.

Now, let's put anthrax in perspective. Although I am not minimizing a single death, the fact is that more people die every 30 minutes from automobile accidents and obesity than died from 10 weeks of the anthrax incidents. The fact is that even if people were exposed to anthrax, there is more than enough time for them to be treated. Yet people were buying rubber gloves to check their mail, if they were brave enough to check it at all, but they don't have any problems walking into a donut shop, or driving to the donut shop, for that matter.

What this says about our society and terrorism is that we can accept major monetary losses, major nuisances, and even death as a matter of fact, but we have an irrational fear at the slightest possibility of death caused maliciously. It is this irrational fear that terrorists want to exploit because it is most likely to cause us to change our behavior.

Causing computer damage, especially where the average person has no control over those computers, means that there is no behavior for them to change. On the other hand, checking mail is a very purposeful behavior that people perform on a daily basis. The threat that a daily behavior can cause intentional death is an extremely effective act of terrorism, no matter how minute the threat is.

The Spies Among Us

Don't get me wrong, though. Computers are of very significant interest to terrorists. Computer attacks can amplify physical attacks. More important, computers aid the planning of physical attacks. Computers allow for the laundering of money. The Internet provides lots of generally irrelevant information that actually provides terrorists with details of their potential targets. The part that freaks people out most is that terrorists walk among us on a regular basis while they wait for the rare opportunity to commit any act.

As this Introduction previously states, terrorists are a miniscule concern in the grand scheme of our daily lives. They exist, but compared to the other threats individuals face from malicious people on a daily basis, terrorists are inconsequential—except, of course, for the people directly or indirectly affected by the very rare terrorist attacks. There are many more people who directly and negatively impact your life on a daily basis.

One time, I had a friend who had a reason to be concerned about her personal safety. I decided to have her meet with my friend Stan so that he could tell her how to detect whether she was being followed and what to do if she did detect something. Stan is one of the most successful GRU agents in that agency's history and defected to the United States in the early 1990s. He was a spymaster and full colonel in an organization frequently referred to as the KGB's evil twin.

Stan described the basic procedures of surveillance detection and evasion, as it is known in the trade, and talked about several incidents in which he used the skills personally in the local Washington, D.C., area. The woman sat there amazed that areas she traveled on a daily basis were the location of international intrigue. When we left Stan, she commented that she just realized that there seems to be an alternate universe coexisting with the real world that we all know.

At other times, I describe my friends to other people. They are amazed that I know many Navy SEALs, Russian spies, CIA operatives (including one who appeared in Playboy magazine as the "Spy Who Took Her Clothes Off"), FBI agents, and so on to the point that I am not phased by any of it. The fact is that thousands of people know my friends as well and don't realize that they are talking to a person on the front lines of international and corporate espionage.

As the people who design the over of this book will likely write, I regularly steal billions of dollars from some of the largest companies in the world. I simulate terrorist attacks. Later chapters describe this process in detail. A shocking fact that comes out of my "penetrations" is that approximately 40 percent of the time, I find evidence that other malicious people have been there before me.

When targeting a multinational manufacturing firm, I found evidence of a Chinese intelligence operation targeting the company from across the street of the company headquarters. When targeting a construction company, I found proof that someone stole the plans of a nuclear reactor. While stealing the product lines of a pharmaceutical company, there was evidence of insider hacking of company computers. While hacking into a bank, I found evidence that one of the bank's computers was compromised and was being used to hack other companies. When investigating a known bank robbery, I discovered that there were at least a dozen other attacks that the bank didn't know about.

This is just a sampling of espionage and otherwise criminal incidents that I was involved in discovering. Other espionage incidents occur around the world on a regular basis. All pharmaceutical businesses are targeted by their competitors as well as foreign intelligence services. Automobile manufacturers target each other on a regular basis. Boeing and Airbus Industrie regularly accuse each other of espionage. Even a paper manufacturer such as Avery was targeted by foreign intelligence services. Companies that offer low-price guarantees regularly spy on their competition so that they know they are offering the lowest prices.

All these cases are clearly notable because of the size of the companies involved. However, every organization and person, large and small, falls under the eyes of someone wanting to compromise personal or corporate information. For example, the telephones at Grand Central Station in New York City are closely monitored by criminals to steal the calling card and credit card numbers from people using those phones. Identity thieves regularly go through mailboxes to steal personal information. Most people have unfortunately experienced firsthand a coworker who is trying to spy on them to make them look bad or stay ahead of them.

Although everyone fears a terrorist attack, we accept as a given the losses caused by other malicious people, losses that we experience every day. There are unfortunate people who have been directly affected by terrorists, but they are rare. For the rest of us, the many small losses add up to huge losses.

Although people think of spies as an elite group of people who go through years of training at government agencies, the fact is that many people use techniques that are traditionally associated with spies. The average criminal is clearly nowhere near as skilled in the techniques and will in no way master espionage techniques. Unfortunately, the average criminal can still be extremely effective, or at least effective enough.

For example, CIA operatives receive years of training to get people to betray their country under penalty of death. That clearly takes infinitely more skill in manipulating human interactions than getting people to divulge their credit card number. Unfortunately, simple con artists know enough. The basic techniques, though, are the same.

Here is a computer-related example: The National Security Agency clearly has tremendous skill in compromising extremely complex networks and systems. Although stories of computer hackers amaze the average person, the skill required to perform their computer break-ins is actually minimal. They simply download tools widely available on the Internet.

Again, the level of skill required to accomplish criminal actions is nowhere the level of skills required of spies, but the fundamental techniques are similar and the criminals are still very successful. The question then arises as to how to know whether the spies among us affect you.

If you work in a large company, you are a target. Your company has competitors and generally has a great deal of money and information of value to many, many people. If you have a credit card, you are paying higher interest rates because of credit card fraud. Similarly, if you have been a victim of a personal crime, you have been targeted. These types of crimes include identity theft, by which, according to U.S. government figures, 10 percent of the population is victimized. Tens of millions of credit card numbers have been stolen off the Internet.

Also relating to computers, if you have ever received a spam message, you have been targeted. If you were infected by a computer virus or received a virus-laden message, you were targeted. Major airlines and bank ATM networks were crippled by computer viruses, which in turn affected millions of people. Example after example leads to the conclusion that just about everyone has been and will be the victim of many spies among us.

There are clearly some James Bond types out there. However, the clear majority of the people employing espionage and criminal techniques are opportunists who rely on people's being overly concerned about a mystical terrorist attack instead of taking basic precautions against the common losses we experience everyday.

The Good News

I received a great deal of training in espionage techniques and commercially used those techniques to simulate the worst possible crimes, as well as investigate actual cases of espionage. What people are most surprised to hear is that despite the fact that I have stolen billions of dollars, broken into banks, and stolen nuclear secrets, as well as seen how criminals and spies do the same for real, the methods used are surprisingly basic. Even more important, the incidents could have been prevented with even more basic countermeasures.

For example, most major power blackouts, including the 2003 blackout that put 50,000,000 people in the dark and cost the economy billions of dollars, result from overgrown trees. As Chapter 5, which discusses computer vulnerabilities in more detail, makes clear, software easily available on the Internet is the source of almost all computer attacks, including those performed by spies and hardened criminals.

The Eligible Receiver exercises best demonstrate this. Eligible Receiver was a code name given to a series of information warfare attacks performed against U.S. military facilities by the National Security Agency and some military units. Despite the fact that the attackers had some extremely advanced tools and techniques, they were limited to using only tools and techniques widely available over the Internet. Year after year, these attacks, which simulated possible real-world attacks such as North Korea attacking the Pacific Fleet, were extremely successful. Within two weeks the NSA experts seriously damaged the military's ability to wage war. Again, it used only widely available attacks. Although these people are better organized than just about all other attackers, any other people could have theoretically achieved the same success.

Even the Defense Information Systems Agency determined that 97 percent of all successful attacks against the U.S. military were preventable. In the civilian world, statistics indicate that more than 99 percent of successful attacks are preventable.

So the good news is that terrorism is generally an insignificant concern. The bad news is that we experience incidents far worse than terrorism on a regular basis. However, even this cloud has a silver lining. The attacks, and more frequently the accidents, we experience are preventable with very simple countermeasures. The big problem is the awareness of how easy the incidents are to accomplish and how easy it is to prevent the incidents in the first place.

At this point some readers may realize that the title *Spies Among Us* is slightly misleading. Yes, there are actual spies walking among us on a regular basis. However, more frequently these spies are actually typical criminals who use basic espionage techniques. This may be disappointing at first. However, Part I teaches you the same information that spies learn to perform their craft. In Part II of this book, there are some great real-life spy stories to satisfy your curiosity. Part III then goes on to tell you what you can do to stop even the greatest spies in the world.

More important, you learn how to prevent yourself from falling victim to these amateurs. Although it may be forgivable to be taken by a real-life superspy, would you forgive yourself for leaving yourself vulnerable to the Hamburglar?

Spies Among Us

How to Stop the Spies, Terrorists, hackers, and Criminals You Don't Even Know You Encounter Every Day

Part

I

ESPIONAGE CONCEPTS

We know the enemies of freedom use the same technology that hackers do, that we do.
—Tom Ridge, Former Secretary of Homeland Security

People associate espionage tactics with spies; however, such tactics are in use everywhere—whether by a real intelligence operative tracking terrorists around the world, a terrorist planting a bomb, a hacker stealing credit card numbers, a member of a drug cartel avoiding the Coast Guard, a petty criminal casing an old woman, or a teenage girl trying to find out whether the boy she likes returns the feeling. Clearly, some of these people are more skilled in using these tactics than others are. This section of the book discusses who those people are and how they accomplish their deeds, or misdeeds depending on whose side you're on. More important, you'll learn how they think. When you know this, you can start to protect yourself.

Part I takes you through the fundamental concepts of espionage and crimes, and discusses preventing them. Chapter 1 takes on the myth of spies and criminals in general as some sort of unstoppable geniuses and puts them in the proper perspective. Chapter 2 introduces the way you should start to think about risk and security. Chapters 3, 4, and 5 respectively take you through what a person and organization has that others value, who or what is actually out to get you, and how you let yourself be vulnerable. These chapters describe the problem and form the basis for the rest of the book, including addressing the problems.

1

How to Be a Spy

J ames Bond is the second worst spy in history; the first worst spy is
Sydney Bristow from the TV show *Alias*. They do everything people
want a spy to do: They travel the world in seconds. They blow things
up. They easily beat up anyone who stands in their way. They kill people.
Their enemies fear them. Why then do they suck as spies?

They always seem to get caught. Because they blow things up, beat
people up, and leave dozens of bodies in their wake, their enemies know
who they are and try to kill them on a daily basis. Sydney Bristow can't
even make dinner in her home without having to kill her roommate.
Sure, this makes for an exciting life, but it violates the prime rule of
espionage: *Never get caught*.

Stolen information and property often become worthless, or even
liabilities, to the spy or thief when the victim discovers the theft. If you
learn that terrorists plan to smuggle uranium into the country, and the
terrorists find out that you know, they'll find another way to smuggle
the uranium. Or they could booby-trap the smuggling device to kill
the people intercepting the package. They might also discover how you
learned the information, which stops you from getting more information. Even worse, the terrorists can feed you bad information in the
future to manipulate you. Because compromises of "sources and methods," as it is called in the intelligence field, can be that devastating, there
are many cases in which valuable intelligence was not acted on, even
though that inaction caused the loss of life. All this is why not getting
caught is the critical factor in determining the skill of a real spy.

Killing people and blowing things up tend to upset the real world. It not only serves as a clear announcement that something has occurred but also creates international incidents and alienates friendly countries. At the very least, the sponsoring government must pay millions of dollars to the victims and the country affected. Investigations arise that could expose sensitive intelligence operations. So unless the mission explicitly calls for killing people or blowing things up, spies don't do these things, and they would probably be fired or at least removed from their position if they did.

Criminals use espionage techniques as well. So, what's the perfect crime? It's a crime that nobody knows occurred. If nobody knows a crime was committed, the criminal is never even suspected in the crime. Sadly, even many victims prefer it this way.

For example, if someone steals a credit card number and uses it, banks prefer that the victims overlook the charge, because the banks make a profit on the transaction. Investigations are also costly, and more frequently than not, the perpetrator goes free and the bank has little chance of catching him or her in the future.

Let's consider another example. Almost all businesses experience white-collar crime, such as accountants manipulating the books and stealing money. If the crime is detected, the company does not fire the employee or have him or her arrested. It generally works out a deal with the employee, whereby the employee leaves the company quietly and pledges never to disclose the incident. Companies claim that the cases are difficult to prove and they don't want the inevitable lawsuits; however, the reality is that they don't want word of the incident getting out.

Types of Spies

When people think of spies, they usually picture James Bond or Sydney Bristow and think that movies such as *XXX*, *Mission: Impossible*, or *The Recruit* reflect the reality of being a spy. In TV shows such as *Alias* and *Jake 2.0*, CIA and NSA agents travel the world performing covert missions. The reality of the espionage world, however, is completely different. NSA and CIA are much more the land of Dilbert than the land of Bond.

Agents

Most people believe that an *agent* is someone who works at the CIA or NSA performing espionage. In the world of espionage, being an agent actually has two possible meanings.

A *special agent* is a law-enforcement officer, such as an FBI or a DEA officer. Special agents also exist in the military and intelligence agencies, as well as at the U.S. Postal Service and the Customs and Immigrations Agency, for example. They perform law enforcement or counterintelligence. They stop and arrest bad guys. This use of the word *agent* does not, however, reflect a traditional intelligence agent.

An agent is a person who has access to information that an intelligence operative wants and who is recruited to provide this information to an operative. In movies, agents are usually portrayed as schmucks who have some sort of mental weakness, such as stupidity or malintent. They provide information to the bad guys, usually without knowing it, and end up dead. With the exception of the ending up dead part, this is largely true in the real world.

In the world of espionage, agents are people who betray their country and who frequently risk death if caught. Given the current state of international affairs, in which there is no major nation versus nation military action, people are more willing to give up information. Sometimes they knowingly give information to a foreign operative; other times they don't even know they are providing information to a spy.

That last statement might sound ridiculous at first. It is, however, true. For example, I could approach a pizza-delivery person who delivers to a military base and tell him that I invest in stocks. I could ask him how many pizzas he delivers to the base during a normal shift. I would then offer him money to tell me if there is ever a substantial increase in the number of deliveries to the base on a given night. (If you know what the base does and that more people are working on a particular night, you can more easily detect intelligence events.) I could justify wanting this information by claiming that if one military base were having more pizzas delivered, others would be ordering more, too, so the value of pizza company stocks would rise. No matter how stupid the reason sounds, do you think a pizza-delivery person would turn down $20 for just letting someone know that he is making more deliveries?

In Chapter 9, I discuss the case of several Ericsson employees in Sweden who provided information to a friend whom they thought was just trying to learn enough to start his own company. They had no clue that the information they "copied" was actually provided to Russian spies.

Cases in which agents knowingly provide information to a foreign operative are more common, though. Although statistics aren't generally available, people familiar with this field tell me it is most common for people to approach the foreign country, or, in an industrial environment, a competitor. When a potential agent offers information or services, the potential operative must determine whether the agent is legitimate and worth using.

For example, the operative must determine whether the agent is too unstable, because that could compromise the whole operation and create more serious problems in the future. Operatives must also determine whether the potential agent is a *double agent* who is approaching them to offer false information or compromise the entire operation.

A friend in the pharmaceutical industry told me how one employee contacted a competitor to sell information about the top drug in development. The employee's company found out when the competitor went to the police. The managers of the other company apparently considered the person's offer for three days before deciding the person must be part of a sting operation. They were actually upset when they found out that the offer was legitimate, although illegal, and they missed the opportunity to buy the information.

More sophisticated intelligence agencies always examine any unsolicited offers of information carefully and never rely on these sources completely. Agents who are recruited by operatives are much more reliable. This process is discussed in the next section.

Operatives

An *operative* is a person who works for an intelligence agency and is responsible for collecting human intelligence. Put simply, an operative gets information from people. As discussed earlier, operatives find agents who provide them with information. In many cases, the operatives inherit agents from a departing operative when they arrive at a new assignment; however, they are generally graded by the number and quality of agents they recruit.

The key word is *recruit*. Typically, an operative is assigned a diplomatic cover, performing, say, a job at an embassy while simultaneously, in his or her spare time, trying to find new agents and exchange information with current agents.

There are also people in non-official cover (NOC) positions. Their cover does not give them diplomatic immunity; they work as journalists or businesspeople or pose as tourists. Sometimes large companies who cooperate with the government employ them. Sometimes they work at a front company. At the CIA, a standard operative is generally recruited when young and is placed in a cover position. NOCs are frequently older and have extensive, real-world business experience with a legitimate resume, making them more believable in their cover. Contrary to how they are portrayed in the movie *The Recruit*, these are not super spies but people who fit more easily into an NOC position. (And I must point out that the cover of an NOC would not be as a CIA employee, as shown in the movie.)

Also contrary to what you see in the movies, operatives are not primarily trained to perform paramilitary operations and bug houses. Although they receive a small amount of that type of training, most of the trainees' time is spent learning how to find and manage agents and exchange information with them. In addition, they receive extensive training in surveillance, surveillance detection, and surveillance avoidance. After an operative recruits an agent, the operative then trains the agent on how to safely exchange information and avoid surveillance. To put it simply, an operative is much more of a puppet master than a spymaster.

In addition to exchanging information and detecting surveillance, operatives must make sure that the agents know how to avoid getting caught if they steal information. If an agent is caught, that capture most likely exposes the operative, too. Additionally, the operative may have to coach an agent on how to get access to extra information. This could include providing the agent with training or equipment to steal more information and conceal his or her crimes.

Operatives keep their distance from the real action. They must have clean hands, so they let the agents commit the criminal acts. This also means that they must be able and willing to let an agent be compromised and suffer the penalties.

Infrequently, operatives may be called on to collect information directly, as opposed to using agents to get the information. Perhaps an opportunity to photograph something arises and they need to act on it. The key principle for operatives is that they are not out committing illegal acts.

Recruiting Agents

Operatives must put themselves in social situations in which they might find people with access to information. They go to parties. They attend cultural and social events. They join clubs. When I asked one former operative what he did, he said he rode the ferry. He was assigned to a city where many businesspeople took the ferry between work and home, so he rode the ferry back and forth for the entire morning and evening rush hours. A good operative creates as many opportunities as possible to meet people. The case study in Chapter 6 demonstrates how to create a situation that attracts potential agents.

As mentioned previously, agents betray their country under penalty of death. In the commercial or criminal world, they violate long-term trust relationships in ways that could land them in jail or dead—depending on whom they get involved with. So, what mental weaknesses make someone a potential agent? The answer is MICE, which stands for money, ideology, coercion, and ego.

- **Money.** This is fairly obvious. People want and need money, and those in dire financial straits may very well be tempted to take money to improve their situation. Operatives look for people who either want significantly more money than they have or need money critically.

- **Ideology.** People sometimes feel compelled to put themselves at risk for a cause, which is how Al-Qaeda and other terrorist organizations recruit their members and why many agents from communist bloc countries became agents for the United States. Terrorist organizations know how to identify people with the potential to kill others for their causes. They then use brainwashing techniques to maintain control over the recruits. Terrorists tell their recruits, for example, that they are doing God's work, which appeals directly to the recruit's ego.

    It is similar in the espionage world. Operatives find agents with sympathetic ideologies. They are then trained to make the agent a money- or ego-based agent because with changing world events, ideology gets confusing and an agent motivated by more personal concerns is easier to control.

- **Coercion.** This is basically blackmail; however, MIBE isn't as catchy as MICE, so it is easier to remember coercion. Operatives find agents who can be coerced into providing information, a tactic typically associated with communist bloc countries, drug cartels, and organized crime. Operatives might threaten an agent's life or his family's; they might blackmail people because of their sexual activities or threaten to expose past criminal indiscretions.

   Coercion can seep into any operative–agent relationship. The fact is that after an agent provides an operative with any information, the operative can then use that information to blackmail the agent in the future.

- **Ego.** It is no coincidence that most agents think they are smarter than everyone else. They think they deserve more than they are getting. They want revenge on the people holding them back or failing to reward them as much as they think they deserve. The current environment of corporate downsizing is spawning many potential agents who need money and want revenge.

An operative must be able to identify these weaknesses in a potential agent; however, it can be hard to find someone with the right information who is also susceptible enough to these weaknesses.

Desensitization

An operative doesn't approach a potential agent and tell her that he wants her to betray her country under penalty of death. The operative slowly befriends the agent, gradually convincing her to provide information. An operative might ask a potential agent for a small favor that is not sensitive in any way; for example, he might ask for the telephone number of someone she works with. The potential agent is then rewarded with a sincere thank you and a token gift.

Over time, the requests and gifts become larger. A single telephone number eventually becomes a telephone directory and then sensitive or classified documents. Before the agent realizes what she is doing, she is at the point of no return. She relies on the money the operative is giving her, and she can't turn in the operative without betraying herself. The slowness of this process not only sucks in the agent and reassures her as she begins to steal even more valuable information, but also allows the operative to verify that the agent can do what she says.

Good operatives help their agents rationalize their actions. "You're not stealing anything ... you're just making copies of it. Nobody will know what you did. This isn't going to hurt anyone. The money helps your family. The company doesn't pay you what you deserve. It's not a crime; it's a hobby. It shouldn't be a crime in the first place." They recast the acts so that they sound innocuous. Although the words are hollow, they help agents deal with their regrets.

Black Bag Operations

James Bond and Sydney Bristow go on special missions and infiltrate places to blow them up or steal things and information. A small part of the intelligence community (and I stress the word *small*) actually performs these types of operations. They're called *black bag operations*.

Performed by a well-trained operative, a black bag operation might be called for when you know an opportunity exists to collect incredibly valuable information and you have no agents to do it for you. For example, you might discover that a government official staying at a hotel will leave his laptop computer in his room for an hour. You believe that the computer contains details of terrorist operations and you don't have a hotel employee who can copy the data from the computer. Or perhaps you want to bug his room.

The most publicly disclosed case of a black bag–type of operation was when the CIA rescued American diplomats trapped in Iran during the Iranian hostage crisis of 1979–1981. These Americans were in hiding and their lives would have been in serious danger if they were discovered. Brilliant CIA operatives created a fake Canadian film company and traveled to Iran to supposedly scout filming locations. They created fake identities and paperwork for the diplomats, and the diplomats left Iran as part of the film crew.

Although these examples are scarce in the real world, they do exist. But before you rush off to join the CIA to specialize in black bag operations, you should know that although some operatives work on black bag operations, these operations are typically performed by current and sometimes former military special forces assigned or detailed to the CIA. The special forces, such as Navy SEALs and Green Berets, actually perform more covert work—both for military and intelligence purposes—than the general public imagines.

It can be argued that undercover law enforcement agents, such as those in the DEA and FBI, perform black bag operations. I really don't want to argue semantics in this case. These are truly heroes who put their lives on the line on a daily basis and can call what they do whatever they want in my book.

So if you really want to grow up to be James Bond or Sydney Bristow, you are better off joining the military and trying for special forces, or joining law enforcement and going undercover. It sounds simple, but it is infinitely more difficult than you might imagine.

I perform, or more accurately simulate, black bag operations. For instance, I might walk into a company, assume a fake identity, and steal billions of dollars' worth of information. I take over banks or steal nuclear reactor designs, all within hours. I stumbled into performing commercial black bag simulations, and there are probably only a handful of people who actually do what I do—although the media, who tried for months to find others who perform the same work, say that I'm the only one.

The Intelligence Process

I've compromised organizations, helped secure them, and investigated their multimillion-dollar crimes. I'm convinced that a basic understanding of the intelligence process—that is, the gathering of information about organizations and individuals—is essential to implementing effective countermeasures. If you want to foil their plans, you've got to think like the bad guys sometimes. Doing this will equip you to better evaluate your own corporate and personal vulnerabilities so that you can choose the best countermeasures for your organization. These concepts are basic, but they are critical to understanding how spies collect information.

Intelligence is a science. Planning, preparation, and execution distinguish the amateur from the professional. Unfortunately for corporations, a little planning allows even the most inept, would-be spies to be successful.

The intelligence process is a strictly codified procedure, and it's hardly endemic to the intelligence community. Street criminals demonstrate their own version of the intelligence process every day. When a crack addict needs drugs, for example, he calculates the amount of money he needs to make a buy, makes the decision to acquire the necessary funds through robbery, performs reconnaissance of possible victims, chooses one that appears to be the most vulnerable, commits the robbery when the right opportunity presents itself, and makes off with everything of possible value. After escaping with the goods, he then evaluates the approximate value of everything stolen to determine whether it will, in fact, pay for the drugs he needs. If he finds his take to be insufficient, he determines how much more he needs, and the process begins again.

The intelligence process is typically divided into four phases:

- Definition of requirements
- Collection
- Analysis
- Evaluation

These activities are circular in nature (see Figure 1.1): Evaluation of collected intelligence begets new requirements, and each phase of the process requires that the previous phase be well executed. When intelligence gatherers begin collecting information without first developing detailed requirements, their actions tend to be unfocused, which makes them much more vulnerable to detection. These would-be spies end up grabbing everything they come across, and they often never find any truly valuable information.

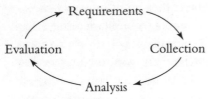

Figure 1.1 The intelligence process

The next four sections discuss each phase of the intelligence process in greater detail.

Definition of Requirements

Clearly defined requirements provide the foundation. When spies know exactly what they are looking for, they do a better job of finding that information. The more specific and refined the requirements, the better the results.

Well-defined requirements are not easy to develop. Let's say the members of a foreign intelligence agency decide that they want a missile system that is in development at an American company. This requirement is too vague. Do they want one of the actual missiles? Or do they want to know the missile's performance capabilities and to understand the underlying technology so that they can defend against the missile or improve their own weapons system? Maybe they want to sell the technology to another country. These requirements have critical differences. It is almost impossible to obtain a prototype of a new weapon, yet there are hundreds of sources for performance and technical data and possibly for design information.

Defining requirements can be just as tricky in corporate espionage situations. The automotive industry is extremely competitive, and each manufacturer wants to know exactly what the other is up to. Accordingly, automobile manufacturers go to great lengths to hide the details of their new car models during the months before their release: They camouflage the cars, test them only at night, and so on. Their competitors (and car magazine writers) go to equally great lengths to unmask the latest model: They pay people to surreptitiously photograph the cars, they rent airplanes to observe and photograph the cars from the air, and they even infiltrate the testing grounds to plant cameras.

First and foremost, intelligence requirements must be realistic, taking into account the available data, resources, and potential risk. Most corporations would like to know everything about their customers, competitors, and suppliers. They might also like to know what the government is up to at any given moment, because pending legislation or regulations can drastically affect them. Available resources, however, rarely allow for such omnipotence, so companies tend to focus their espionage efforts rather narrowly, very often on specific customer concerns—anything that could affect market share and customer satisfaction.

In some cases, initial intelligence requirements can be broad. "Tell me what I don't know" seems to be too vague an objective, but it's often the basis for spirited espionage activity. Usually fewer resources (people, money, time, and so on) are involved in this kind of information-collection activity, and low-risk tactics are employed. After these fishing expeditions, organizations can develop more targeted requirements.

Requirements determine the tactics used and the level of risk assumed. Using the previous example, "Tell me what I don't know," intelligence organizations tend to stick to reviewing information that they already have and searching publicly available databases. They also search business journals, newspapers, and magazine indexes for useful information. These activities are extremely low risk, and most companies—and all intelligence agencies—engage in this kind of straightforward intelligence gathering on a regular basis.

The quality of information gathered in this way varies, but it can be outstanding. An interview with, say, the target's chief financial officer (CFO) offers even a greater potential for reward; however, the risk is also much higher. A face-to-face interview potentially exposes the whole operation, whereas a public data search is almost undetectable.

Requirements define the kind of information that has value to the organization *launching* the intelligence operation; this information might not even be considered valuable by the company that possesses it. A restaurant's reservation list is practically worthless—unless a terrorist organization wants to assassinate someone dining in the bistro. Knowing when the target will be at the restaurant provides the terrorists with crucial information. Likewise, an old expense report can give a competitor an indication about a potential marketing lead.

Collection

When most people hear the word *intelligence*, they automatically associate it with collection. To many, espionage is the collection process. However, collection is just one (albeit the flashiest) phase of espionage.

To satisfy the requirements defined in the first phase, information must be collected. To experienced spies, the information-collection process is highly intuitive. After they understand the requirements of the assignment, they usually know where and how to obtain the desired information. For example, if I wanted to learn about someone's personal habits, I would look at credit reports and credit card statements, follow the person for a period of time, and talk to the person's friends and coworkers. I might even talk to the person directly. If one of the requirements of the project is to keep the effort a secret (not always necessary), I know to avoid people. These activities are second nature to me.

Sometimes the information is already available. If I wanted to locate someone, for instance, I might be able to find the person's address through a variety of computer resources, such as the Internet. Many supposedly long-lost people have been found on the Classmates.com web site. Search engines such as Google can often find this information.

There's no need for a lot of legwork nowadays; trips to courthouses or exhaustive interviews of friends and family are no longer necessary.

Hundreds of databases in cyberspace provide open-source information. Some organizations, such as large companies and foreign intelligence agencies, have their own massive databases, which are stuffed with information about people and companies.

Although it may sound more like an art, collection is—like the intelligence process it is part of—a science. People have predictable vulnerabilities, and what makes collection an intuitive process is that spies understand this. They study techniques for years. Although some people are obviously better at collecting than others, you can train people to be collectors.

TYPES OF INTELLIGENCE

Notice that I refer to those who gather information as *collectors*, not *operatives* or *agents*. The reason is that those are terms specific to Human Intelligence, or HUMINT, which is just one type of collection among many. Depending on what is being targeted, the other intelligence disciplines can produce much more effective results. Signals Intelligence, or SIGINT, is the collection of communications signals, including telephone and radio signals. The collection of Internet traffic generally falls into this category. Imagery Intelligence, or IMINT, involves taking images and interpreting those images. The word *images* is used instead of *photographs* because there are many high-tech types of images well beyond traditional pictures. Open Source Intelligence, or OSINT, involves searching through publicly available information. There are many other disciplines, such as TRASHINT, which are important but used less often than the ones mentioned here.

The type of intelligence collection chosen depends on the requirement. It is not unusual to task multiple intelligence types for a single requirement. In many cases, it is actually preferable, because one form of intelligence can confirm another. For example, HUMINT can gather information, but it may be partial or fake. SIGINT can overhear people talking about faking the information. IMINT can take pictures confirming the results. So a good intelligence operation looks for everything and then analyzes and evaluates all of it.

Spies use a set of well-established collection methods. Some of those methods are scientifically complex, but the vulnerabilities they exploit are basically the same ones that petty criminals take advantage of.

Experienced spies often have a better idea of the actual value of the information they're seeking than do their targets, who typically take the information for granted, leaving it unduly exposed. Frequently, there's simply no reason to resort to expensive or complicated acquisition methods; the targets make it so easy.

An effective intelligence collector finds the location of the information in question before beginning any other tasks. Sometimes the location is obvious; sometimes it is not. If a specific source of information is unknown to collectors, they target potential sources. Only when the true source is identified does the real collection effort begin.

In some cases, surreptitious information collection is an ongoing process. Pierre Marion, the former head of the DGSE (the French intelligence agency), for example, has acknowledged placing people inside numerous American high-tech firms. The DGSE believes that by establishing an agent as a long-standing employee within a targeted company, it creates a breach that pours data for years. Although this farsighted approach yields varying degrees of success, the rewards are usually tremendous.

Long-term collection efforts are rare outside national intelligence organizations, large corporations, and organized crime. These groups have the money required to place and fund people for long periods of time. They also have the resources required to identify possible agents who are likely to volunteer information.

Well-funded organizations can afford what you might call espionage luxuries, such as paying insiders, establishing and monitoring long-term telephone bugs and wiretaps, and securing the cooperation of regular informants. Large companies are also better able to distance themselves from espionage activities. They can monitor the competition by paying people to pay people to pay people to get information. Organized crime is adept at this kind of layered espionage activity.

Disinformation

Disinformation is a common practice among smart organizations. These groups try to mislead would-be spies by providing them with false data that is not only worthless but also sometimes used to unmask the thief. One of the most common examples of this kind of disinformation may be found in your local telephone directory. Telephone companies place fake listings in their directories to catch rival publishers violating their copyrights. The practice is called *seeding*. Whenever one of the fake listings in the "official" telephone directory turns up in another directory, the company has clear evidence of an illegal copy.

Disinformation can also damage the recipient of the collected information. The so-called Star Wars defense program of the 1980s is an excellent example of this side effect. During that time, all indications were that the United States was putting together a system that shielded it from all incoming missiles. Government officials talked to the press about it, and known Soviet spies likely were fed information indicating that the United States had the required technology to accomplish such a plan. Feeling it had to respond, the Soviet Union nearly spent itself into bankruptcy trying to account for the Star Wars program. As you know, the program never materialized to any significant degree. How many companies have done the same to their competitors?

Sometimes disinformation is used to discredit people or organizations. White supremacist groups print their own version of the Bible to claim that God supports their ways. Terrorist groups use disinformation to incite people to commit suicidal acts. The Soviets used disinformation to turn people against the U.S. government and Americans in general. For example, they spread rumors that American missionaries' real purpose in Third World countries was to find organ donors. Sometimes people use the Internet to discredit people just for the fun of it, by spreading fabricated rumors.

One security countermeasure, known as the *honeypot*, involves placing made-up information that looks very valuable into an otherwise unused area of a computer. The information is sometimes not only incorrect but also damaging to competitors. Because no valid users belong in these honeypots, any intrusions sound an alarm.

When you use multiple sources of intelligence, you are likely to see through the charades. Experienced intelligence and business professionals know to see all the facts from all the sources before acting on intelligence.

Analysis

After the information has been collected and delivered to the sponsoring organization, the analysis phase begins. At this stage of the process, analysts pore over documents and comb through reams of data, sorting out the pieces into useful reports. This can involve translating information from foreign languages or computer formats. When the requirements are clearly focused, this process is straightforward.

Intelligence analysis falls into two major categories: standard intelligence analysis and traffic analysis. *Standard analysis* involves the examination of the actual content of the collected data to determine its potential value. *Traffic analysis* is the process of examining data flow. Information flows through a variety of media, including telephone systems, computer networks, and the mail. If I watch someone's mail over time, just reading the envelopes, I can learn an incredible amount about that person. Return addresses on letters can reveal employers and religious affiliations. Magazine subscriptions indicate personal interests. A credit card bill can reveal something about a person's income status. Children's magazines indicate the approximate age and number of children in the household. Letters from colleges give an educational history.

Even airline reservations provide valuable information. From a corporate perspective, knowing which companies visit which research facilities can tell me which companies want to commercialize the latest research. Seeing who stays at a hotel close to a research facility can point out likely licensees of their latest technologies. Trips by a researcher to other companies can reveal an unhappy employee who is trying to find a new job—a potential agent.

The more effort an intelligence organization puts into collecting data, the more effort it must put into the analysis of that data. Spies involved in long-term efforts constantly feed information to their primary organizations. It takes experienced analysts to know what information is valuable and where to find it within the flood of the collected materials. The driving concept for the analysis effort is value. Analysts must know what is valuable to the people they report to, and more important, what could be valuable to them. Good analysts always look beyond the scope of the current collection effort and strive to get the most value from whatever is collected. While searching for one chemical formula, for example, espionage analysts might stumble onto even more valuable formulas.

The final products of analysis are written reports that organize the information into a useful form. Writers of these reports tailor them to the needs of their recipients.

Evaluation

After analysis comes the evaluation phase. Although it sounds a lot like analysis, evaluation is quite distinct. Evaluation refers strictly to the process of determining how well the information collected meets the particular requirements of the espionage effort. If the information satisfies all requirements, then all collection efforts may stop because the spies got what they were after. If the evaluation is part of a long-term collection project, then requirements are adjusted as they are satisfied, and new information is evaluated.

A good evaluation also notes when the collected information uncovers other potentially valuable targets. After providing their customers with their desired secrets, good industrial spies market this extra booty to new customers. They also use the additional information to entice their current clients to do more business with them.

Evaluation also serves another purpose: It is the reality check for ongoing espionage activities. Only through careful evaluation can ineffective collection efforts be stopped. On the other hand, highly successful activities receive increased resources at this phase and may go on forever.

COOKING THE BOOKS

Sometimes people tamper with the evaluation process because of personal biases. This is known as "cooking the books." Spies have pet projects, and they hesitate to reduce their resources in the face of a negative evaluation. Others might hate a particular project and search for any excuse to terminate it. Sometimes the biases result from pressure on analysts from above. That is a claim made against the Bush administration for calls to go to war against Iraq. Many people contend that analysts were forced to provide only information that concluded that Iraq was developing weapons of mass destruction.

Whatever the impetus, cooking the books hurts the people who act on the information. Fortunately for potential victims, tainted evaluations occur frequently, causing fruitful espionage efforts to be canceled and bad ones to continue, draining valuable resources.

Basically, evaluation is a determination of value. The evaluation process focuses on whether the requested value has been attained, as well as whether something else of value has been discovered. Value puts the whole process in motion and can stop it in its tracks.

The Intelligence Process in Action

Early in the previous section, using the example of a junkie finding money for a fix, I noted that the intelligence process is a codified procedure used both within and outside the intelligence community. Here are some other common scenarios that demonstrate how the process is used:

- A girl wants to know whether a boy likes her. She tells her friends that she wants to know this information. Her friends decide to ask the boy or his friends. They get an answer and determine whether the boy likes her. The girl evaluates the information and then decides whether she needs more information.

- An employee wants to find out whether he will receive a promotion. He determines which secretary fills out and submits the paperwork. He can then try to talk to the secretary and ask her whether she knows anything. He can also try to access her computer while she is away from her desk, or go through her desk to look for copies of the paperwork. After finding information, he sees what the information indicates. If he does not find what he wants, he tries other methods.

- A company's managers want to find out whether their competitors are developing a product similar to what they have in development. They read trade journals. They talk to their clients to see whether they were approached by the competitor. They can hire a third-party firm to see whether they can collect other information in ways that they don't want details about. They review all the collected information to see whether they have a clear answer. They determine that the competitor does have something similar, and then they want to find out how similar.

- The U.S. government wants to see what another country's position is on a treaty. It could task NSA to listen to telephone communications. It could get the CIA to see whether that agency's known agents have access to the information. A preliminary answer is determined on some points, so the intelligence agencies are retasked to collect information specific to those points.

As you can see, there is always an initial requirement, a collection effort, an analysis, and then an evaluation as to whether the requirement has been satisfied. This is a repeatable process, a science, that is used in all intelligence-gathering activities.

Information Is Information

When I perform penetration tests, my basic goal is to grab a company by its neck and squeeze. Simply stated, I want to steal something that is so valuable to it that it cannot ignore the results. You will notice that I specifically do not say that I want to hack the company's computers, climb up the sides of buildings, or bug offices. I really don't care how I get something, as long as I get it.

If a crook gets your credit card number, does he really care whether he hacked it off your computer, picked up an old receipt from the garbage, or tapped into a telephone line to overhear you order something? Clearly not. Likewise, do you really care how he did it? I'll bet you're too busy worrying about stopping him and cleaning up your credit report.

It's the same in the business world. If a pharmaceutical company wants a competitor's new drug formula, is the result different if it hacks a computer, buys the information from an insider, or finds a draft document in the garbage? Information can be obtained verbally, electronically, physically, or visually. It can be snatched from computers, certainly, but a well-placed bribe can be just as effective. Information is information. To a spy, the form the information takes is irrelevant; the content is what matters.

Spies might not care how they get the information, but they do care about getting caught. They target the information and determine the easiest way to get it given the resources they have available while not getting caught. Espionage, and crime in general, is goal oriented.

The problem, though, is that most people and companies worry about specific types of criminal attacks that are usually overly hyped, such as computer hacking. This leaves information very vulnerable to anyone interested in looking beyond the obvious. Don't get me wrong, though: Computer hacking is a very useful way of getting information. Despite the hype, computers are generally poorly protected; hackers can easily remain anonymous and not get caught.

In the business world, information in the wrong hands can destroy a corporation, put people out of work, bankrupt local merchants, and devastate shareholder families. If your competitors want your company's strategic plans, they don't care whether they get them from your computers or your garbage. Information is information. The form it takes is irrelevant—the content is what matters.

Forms of Information

When I use the word *information*, what exactly am I talking about? The classic definition describes information as organized data, but that's not really very useful in our present context. Here, *information* refers to any piece of knowledge that could hurt you or your organization or help your competition if it were to fall into the wrong hands. That piece could be great or small. It could be a business plan or a phone number, a set of blueprints or a computer password, a high-tech prototype or a business card, your social security number or your mother's maiden name.

Although the form of information is irrelevant from a spy's perspective, it is extremely relevant to knowing how to protect yourself. The following sections describe the various forms of information and how they might be obtained.

Computer-Based Information

Almost every piece of information generated by a modern company or other organization eventually finds its way onto a computer somewhere. Information is either recorded on a computer to formalize it or actually created in a computer environment. Nowadays, most executives type their own messages and correspondence directly into computers; the dictation-taking secretary is an anachronism. Computers are used for spreadsheets, databases, project design, and tons and tons of e-mail.

E-mail is one of the most potentially vulnerable types of computer information because most people don't think much about how they're using it. In modern corporate America, most organizations are drowning in e-mail. People use e-mail to convey virtually all types of corporate information, from the most banal interoffice memos to the most sensitive project details. The corporate e-mail conversation is dense with information about company problems, personnel issues, and project status. Stop and think about the e-mail messages you have sent and received during the last week. What would happen if they were intercepted by an unfriendly party?

Individuals also have their own computer information to worry about. As computers become ubiquitous to our everyday lives, more of our critical information is on our computers. Quicken has our bank accounts and credit cards. Your computer has instant access to log in and commit bank transfers. PDAs have the essence of a person's life stored on them.

Nearly everyone understands the importance and potential vulnerability of computer-based information. Most people do take steps to protect their most sensitive computer documents. However, many do not realize how damaging their supposedly nonsensitive computer information can be. E-mail discussing travel plans can compromise potential mergers. Informal notes usually contain as many details as finished documents. Computer-based information is an extremely fruitful source of information to spies.

Formal Documents

Companies generate many kinds of formal documents for a variety of purposes. Strategic plans, contractual status reports, manufacturing specifications, and production reports must be printed and kept as hard-copy documents. These reports contain critical information that could ruin a company if it were compromised. Most people recognize the value of formal documents and take appropriate steps to protect them.

Draft Documents

Although people instinctively recognize the value of formal documents, they often treat the draft forms of those documents as worthless. They seem to assume that when a finished document is available, the drafts are outdated, inaccurate, and therefore unimportant. Although the draft document itself might be of little use after the final draft has been issued, the information it contains is hardly worthless. Much of it is very valuable indeed, and corporate spies know it. Typically, the draft documents contain the same hard facts as the final document; only the presentation changes significantly. As often as not, the first draft of a document is as valuable to a competitor as the thirty-fifth draft.

Working Papers

Much of the information contained in formal documents and their earlier drafts can be found in the working papers that are part of your day-to-day business routine. Project teams produce action lists, status reports, research summaries, business correspondence, and product specifications. Although the distribution of these documents is generally limited, they aren't usually thought of as sensitive, even though they can contain critical information about specific aspects of a project or organization. Often, these working papers are not controlled in the same way as formal documents, and people frequently lose track of them.

Scrap Paper

In the process of performing work, people inevitably record thoughts and notes on hundreds of bits of paper. We scribble on note cards, appointment calendars, and cocktail napkins, writing down anything from a grocery list to the invasion route for a military campaign. These bits of scrap paper are usually ignored. We don't give a second thought to that Post-It with our computer access code or the telephone message slip with the project supervisor's e-mail address. Yet, once again, these seemingly unimportant carriers of information can contain the same sensitive data as the formal documents that we tend to protect.

Other pieces of paper with potentially unnoticed valuable information include travel tickets, credit card receipts, invoices, and shipment manifests. For example, the "Good Morning America" producers invited me to be on their show to talk about credit card fraud, and they purchased tickets for me to fly to New York. When I arrived at the airport, I received a copy of the receipt, which had the "Good Morning America" credit card number embedded in it.

Papers that are otherwise pieces of scrap may not give a competitor the big picture, but they can help to fill in the pieces. They can give a spy a sense of where to direct attack efforts. A purloined appointment calendar can show me that an important executive meets frequently with an individual from another company, which could indicate a possible merger or joint venture in the offing. That's extremely valuable information. With enough scraps like this, I can put together all I need to know to cause a lot of damage.

Internal Correspondence

Internal company correspondence contains an incredible amount of information. Companies produce their own newsletters, policy documents, and meeting minutes, filled with project data, details about people, company status updates, and a variety of other information. Often, the people producing these documents have no idea they are generating sources of sensitive information. They don't anticipate the numbers of people who will eventually see the documents.

For example, my work involves identifying vulnerabilities in many publicly known companies, so I use code names for my clients in most of my documentation. Only those people who need to know the client's real name should have that information. That is why I was extremely concerned when a purchasing officer distributed a memo that put a code name together with the client's name. The information leak could have been disastrous. Fortunately, I was able to recover all copies of that memo.

Legal and Regulatory Filings

Government agencies and regulations require organizations to publish a variety of information. Companies produce annual reports, patent applications, FDA filings, and a wide range of other documents that are required by law. The content of these filings and releases is usually specified by the relevant government agencies, both foreign and domestic. However, many companies go beyond the scope of these requirements, releasing much more information than necessary.

This situation has spawned the growth of a new industry made up of legitimate businesses that provide a specialized checking service. For a fee, these services check new government filings on a daily basis, searching for useful information and passing it along to their sponsors. Of course, industrial spies check these records, too, or they use one of the commercial services themselves.

Other Records

Almost every action leaves a record somewhere, especially in the business world. When you travel, you generate records at hotels, airlines, and car rental companies. When you take out a library book, your selection and its due date appear in the library computer. Monica Lewinsky's bookstore loyalty records were subpoenaed. When you place a telephone call or receive one, the action is recorded. Telephone records reveal many marital affairs. When someone pages you, when you log on and off a computer system, and when you browse an Internet web page or look at Internet newsgroup messages, *all* of it is recorded. Depending on the security enforced on your computer system, each and every one of your actions may be recorded.

These types of records have been used to convict people of crimes, to provide leads to corporate secrets, and to compromise the most sensitive operations. In many cases, accessing these types of records is completely legal.

The Press and Other Open-Source Information

Spies and criminals in general don't need to engage in illegal activity to begin to compromise information. The data they need to get started can often be found in newspapers and trade magazines. Also, many publicly available databases have a tremendous amount of information, most of which is available to anyone with Internet or library access.

Anything that is publicly available is typically referred to as *open-source* information by the intelligence community. These resources search for or contain important industry news. They report who wins major contracts, list which executives are moving to which projects, and supply a wealth of other information that can be quite useful. Every little piece of information helps give a spy a bigger picture. In some cases, spies are able to secure everything they need from open sources without ever resorting to aggressive activities.

Corporate public relations and marketing departments play a key role in the dissemination of this kind of information. They quite naturally want to give out as much news as possible about their companies to help increase sales and profitability. That's their job. Unfortunately, they tend to go overboard, releasing too much information. This information makes its way into a variety of public and private databases, which are widely available to anyone with a computer account. Databases such as EDGAR contain complete Securities and Exchange Commission (SEC) filings. There are special-interest Internet newsgroups, where people interested in specific companies or market sectors can post anything that they come across dealing with their interests.

The term *googling* is now in many dictionaries, as in googling someone to get personal information. People leave traces all over the Internet. They post personal issues to newsgroups. Many people have web logs, or *blogs*, that detail their lives. People have detailed Instant Messenger profiles. Some people just give all their information away.

Formal Meetings

Most organizations hold some kind of formal meeting in which its members discuss a variety of corporate and project issues. The information discussed at these meetings is frequently very sensitive, whether the participants are senior officers or line supervisors. Typically, someone prepares a meeting agenda and materials. Someone else prepares the minutes of the meeting, which summarize everything that went on during the meeting. All these materials contain information of great value to corporate spies. This does not even address what could happen if the meeting room is actually bugged.

In one case, I performed a penetration test on a very large company that makes commodity trades. I walked into a meeting room at 9:00 P.M. and noticed papers neatly laid out in front of every seat. When I picked up one of the sheets, I saw that it listed all the trades the company intended to perform the next day, including specifically how much and when. People familiar with the concept of market timing would be able to make a fortune making trades in anticipation of the large trades my client would make. I discovered that it was a regular practice to print these documents the night before so that all the traders could meet first thing in the morning to be aware of the plan.

Informal Meetings

Any time employees get together and talk about work, either in person or over the telephone, that gathering could be considered a meeting. The sensitivity of the information discussed at these informal meetings varies greatly. Telephone conversations in particular contain a great deal of very sensitive information. There's something about the device that causes people to relax and let their guard down. Many industrial spies make it a point to tap telephone conversations so that they can pick up useful bits of conversation.

Casual Conversations

Perhaps the most overlooked source of valuable information is the casual conversations that take place both inside and outside the office every day. People can't help talking about their work. Sometimes they're just getting together with coworkers for a few beers, and work is the natural topic of conversation. Sometimes they're trying to impress others by talking about sensitive company matters. The smoking areas outside major office buildings are great places to pick up information through casual conversation. I've heard of spies taking up smoking specifically to exploit this vulnerability.

Here are some real-life examples of how information can be gleaned for conversations:

- My friend Stan, the Russian defector, makes a habit of finding the smoking areas and lighting up with everyone else. He becomes just another one of the guys. Within a few hours, he has a grasp of most things going on inside the company. Since these smoking areas are frequently at loading docks or near side entrances that aren't monitored as well as the front doors, Stan's new friends usually hold the door open for him as they all supposedly go back to work.

- While consulting for a major New York investment bank, I took its employee shuttle from the Financial Center to an uptown office. I couldn't help overhearing two employees sitting nearby discussing an upcoming major merger between two large firms. If anyone else overheard them and used that information, the bank could have been accused of insider trading.

- A secretary I know was having dinner with her husband after work in a restaurant, where she overheard a couple of sales executives from her company talking at the next table. She heard them laying out the details of the sales plan for a new product. This was very sensitive information that was overheard by possibly 40 people.

- Bartenders near the headquarters of one of the largest companies in the world regularly overhear some of the most critical business deals in the works at the company in question.

These kinds of conversations are common. Good, patient spies know how to exploit them, and over time, spies can get a lot of information just by being good listeners.

Conclusion

You now know the basics of being a spy. Sadly, the same techniques that make someone a master spy make a petty criminal successful. When you put yourself in the place of a spy or criminal, with the perspective that the only thing worse than being unsuccessful is getting caught, you can appreciate why the successful spies proceed slowly and carefully.

The successful spies and criminals make sure that they have clear goals and then go through the constant process of collecting and analyzing information and evaluating those goals. They determine what information or other end goal is the most vulnerable to them; then they target that information.

This is not to say that the less skilled and narrow-minded criminals are not successful. They can be successful enough when people leave information, or something else, poorly secured. At face value, this might seem to be just luck. The fact is that people leave themselves and their companies vulnerable in many ways. The "good" spies are those who are prepared to act quickly to obtain whatever information is left vulnerable, in any form that it takes. They take the path of least resistance.

The good news is that you can stop the spies, in all the forms they take. Whether they are truly spymasters, terrorists, criminals, or nosy neighbors, they all target information. If you protect that information appropriately, you stop the spies.

2

Why You Can Never Be Secure

The title of this chapter seems to directly contradict the message of the book; however, it is accurate. It's true that you can never be 100 percent secure. The only people who claim they can provide you with complete security are fools or liars.

However, you can be secure enough. That is the key principle. You will always have an element of risk in everything you do. The only way to avoid risk is to not do anything. (But consider that if you sit at home locked in your room, a meteor can strike your house or an electrical fire can start.) In reality, people and companies cannot avoid risk. The only way to not assume risk is not to do business.

Unfortunately, companies and people tend to ignore all risk and charge ahead. For example, many companies want to do business on the Internet because of all the potential financial benefits. However, they ignore the fact that there are dangers, or risks, that incur costs they are not familiar with. Frequently these quick movers think they are too small for anyone to want to attack them. As you should know from reading the previous chapter, this company is now the perfect victim. Companies want the benefits without acknowledging the costs.

Would a business buy a delivery truck and not get insurance or fail to maintain that truck? Of course not, because it presents too much risk, and it just goes against all notions of common sense. People know that there is a cost to pay to get the potential benefit of having a delivery truck. However, people completely ignore this concept when it comes to the Internet and computers in general.

The Risk Equation

The core of the intelligence process, described in Chapter 1, is compromising vulnerabilities and avoiding countermeasures in the pursuit of valuable information. It's about determining needs and satisfying them. Another word for this process is *espionage*. When a company is the target of intelligence activities, the process is called *industrial espionage*. The chances that an intelligence operation will breach your company's security and compromise something valuable is called *risk*.

Risk is the driving consideration of all corporate espionage activities. The strategic decisions of those who would attack your organization are driven by it; the types of counterintelligence measures, or security countermeasures, you put into place depend on it. You can't take appropriate steps to protect your personal information without first understanding the concept of risk.

In emotional terms, most people think of risk as their chance of experiencing pain. They manage their risk by balancing their chances for pain against their chances for pleasure. Unfortunately, many organizations base their corporate risk management decisions on emotion rather than on sound research. "It wouldn't happen to me" or "I have nothing that anyone would want" are all-too-common beliefs floating around the business world, with no solid foundation. This head-in-the-sand attitude increases the risk to companies of all sizes, leaving them vulnerable to major losses.

The other extreme is to overreact—to spend money on trendy countermeasures that are not appropriate and deplete resources without reducing risk at a reasonable cost. It doesn't make sense to spend more money and effort protecting information than the information is actually worth.

The post–September 11 hysteria is an example of inappropriate risk management. People ran out and bought gas masks. Somebody even bought enough plastic sheets and duct tape to seal his entire house. The news media rushed to the middle of nowhere to feature this idiot. So what's wrong with these countermeasures?

Gas masks provide protection against gas attacks. They are basically useless against most real chemical and all biological attacks. You actually need a whole suit for that. Also, gas attacks are a significant threat only in closed spaces, yet most people who bought gas masks didn't take them along to their visits to such places; most kept their masks at home. So gas masks sound good but do little to save a life even in the most likely attacks.

Plastic sheets and duct tape are a countermeasure to potential biological and chemical attacks. However, those types of attacks are usually limited to a very small area. The likelihood of some terrorist targeting farm country to attack the person who covered his whole house was infinitesimal at best. At the very least, this irrational act attracted attention to the person in the first place, which put him at greater risk. More likely, he would suffocate himself and his family because no fresh air could come into his house.

Fortunately, you can disregard the hype and madness and use a scientific way to define your personal and organizational specific level of risk. This formula, called the *risk equation*, has been used by statisticians to establish insurance-related risks for decades. The risk equation (shown in Figure 2.1) includes four essential components: value, threat, vulnerability, and the countermeasures.

$$\text{Risk} = \left(\frac{\text{Threat} \times \text{Vulnerability}}{\text{Countermeasures}} \right) \times \text{Value}$$

Figure 2.1 The risk equation

- **Value.** This refers to the worth of your information or other assets, both monetary and otherwise. The value of your information must temper the funding and allocation of your espionage countermeasures. You don't want to spend more money, time, and effort protecting your information and other resources than it would cost you to lose them. For example, you would not normally pay $3,000 to install a car alarm on a $2,000 vehicle. However, multibillion-dollar corporations cannot protect billions of dollars' worth of information with less than a million-dollar security budget (although many firms have tried). Chapter 3 discusses how to determine the value of information.

- **Threat.** Simply put, threat refers to the people, organizations, and other entities who might be after your valuable resources. A threat can be intentional or inadvertent, manufactured or naturally occurring. Although companies do not always want to acknowledge it, there is always a threat in one form or another. Chapter 4 describes how to identify threats.

- **Vulnerability.** This refers to your organization's weaknesses or what allows a threat to exploit you. If you have no vulnerabilities, a threat cannot exploit you, so you have no risk. Computers connected to the Internet, unlocked offices, employee ignorance, spotty security procedures, and putting a building in a flood zone are examples of vulnerabilities. Vulnerabilities can never be wholly removed from an organization, but they can be managed with countermeasures. Chapter 5 examines vulnerabilities.

- **Countermeasures.** These are the steps, procedures, and devices that you have in place to address your specific vulnerabilities. If your organization establishes a set of countermeasures that fails to address your vulnerabilities, you're just wasting your money. An awareness program that leaves out certain weaknesses in your organization does nothing at all to plug those holes. See Chapter 12 for an extensive list of countermeasures.

All these components affect one another. It is their interaction that determines your risk level. If, for example, you accidentally leave a piece of paper in the public library, the information on that piece of paper is highly *vulnerable*. You have to assume that your competitors are interested in everything about your company, so there is a *threat* that someone wants to find that paper and use it against you. If, however, that paper contains only widely available information—say, the address of your company—it wouldn't have much *value* to a competitor. Consequently, you create *zero risk* to yourself or your business from this piece of paper. Paying a security guard to protect that scrap of paper would not be an appropriate *countermeasure*.

The Risk Assessment Process

Mathematical models of security-related risk can be very useful to a wide range of organizations. Big companies are familiar with creating such models for nearly every business decision, but the process might be new to smaller operations and individuals. Smaller organizations and individuals can step through the process intuitively, without assigning numerical values.

Say that your company is a small manufacturing firm. You have developed a new process for producing a special gear at much less cost than your competitors can produce it. This gear can greatly increase your sales and profits, and it could do the same thing for your competitors if they knew your process. Also say that many other companies produce this particular part. Clearly, you have a threat to your organization that could be called medium to high. Also, you have identified weaknesses in your operation, but not a huge number of them, so your vulnerability is medium. You have high value, medium to high threat, medium vulnerability, and no real countermeasures. Your risk would be medium to high, and you should increase your countermeasures as appropriate, based on the vulnerabilities that are most likely to be exploited.

From the Spy's View

Industrial spies—one of your threats—also use a version of the risk equation. The risks involved in any one information-collection action influence the choice of collection methods. The collection of highly vulnerable information usually involves little risk. The collection of very valuable information, even though it is protected by extreme countermeasures, may warrant a high level of risk.

At one extreme, spies may choose to kidnap an executive to secure extremely valuable and inaccessible information as ransom. Most targets, however, do not warrant such a risky operation or such an enormous expenditure of resources.

Spies also weigh the costs of detection against the possible benefits of securing the information. Unfortunately, most spies face very few effective countermeasures, so *their* risk is often quite low.

What Is a Security Program?

The risk equation actually defines the goal of a security program. Consider that you do not have any control over the assessment of the value, threat, and vulnerability of your organization. In fact, you and your organization want to increase your value as much as possible, which increases your risk as a whole.

No individual security program can completely remove a threat. You cannot get rid of people who want to harm you. You cannot stop an earthquake or a flood from occurring. The United States has still not wiped out terrorism, despite all its resources.

Vulnerabilities will always exist as well. As long as you function in the real world, vulnerabilities can't be avoided.

Your security program is the implementation of countermeasures to address the vulnerabilities. Value justifies the amount of money you spend on the program. Defining the threat helps you determine the vulnerabilities that are most likely to be exploited, as well as the scope of resources the threat may use against you.

Risk Optimization

Only when you understand the real components of risk can you put together an effective and appropriate strategy for protecting your organization and managing your risk. By addressing your vulnerabilities and *optimizing*, rather than *maximizing*, your counterespionage efforts, you can greatly improve your security.

So the goal of your security program is to optimize risk, never minimize it. This is an extremely important distinction. It also sounds counterintuitive to many people.

Think about the meaning of the word *minimize*. The definition is to reduce risk as much as possible, which means that you want to eliminate all possible ways to lose information or other assets. However, a policy that says you need to minimize your risk means that you need to address all risk that you possibly can. That is not realistic from a value perspective.

Consider an automobile. Everyone wants a safe car, but do you want to minimize all risk associated with the car? You can, for example, install more safety equipment. You can be like NASCAR drivers and have a seatbelt that buckles down your entire body. You can install bulletproof glass. You can put a regulator on the car that prevents it from going faster than 30 miles per hour. All that would make the car safer. But would it leave the car usable and affordable to most people? Clearly not.

The Cost/Risk Relationship

Figure 2.2 graphically depicts the cost/risk relationship. The vertical edge of the graph represents cost. The curved line that starts in the bottom-left corner represents the countermeasures you implement for your security program. The curved line that starts at the top left represents your vulnerabilities. The area under the vulnerabilities graphically represents your risk or, more accurately, your potential loss.

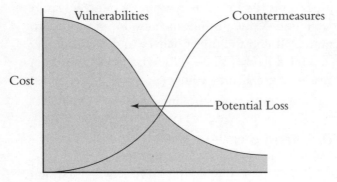

Figure 2.2 The cost/risk relationship

As shown in Figure 2.2, as you start to spend money on countermeasures, risk starts to decrease quickly. Many countermeasures are very inexpensive and have a huge payback. At some point, the vulnerabilities are more difficult and expensive to address, so the payback, or reduction of vulnerabilities, begins to level off.

The graph can extend infinitely to the right. Because you can never have perfect security, the vulnerability line is asymptotic and never hits zero. At the same time, the cost to continue to reduce vulnerabilities, and therefore risk, constantly increases. What is the right balancing point of the cost of countermeasures versus risk? This is risk optimization.

The Balancing Point

Risk optimization is the point at which you appropriately balance the money you spend on your countermeasures, or your security program, with the amount of risk you are willing to accept. Figure 2.3 depicts that point.

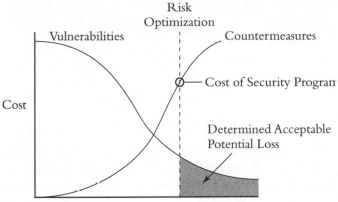

Figure 2.3 Risk optimization

The vulnerability and countermeasure lines are the same as in Figure 2.2. The new vertical line represents a point at which you have balanced the cost you are willing to spend with the amount of risk you are willing to allow to exist in your life or organization.

The point at which the vertical line crosses the countermeasure line is specifically the amount of money being spent. The shaded area below the vulnerability line and to the right of the new vertical line represents the amount of risk you assume by spending that money.

People immediately want to assume that the point of risk optimization is where the countermeasure and vulnerability lines cross in this graph. That is incorrect. The appropriate way to optimize risk is to first determine the amount of risk you are willing to accept. Figure out how big of a shaded portion remains. Again, the value you protect should assist in determining an acceptable level of risk. At that point, you determine the cost for implementing the countermeasures you need to be left with that amount of risk. This should be the decision process.

There is another reason that the point where the countermeasures and vulnerabilities cross is not a good way to choose the amount of risk you are willing to accept. In all but extreme examples, you do not want to invest more money in your countermeasures than the amount of remaining risk. It is not cost effective. Likewise, Figure 2.3 is not a situation that most businesses would implement, for which the money invested in a security program is more than the remaining risk. The optimization point is drawn there only for the sake of clarifying the graph.

Unfortunately, people and companies always seem to first choose how much money they want to spend on their countermeasures (security program), without considering the amount of risk they can accept. The amount of risk you or your company accepts should be a conscious choice.

One question people frequently ask me is, "What percent of my budget should be allocated to security?" I really hate that question, because it demonstrates an ignorance of risk. A security program budget should be determined by examining where your security program needs to be, where you are now, and then how you will get to where you need to be. If you already have a good security program in place, you just need a budget to maintain that level of security. If, however, your security program is lacking, it will cost you more, because you need to spend money to bring your security program up to par. Whatever that costs is how much you must spend to leave only that amount of risk you consciously decide is acceptable.

The concepts here are valid for security programs as a whole, as well as for information security programs.

Risk Optimization in Action

It is extremely difficult to determine an appropriate security budget, even when you are implementing a risk optimization thought process. At a high level, you can look at your potential loss and attempt to determine an appropriate level. For example, if you are in a bank that performs billions of dollars of transactions a day, that is your potential loss. You may then figure out the likelihood of loss, and multiply that by the dollar value of the potential loss. For example, a bank performs $6,000,000,000 of transactions per day. If you assume that there is a .1 percent likelihood of a serious incident, and that there are approximately 250 trading days per year, the overall potential loss is $6,000,000,000 × 250 × .001, or $1,500,000,000 annually. It is therefore not unreasonable for a bank to have a security budget of more than $100,000,000 annually.

At a personal level, consider a home that has $20,000 of belongings. If the owners have insurance with a deductible of $1,000, they have a potential monetary loss of $1,000. It may also be reasonable to include nuisance value to add to potential loss, which you can estimate at $10,000. This means that your potential loss is $11,000. If you assume that the likelihood of experiencing a loss is 3 percent, the estimated loss is $330. Is it therefore logical to add an extra lock on your front door for $50? Or, $300 for a home alarm monitoring service? Clearly there is a psychological component to add to these calculations; however, from a strictly financial perspective, the single lock is a much more reasonable investment than the home monitoring service.

In a more reasonable business scenario, it is best to examine vulnerabilities one at a time. For example, you may decide that losses due to poor passwords cost a large organization more than $10,000,000 per year. You determine that the best countermeasure is an "identity management system." The identity management system costs $1,000,000, and will last three years, for an amortized cost of $333,333 per year. That is a reasonable countermeasure to implement.

Chapter 13 thoroughly discusses implementing risk optimization.

Conclusion

Notice that what I'm talking about in this chapter is *risk management*. Companies functioning in the real world will never be totally risk free. Enterprises must exchange information with employees, suppliers, support organizations, the government, and customers on a daily basis. You can't do business in a vacuum.

Fortunately, you don't need to seal your company in a bubble to keep your information safe. Many highly effective countermeasures are simple, inexpensive, and not particularly disruptive of your day-to-day operations. People are surprised when they learn that the simplest countermeasures often provide the greatest protection.

This does not mean that you should spend little on your security program. The amount you spend must be a conscious decision based on the amount of risk you want to accept.

My editors commented that this chapter seems "light." From a size perspective, that is true. However, from a content perspective, this is the most valuable chapter in the book. When you truly understand the concept of optimizing risk and making a purposeful decision to accept risk, you can actually implement a proactive security program.

3

Death by 1,000 Cuts

Governments act on the perceived priorities of the people. The public willingly accepts millions of slow and lingering deaths from obesity. The public also accepts tens of thousands of deaths a year from automobile accidents. However, a single death resulting from terrorism traumatizes people. Hence, the U.S. government constantly warns us about potentially devastating terrorist attacks, which would affect relatively few people if they were ever realized, but does not tell us about the problems that affect us on a daily basis. These problems, although individually small, add up to more losses than what might result from another September 11-style terrorist attack.

Governments carry this thought process over to the information world. They frequently warn industry and the public about the specter of cyberterrorism, and people, believing the whole concept of terrorism is overblown, become indifferent to any warning about security threats in general. It is this indifference that makes industry and the public overlook the smaller losses that occur daily. Hence, they suffer "death by 1,000 cuts." (Credit for the term and concept goes to Bill Boni.) This analogy means that small losses accumulate to devastating losses. This is true for businesses and individuals.

The implication is that people don't appreciate the true nature of what has value. Nor do they recognize the small but consistent loss of value they experience on a regular basis.

This chapter addresses the nature of value and its implications. Without an understanding of value, businesses and people will not be able to adequately determine their risk and justify the countermeasures that they need to implement.

Types of Value

Determining the value of the information in your business or personal life is an essential first step toward developing an effective security plan. If your information isn't worth anything—monetarily or otherwise—it won't matter how vulnerable you are to attack. No one normally spends time and resources collecting worthless data. Espionage professionals do not define requirements and fund collection efforts if there are no potential rewards for their efforts.

Without perceived value, no basis for analysis and evaluation exists. You could have an open warehouse full of unlocked filing cabinets stuffed with documents, or post your information to your web site with a thousand links to it, and still face no significant risk if the contents of those documents have no value.

Of course, the chances that your information has *no* value to *anyone* are slight. If your business has competitors who want to know what you're up to (and what business doesn't?), then at least some level of risk exists. Often, smaller enterprises face the most risk because their information is valuable to so many competitors. General Motors certainly must protect itself against a few serious competitors, but a small restaurant needs to protect its recipes from thousands of current or would-be restaurateurs.

People don't appreciate the value that they have or represent. Most people think, "I don't have anything a spy or criminal would want." However, consider that your credit card may be worth thousands of dollars. Your computer frequently has your bank account information. An employee ID number or a social security number can allow a spy to steal billions of dollars of information from your company. Your home computer can be used to attack megasites such as eBay.

Individuals and organizations have different ideas about what is valuable. Foreign intelligence services have greatly varying requirements, and almost anything can have value to them. Industrial competitors care only about their businesses' standing and what their competitors intend to do. This would include competitors' manufacturing and strategic plans, production capabilities, and so on. Identity thieves want any small piece of information that can allow them to steal your identity.

As I suggest in Chapter 2, the value of your information must temper the funding and allocation of your espionage countermeasures. You don't want to spend more protecting your information than it would cost you to lose it. But in your calculations, you will want to consider more than just the monetary value of the information you seek to protect. Every business and individual must consider three types of value: monetary, hidden, and adversary/competitor. These values are defined in the following sections.

Monetary Value

When we talk about monetary value, we usually apply the concept primarily to physical assets. Every physical asset has a market value that can be calculated readily in dollars and cents, usually in terms of replacement costs. Cars have resale value. Art has an estimated market value. Houses have an appraised value. Insurance companies thrive on pinpointing these kinds of values and limiting claims to the penny.

However, the monetary value of physical assets to a person or business is much greater than the mere cost of replacing those assets. Unfortunately, this value is often much less obvious and quite difficult to calculate accurately.

For example, when an airline lost my luggage on a flight from Baltimore to Phoenix, the loss cost me more than the price of replacing my suitcase and its contents. There was the cost of telephone calls to the airline to check on the search for my bags; the price of the gasoline to drive to the luggage shop to buy a new suitcase, clothes, and so on; and the cost of notarizing the forms to send to the airline to validate my loss claims. I spent around $1,000 in additional expenses.

When you lose your computer, the cost pertains not only to the value of the computer itself but also of the lost information and the inconvenience. For example, the CEO of Qualcomm had his laptop stolen after making a presentation to a large audience. As reported by trade magazines, the information stored on the computer was potentially worth millions of dollars. As this section later describes, the loss of the proprietary information on the computer could cause a drop in Qualcomm's stock.

Consider the monetary value associated with the destruction of the World Trade Center towers. The businesses located in the towers lost more than their office space. They lost irreplaceable workers. They experienced devastating losses of business, relocation expenses, and computer and other equipment rental expenses. Major transportation lines into New York City were destroyed. Telecommunications capacity was destroyed. Even though the New York Stock Exchange was not directly hit, it closed for five days.

Hidden Value

Information is not a physical asset, which makes the calculation of its monetary value rather difficult. Is its worth found in the time it took to create it? Or is it as valuable as the price someone will pay for it?

People who compile and sell mailing lists to direct marketers know the value of the names and addresses on those lists. It might have cost hundreds of thousands of dollars to compile the lists, but after they are created, they are worth millions in ongoing sales. The value of the laptop on which the list is stored is very low in comparison.

THE VALUE OF YOUR E-MAIL ADDRESS

Spam is a sickening occurrence on the Internet. It costs people and companies billions of dollars in lost productivity to go through it. It costs billions of dollars to buy software and hardware to store and process the extra e-mail generated.

How do these spammers get your e-mail address? Sometimes they just guess your name, but more frequently, you give it to them. They troll Internet web sites for names. If you ever posted a message to an Internet message board or mailing list, it was likely captured. You might have entered a contest and included your e-mail address on the entry form. For the one-in-a-billion chance of winning a small prize, you subjected yourself to a lifetime of spam. Sometimes you give your e-mail address to a legitimate company to do business, and if you don't purposefully click the "opt-out" button, they "share your information with third-party business partners as a service to you."

Many companies carefully calculate the monetary value of their assets without considering their hidden value. You might have a floppy disk on your desk that would cost you about $1 to replace. If, however, that disk contained your company's business plan or the essentials of a key process, how much would it be worth to you then? It might even contain a less-sensitive file that took hundreds of hours to create. What would it cost you to re-create that file? Often, work like this is irreplaceable, which means that the $1 disk is *invaluable*.

The hidden costs of a loss are often the most damaging to an individual or organization. Sadly, the hidden element of value is most frequently hidden from yourself. Although you might not be conscious of hidden value, criminals, spies, competitors, and disgruntled employees often are. They know where and how to hurt you the most. The following sections describe some of the hidden values of information.

Confidentiality

In most cases, *confidentiality* is not considered to be a major value issue. Yet what about information that could hurt you if it fell into the wrong hands? What happens when private information is compromised? When large companies sue each other, they often try to keep the specifics of the suit secret, because such details could hurt them. Some companies don't file a lawsuit at all, or choose not to defend themselves in a lawsuit, because of the possibility that secrets may get out. Inside crimes in many organizations go unreported, because the companies don't want to appear vulnerable or lose the public's trust. In espionage, many spy cases are not prosecuted because of the potential leaking of secrets.

Public or customer confidentiality is of inestimable value to an organization. A study by the University of Maryland revealed that a company's stock prices drop by five percent when information is exposed. Despite the growth of e-commerce, many people don't believe that their credit card numbers and other private information will be safe in cyberspace (never mind that it is probably safer to give out your credit card number online than on a cordless telephone). Distrustful consumers are costing online merchants billions.

In response to many incidents, California passed a law, known as SB 1386, which requires companies to notify people potentially victimized by a hack of a company web site. Wells Fargo was one of the first companies forced to publicly disclose a potential compromise of information under the law. This law actually has far-reaching effects, given that any web site allowing California residents to provide the site with information must comply with the law.

In a more personal context, an article writer in the Winter 2003 edition of *2600: The Hacker Quarterly* (a magazine targeted to stereotypical computer hackers) described how he read his girlfriend's e-mail on her computer and looked at telephone bills in her files to get details of an affair she was having. When people disappear, or commit other crimes, it is standard procedure for police to go through the victim's or perpetrator's computer to get details of his or her life. For example, in the infamous Chandra Levy case, the police found links to directions to places where Levy wanted to go prior to her disappearance.

Integrity

The *integrity* of your information is another hidden value. Whether the data in question has been purposely modified, inadvertently corrupted, or is just plain wrong, the loss of information integrity can cause irreparable damage in many industries and lives.

For example, I stopped in at a small bicycle shop to look for a certain type of bicycle helmet. The clerk checked the store's computer system and informed me that none were in stock. As I headed for the door, I spotted the helmet I was looking for on a shelf. I told the clerk, who apologized and sold me the helmet. I had almost left and spent my money elsewhere. How many other companies have lost business because their computers didn't accurately reflect the state of their inventories? How many companies have promised to deliver products they didn't have?

The Toys " Я " Us chain relies on its ability to track precisely the items in its stores. This is especially true during the period between Thanksgiving and Christmas, when the company sells the entire contents of each store five times over. The company uses a computerized point-of-sale system to manage its inventory. If that system shows that more products have been sold than were actually moved out of a particular store, then the shelves and stockrooms in that store quickly become overstocked; if the system shows that fewer products have been sold than in actuality, then the shelves quickly become bare and sales are lost. Millions of dollars per month in revenues depend on the integrity of the Toys " Я " Us inventory system.

Banks rely on the ability of their computer systems to accurately transfer trillions of dollars a year. More important, the public trusts these systems not to lose any of its money. If that trust were ever lost, the banking industry would collapse, and the banks know it.

On a personal level, people's reliance on information integrity has a huge impact. People rely on the electrical system. Individuals have lost their life savings relying on poor stock information. People have ruined relationships with loved ones because of inaccurate or malicious information from third parties. People rely on the government to provide accurate information. Consider how Richard Jewell's life was ruined when the government portrayed him as the Olympic Park bomber.

Availability

The *availability* of information is another aspect of value. No matter how sensitive, how reliable, or how safe a particular piece of information is, if you can't get to it, it's not only worthless to you, but it's unavailability could cause devastating results. What would happen to a mail-order business if its telephones were to suddenly stop working? What would happen to a manufacturer if its blueprints and schematics were lost? What would happen in a war if missile-targeting information were rendered unavailable?

The SABRE system drives most of the major airline support systems. If the information provided by the SABRE system were suddenly unavailable, we wouldn't be able to make flight reservations or pick up a boarding pass. It could ground planes for all airlines that use the SABRE system, and the airlines and everyone who depended on them would lose millions. If the Toys " Я " Us computer system went down at the wrong time, it would cost the company millions. The shutdown of a robotics system at an automobile factory, even for a short time, would be financially devastating.

Nuisance Value

One of the biggest elements of hidden value is nuisance value. When people experience identity theft, they usually end up not being responsible for the illegal charges. However, the victims spend thousands of dollars and weeks of their time attempting to clear their names.

In some cases, recovery from a loss is impossible. I once received a call from a couple of friends of mine in a panic. They told me that their computer seemed to be hit by a computer virus. The only loss they really cared about was their pictures. They had taken digital photographs during their world travels and stored them on their computer. Hundreds of pictures disappeared and could never be recovered.

INFORMATION RESOURCE MANAGEMENT

Only about a decade ago, companies determined the value of their information systems (IS) department by the estimated monetary value of its computers, peripherals, software, and the salaries of personnel. Typically, IS was considered to be a physical resource that should be managed in the same way as every other physical resource. Accordingly, the IS departments were subordinated to the CFOs.

During the late 1980s, businesses began to understand that the value of the information and the services provided by the computers was greater than the computers themselves. This was especially true in the banking community. The concept of information resource management (IRM) swept the business community.

Most large companies now employ chief information officers (CIOs), who are given strategic responsibility for information resources. A CIO often enjoys status equal to the CFO and sits in on all executive meetings. Companies with CIOs on staff understand that computers represent much more than the monetary value of the hardware, software, and employees. They recognize the tremendous amount of hidden value of information. IRM therefore implies that a security program must recognize this fact when determining value and funding countermeasures.

Even if you completely recover from a loss, there is the tremendous inconvenience of dealing with it. You need to replace what you lost. When the airline lost my luggage, I lost my personal calendar, notes, and clothes. Instead of just claiming my luggage, I had to wait 30 minutes to confirm that my luggage was misplaced. It took me another 20 minutes to file paperwork. I had to buy new clothes. I made regular calls to the airline to see whether my luggage was found. After 14 days, I filed more paperwork to get the airlines to pay me $1,250 for the lost luggage. Although that may seem to be a lot of money, it was nowhere near worth the aggravation.

Businesses lose track of this. Although many businesspeople claim that they are insured from losses, they don't consider the disruption to their day-to-day operations. They look at their business at a high level but don't consider the impact to the individual employees who cannot do their jobs. These small, day-to-day troubles cause the death by 1,000 cuts. For example, a small virus incident costs a typical organization approximately $20,000.

The nuisance value can be more damaging than the monetary value because it affects people's psyche. It prevents them from going on with their daily lives.

Adversary/Competitor Value

Information that might seem totally worthless to your organization can be extremely valuable to a competitor. Broken products tossed out in the dumpster can give a reasonably resourceful competitor an opportunity to reverse-engineer the product, cutting into your market share and profitability. If the competitor is very resourceful, you might find yourself out of business.

Sometimes the value is irrelevant to you but affects the situation around you. When I throw away food and a vagrant picks it out of the trash, I am not affected in any way; I have lost nothing. Some restaurateurs, however, might argue that every meal a vagrant pulls out of a dumpster is one more meal they don't sell, or they might say that the presence of the vagrant scares off customers. Both could result in lost revenues for the restaurant.

I was in a hotel in Amsterdam, and as I checked out, the cashier made a mistake filling out my credit card receipt. She tore it in half, threw it in the trash, and started filling out another receipt. I asked her to pull the receipt out of the trash so that I could shred it. She told me that it was torn in half and couldn't be used. I pointed out to her that the credit card number was still very readable.

How about those credit card applications you get in your mail? You may choose to just throw them out, but criminals realize their value and may go through your trash to find them. Even worse are the unsolicited checks that credit card companies send you. If you simply toss them in the garbage, a criminal can easily take them out and start using them.

Workers inside a company often deal with sensitive information they don't think of as valuable. Items such as price and customer lists fall into this category. All too often, familiarity breeds indifference, and a critical list becomes nothing more than another piece of paper. If people lose that paper, they just print another copy. This casual attitude toward valuable data is commonplace in most businesses, and it inevitably costs companies millions, if not billions, of dollars every year.

Many companies counter this dangerous practice with data classification, in which they classify data by estimating how much damage would result if a competitor were to get hold of it. The U.S. Department of Defense has been doing this for years, classifying information as Confidential, Secret, or Top Secret and criminally prosecuting people who do not treat information appropriately. In the business sector, you can't hold the same threat of criminal prosecution over people for not treating your information appropriately, but you can impress on them the importance of respecting your classification by firing anyone who doesn't.

Calculation of Value

The value of your information is one of the factors in determining how much you should spend on security countermeasures in your organization. You'll want to look at the costs to your company of short-term, long-term, and permanent losses of sensitive data. What you're after is a reasonable balance of appropriate countermeasures and potential losses, or risk optimization, as described in Chapter 2.

Because you need to know what you have before you can decide what it's worth, you start by putting together a list of your information. You'll also want to compile a list of the people who use this information or are affected by it. How many salespeople rely on it? Do any third parties depend on it? Will the loss of this information create a ripple that causes a loss to another company that can sue you? Will the loss of this information cost you the trust of your customers and, ultimately, their business? Will your losses be noticed by Wall Street, causing a drop in the value of your company? Is the information subject to new regulations, such as the Health Insurance Portability and Accountability Act (HIPAA) or the Sarbanes-Oxley Act, whereby mismanagement of the information could result in jail time?

Next, you'll want to answer two important questions:

- Which piece or pieces of information held by your company might have the greatest value to a potential threat?
- How much would you lose if an adversary were to compromise that information?

In an ideal world, you would consider all the information at your company, but in most cases that could be an overwhelming task. Some companies might reasonably base their answers on a worst-case scenario, in which a competitor could put you out of business with the information.

Obviously, the smaller the business, the easier it is to answer these questions. But remember, the harder the question is to answer, the more important it becomes. Take care to consider your answers carefully, taking into account monetary, hidden, and adversary/competitor values.

Many people contend that the entire value of your company is at stake, no matter what information is threatened. In reality, the losses are usually not that dramatic. For example, a descendant of the inventor of Coca-Cola was rumored to be considering selling his family's secret formula. Although the Coca-Cola Company has relied for decades on this secret formula to make its featured product, the company would not crumble if the recipe were to get out. Coca-Cola has name recognition, promotional resources, and other products. The company might lose some market share, which could amount to millions of dollars, but it would survive.

Individuals can calculate value less formally. On most occasions, you need to determine only whether something has value. Then you can decide what constitutes adequate protection. For example, as you go through your mail, you can decide whether your mail has value to anyone. If it does, you can shred the mail instead of tossing it in the trash. Deciding what to do to secure your home can also be as simple. For most people, the value is lost primarily through accidents or random crimes. To protect your home computer, you can take practical and cost-effective security precautions (see Chapters 12 and 13 for recommended security measures).

All companies, no matter what their size, have competitors who want their information. Criminals and spies target any individual who crosses their path. By determining which information they want the most, you help to define the threats you and your organization face. Value is the reason most of those threats exist.

Conclusion

People and companies are woefully ignorant about the concept of value. They focus on the obvious losses and the media-generated hype.

There are many aspects of value to consider that go well beyond the obvious.

The value that you don't consider is what you tend to leave most exposed, and is then most likely to be compromised. These are the little cuts that you experience on a daily basis. If you are not careful, those cuts become infected. Eventually you will bleed to death.

4

Spies and Their Friends

T his was the most interesting chapter to research and the hardest to write. I was honored to interview a wide variety of insiders to achieve a sufficient breadth of background on a very dynamic subject. Some of the people I interviewed include James Woolsey, the former director of both the FBI and CIA; Ken Minihan, the former director of both the NSA and DIA (Defense Intelligence Agency); Ron Dick, the former director of the National Infrastructure Protection Center and who is currently with Computer Sciences Corporation; Victor Sheymov, a former KGB officer; Christopher Painter of the Department of Justice Computer Crime and Intellectual Property Section; and John Nolan of Phoenix Consulting Group. All these people have a deep and well-thought-out perspective on the threats that we face on a regular basis. Each also had a unique perspective concerning the best ways to frame the threat. What follows is my combining of their synergistic but differing paradigms. I also made sure to highlight the frequent threats to individuals.

Terrorists are the top fear on people's minds. These are the people our leaders say we have to worry about. They are ready to strike at any minute and cause us devastating losses, the likes of which we can only imagine. Unless you ignored all other pages of this book to this point, you know that I am being facetious here.

Actually, I believe that people are tired of hearing about terrorists. As a matter of fact, in the proposal phases of this book, the publisher wanted to steer the focus away from terrorism because of the idea that people don't want to read about terrorism anymore and the government cries wolf much too often. I agree that terrorism is an overly hyped issue and should not be obsessed over. However instead of turning their focus to infinitely more likely threats, people ignore threats completely. When this ignorance exists, people are left completely vulnerable.

Although people aren't consciously thinking about the risk formula, they intuitively know that if you don't have anyone after you, you do not have risk and you do not have anything to worry about. Unfortunately, there is always a threat present.

Threats target individuals and organizations. Both groups have threats. A threat can be a drug addict looking for money to score some drugs, a coworker trying to undermine you, or an anonymous teenager with a computer trying to get your social security number. It can be a terrorist organization or an employee upset about being passed over for promotion. It can also be a hurricane or a power outage. Threats exist everywhere and they increase your risk.

The threats can target you directly, or they may target you to get to a third party. Your organization might possess information about another targeted group, which could make you a secondary target. The chances of someone breaking into an online merchant to steal a rubber raft are minimal when you consider that the criminals also have access to thousands of credit card numbers. A smart crook might steal a woman's purse to get the keys to her office building, and then use the access to attack a neighboring organization. Your suppliers might be attacked because of the records they keep about your operation.

Human Errors and Accidents

Although people want to hear about terrorists and hackers, the fact is that the largest losses are from the people in the mirror: In everyday life, people cause themselves the biggest problems. Human error creates more problems than any malicious entity ever will. Poor security awareness leads to what would be considered mighty dumb mistakes after the fact. Losing a disk, leaving a laptop computer at airport security, spilling water on a computer, losing a check book—all are accidents that inevitably affect your well-being.

In the corporate world, the most deadly source of error is within the ranks of a company's own employees. This is the most basic kind of threat your organization is likely to face. People make mistakes, and those mistakes are the most likely things to hurt you. The majority of the errors made by employees are the result of poor training, but some highly trained personnel also screw up from time to time. Highly trained workers have more privileges and responsibilities, so they can do more damage when they err. Computer files are accidentally deleted with frightening regularity in almost every organization. Most of these incidents are minor, because most users have access to only a limited number of files; when a systems administrator clicks the wrong button, however, he or she can delete every file on the computer system.

The Hubble Space Telescope was rendered partially useless, and required tens of millions of dollars to correct the problem, when a mathematical calculation was off by a very small amount. A NASA Martian probe was destroyed, costing tens of millions of dollars and destroying a once-in-a-lifetime opportunity, because one set of development engineers used imperial measurements and another set of engineers used metric measurements. Although space missions represent the extreme, small mathematical and programming errors result in incredible losses. Bookkeeping errors create millions of dollars of problems. Wall Street scandals result from experts making errors and miscalculations. Small programming errors result in major systems crashes taking businesses offline, costing them millions of dollars.

In the physical world, military officers have accidentally left classified materials on a bus. Automobile accidents put people in hospitals, if not kill them, before critical deadlines. People leave their credit cards behind at restaurants. If it can happen, it has happened and will happen again.

Human error and accidents in general cause hundreds of billions of dollars a year. When not appropriately anticipated, incidents can literally destroy a life or a company.

Acts of God

Next to human errors, acts of God are responsible for the greatest financial losses to businesses in this country. You can talk about the greatest crimes in history; however, floods, tornados, earthquakes, lightning strikes, fires—such events cause billions of dollars worth of damage every year, including losses from damaged equipment, lost productivity, and lost and corrupted data. The four hurricanes that hit Florida in 2004 caused more than $15 billion in damage. Lives were lost, businesses destroyed, and major inconveniences arose all over the country. Earthquakes hitting major cities also create billions of dollars of damage in a single incident.

In this case, I am not just talking about the United States. Forty thousand people were killed in a 2003 earthquake near Bam, Iran. Hurricanes in 2004 killed thousands of people in the Caribbean. The economic damages are severe, but they take a back seat when poor preparation causes so much death.

Even something as simple as an overgrown tree can cause tens of billions of dollars of damage. The 2003 power outage that knocked out power to a significant area of the U.S. Northeast and Midwest resulted from overgrown tree branches and caused tens of billions of dollars in losses. Trees also caused the 1996 blackout in nine states of the Pacific Northwest.

Although not an act of God, poor facilities can also wreak unexpected havoc. Damaging power outages can result from bad wiring or from exceeding the power limitations on inadequate electrical systems. I once gave a computer hacking demonstration to a German news crew in a laboratory that was running more than a dozen computers simultaneously. The cameraman plugged his high-wattage power converter into a wall socket and overloaded the electrical system. The entire lab went dark. Critical systems on uninterruptible power supplies (UPS) continued to function, but several usually less important systems that were not on a UPS crashed. Hours of work were lost, and hours were spent on repairs and recovery. The loss in manpower amounted to more than $1,000 for this relatively small incident. These kinds of accidents occur daily throughout the country, and the cost adds up quickly. Fires and floods can pose a significant threat, depending on the region or country in which your business is located.

Flood damage can result from heavy rains and hurricanes as well as from water pipe breaks, sewer backups, and sump pump malfunctions. In some regions, heavy rains can create damaging mudslides. When the loss of equipment from such natural disasters is combined with the loss of information and productivity, the total can easily reach billions of dollars.

Hours and even years of work are lost to acts of God every day. In most cases, these natural disasters are not utterly ruinous, but they are costly in almost every case. Consider carefully the geographic location and physical facility of your organization. Bad weather and bad wiring can represent a significant threat.

When dealing with individuals, the scale may not be as large but the problems can be more devastating. People lose their homes and their lives. When people start to think about protecting themselves, they must first consider the natural events that could damage them more than any criminal ever could.

Common Criminals

I have to admit that I am happy when I read stories about identity theft, credit card fraud, phishing, and the like in the media. I am not happy that these crimes are occurring but that the stories are actually being covered. These stories need to be covered more than terrorism and similar issues, because these crimes hit people on a daily basis.

According to the U.S. government, more than 25 percent of the U.S. population has been hit by identity theft in one form or another. This theft ranges from a criminal's committing crimes under another person's name to misuse of a credit card. Other statistics indicate that the average Internet user is subjected to 17 phishing attempts a day. Make one mistake and you have given criminals everything they need to abuse your good name. The following subsections break out a sampling of these threats and discuss their basic methods. Some of the attacks are elaborated on in Chapter 11. There will clearly be some overlap with the other threat categories I discuss in this chapter; however, I want to identify the specific threats to individuals.

Identity Thieves

Everyone has been or knows someone subjected to identity theft. Frequently it involves fraudulent credit card use. Other times it is as extreme as assuming someone's life. Although strangers typically commit this crime, it frequently also involves relatives who have easy access to information.

All someone needs to steal an identity is a name. From that point, with the right access to the Internet and the knowledge of the right web sites, an identity thief gets all the information he or she needs. To give you an idea of how this works, Phil Cummings, an employee of a company called TCI in New York, was a help desk operator. TCI has access to credit reporting agencies, and Cummings had access to the credit reports of just about everyone in the United States. Over a short period of time, he downloaded the credit reports, with social security Numbers, credit card numbers, and other identification numbers, for 30,000 people. It takes just one person with the right access.

Identity thieves also drive through neighborhoods and go through mailboxes to take mail out before the legal recipients do. The mail has all the sensitive information that they need. Identity thieves also go through people's garbage and find the same mail that they didn't get from the mailboxes. You can find everything from bank statements to credit card offerings in the trash for the taking.

Credit Card Fraudsters

I want to distinguish criminals who focus on credit cards from straight identity thieves, because most credit card fraud lately is conducted through the Internet. These people focus specifically on abusing valid credit cards, as opposed to specifically targeting a person and stealing additional information about that person.

Although some of this fraud occurs through stolen mail, it is increasingly due to theft of massive numbers of credit cards from Internet web sites. In Chapter 10, you read about Alexey Ivanov and how he stole more than 50,000 credit cards in six months. That is actually small compared to cases in which a single computer compromise can result in the theft of hundreds of thousands of credit card numbers. From this point, the criminals either sell the cards in blocks of hundreds or use the cards to order merchandise. You bear the aggravation of clearing it all up. There is little an individual can do to stop the computer hacking, except in your choice of which sites you divulge your credit cards to.

Sometimes you actually hand over your card to your thief. People can buy a small device on the Internet that reads credit card strips. These devices are then attached to a common PDA, such as a Palm Pilot, or even a cell phone. There are many instances in which waiters and department store clerks take a customer's credit card and run it through these criminal readers away from the customer's vision. Given that many people don't know what is actually going on, this can happen right in front of them. At the end of the day, the friendly waiter downloads the information to another device that creates a credit card with the same electronic strip as your own, which can then be used anywhere that requires no additional verification.

Spammers

The average Internet users receive dozens of spam messages a day. On a basic level, the cost is in lost productivity. It takes time to go through all that e-mail. Spam controls also cause valid messages to be deleted and costs companies millions of dollars a year to deal with computing resources to deal with the 70 percent or more of daily e-mail messages a day that is spam.

For individuals, the biggest problem is the fact that most spam is fraudulent. People who are gullible enough to reply to spams perpetuate the problem and are likely to get garbage. Frequently, spam messages serve the sole purpose of stealing credit card numbers.

Lately, though, spam is being combined with more damaging attacks. Spams have spread viruses. They are also used to spread spyware and other malware, which monitors your actions, steals your information, and can sometimes take full control of your computer.

Viruses and Worms

Computer viruses and worms cause billions of dollars a year. These types of computer programs basically spread themselves, causing damage in their wake. Viruses require a person to take some action, such as open an e-mail. Worms spread themselves automatically without requiring any manual actions. These malicious programs have caused banks and airlines to go down. ATM networks have been rendered useless. These are not exaggerations in any way.

Viruses spread primarily through e-mail but can also spread via malicious web sites or legitimate sites commandeered by a hacker, Instant Messaging, or other surreptitious means. It's impossible to downplay the damage these things cause and the methods that can be used to spread them.

Virus writers tend to be unique from hackers. A stereotypical hacker tries to break into systems. Virus writers never have to go near any computer except their own. Although virus writers would seem to have to be creative in that they write their own software, virus-writing kits are available on the Internet that allow even someone with minimal knowledge to create one. Although a dozen or so viruses a year actually make the headlines, thousands of new viruses are released to the Internet every year. As to what the writers' motivation is for wanting to cause as much anonymous damage as possible, the only thing that makes any sense is a desire to feel powerful. They choose to exercise this apparent need through damage.

A growing number of virus writers are writing viruses to create zombies to forward spams or commit further malicious acts for profit. However, most virus writers by far apparently do their deeds to stroke their own egos.

Phishers

As previously stated, people receive phishing attempts everyday. Phishers basically rely on spams blasted to as many people as possible. The messages claim to be from your bank and state that a problem exists with your account. The message contains a link to a web site for you to go to so that you can clear up the problem. The site appears to be legitimate and requests your account information, including your account numbers (sometimes a credit card number) and personally identifiable information, such as mother's maiden name and social security number. The phishers then use this information to steal money from your bank accounts, abuse the credit cards, and sometimes to open new accounts. Although many people wonder who would respond to these messages, statistics indicate a 5 percent response rate to these messages, resulting in $2.4 billion in annual losses.

Spyware and Other Malware

Spyware is surreptitiously installed on your computer and watches your actions. It is frequently used by advertisers to put pop-up ads on your system as you use the Internet. It can also be used to steal passwords and personal information. Sometimes the software is installed by legitimate web sites when you visit the site. Congress enacted laws in October 2004 to make this practice illegal.

Other types of malware sits on your computer and can take control of your computer. After this software has been surreptitiously installed on your computer, it reports back to its master about the success. It then sits there waiting for commands. One report stated that there were 30,000 networks of these zombie computers that can be used by any person with access to them. This access is traded among a variety of groups.

Zombie networks are frequently used in denial-of-service attacks, in which they bombard web sites to take them down to extort money from the victims. The most common use of the zombie networks is to send spam. Your home computer can be used to commit these crimes, and you likely have no idea of it.

Insiders

Although acts of God and human errors cause much more damage than corporate spies ever will, attackers do cost U.S. firms well over $100 billion annually. You might not realize it, but the most deadly of these spies are company insiders, most often your own employees.

People with physical access to your company pose the greatest threat to your security. They have the time and freedom to search people's desks, read private memos, copy documents, and abuse coworker friendships. They know things about your operation because they're on the inside. They typically stick to low-risk espionage activities, and if they're smart, careful, and patient, they're rarely caught.

Most important, these people know where and how to hurt you. They know your prized secrets, they know your competitors, and they usually know how to hide their actions. Insiders constitute a formidable threat that is much too common. What is perhaps most damaging about insider espionage is that it goes unnoticed.

Although insiders do things for their own reasons, they are frequently the pawns, wittingly or unwittingly, of the other parties you will read about in sections that follow. Their access as a whole makes them valuable to many.

Employees

Current and former employees can pose the most destructive threats you will ever face. One of the things that makes them so dangerous is that they're often very difficult to spot. Two documents were pointed out to me by an observant coworker when I was working at NSA that illustrate exactly how difficult detection can be. Both documents described a worker as follows:

- Shows an interest in what coworkers are doing
- Always volunteers for extra duties and assignments
- Works late hours
- Rarely takes vacations

One of the documents, written by the personnel office, was giving advice on how to get promoted at NSA; the other, written by the office of security, was listing the signs that a coworker might be a spy. In almost all cases, a spy appears to be one of your hardest workers.

Employees turn on their employers for many reasons. They do it for money, for love, to get even for perceived wrongs, and even because of political ideologies. Although the MICE concept I discuss in Chapter 1 applies to how to identify and recruit a spy, it also implies why a person would commit malicious acts in general. They can be cool, sophisticated pros or petty criminals.

When greed is the motive, companies that perform large volumes of automated electronic funds transfers are frequent targets of employee theft. The general public would be surprised at the number of companies that perform these kinds of transactions. Retail store chains, direct marketers, large wholesalers, insurance companies, and investment firms, among others, regularly send millions of dollars through computers around the world. Embezzlers create false accounts to move money to private accounts. This occurs in the Pentagon, large companies, and mom-and-pop shops. Although diligent auditors and computer administrators may discover the problem, sometimes the only indication is when a company goes bankrupt.

There are many cases in which a mole is planted inside a company by a competitor. Sometimes this is done for national security purposes and the mole is a member of a foreign intelligence agency. Other times the mole is serving a domestic competitor. These cases are generally not intentional. However, when companies see that their competitor has job openings, they sometimes get someone to apply for a position. That person is tasked with trying to find out as much information as possible during the interview process. On some occasions, a person is actually offered the position, and in many cases, the current employer offered to pay the departing employee to continue to provide information from the new company.

Throughout the country, there are hundreds of cases a year, which never make the headlines, involving insiders trying to steal money and information from their employers. The following sections describe the various types of employees who may be a threat to your organization.

Disgruntled Employees

Many employees feel that they deserve more recognition and respect than their employers show them. The disgruntled employee is almost a cliché in this country, but a frustrated worker can pose a real threat to your organization. It's usually not about money for these folks—what they want is to feel important, and that makes them dangerous.

Disgruntled employees are easily manipulated by outsiders and are considered an important resource among professional spies. Such employees commit industrial espionage for the specific purpose of stroking their own egos. They seek approval and respect, and their handlers know how to give it to them. A good spymaster will tell disgruntled workers that people as important and smart as they are can get their hands on anything in the company. To prove their worth, these employees will often go to extreme lengths, compromising some of the company's most valuable information.

In many cases, employees with an ax to grind just want to hurt their employers. They're mad at the company for a variety of reasons: they're not getting paid enough; they find working conditions to be unsatisfactory; they don't get along with coworkers; or they don't like the boss. What they want is revenge. They plan their attacks meticulously and focus on how best to hurt their employers. In some cases, their revenge involves selling information to a competitor; more commonly, it manifests as acts of sabotage.

There's a popular story in computer security circles that serves as a good example of the potential damage a disgruntled employee can do. It goes like this: A computer programmer, anticipating that he will be leaving his job under unfriendly circumstances, modifies a computer program that does the company payroll. When the program runs, it checks to see whether the programmer is on the payroll. If he's not, it deletes all employee records.

According to John Nolan of the Phoenix Group, who typically investigates these types of incidents, about 2 percent of employees in any organization are willing and witting to commit malicious acts. They do what they know how to do best to hurt your organization.

Thrill Seekers

Sometimes what dissatisfied insiders crave is excitement. They commit espionage for the thrill of it, to break the routine of their boring lives. The prospect of secret meetings, dead drops, and the like captivates these wannabe James Bonds. Whenever I give talks about the espionage simulations I do, many attendees volunteer to work with me for free. After my articles about the work are published, I receive résumés and calls about possible job openings. This type of work intrigues most people, but few are willing to cross the line into genuine espionage activities. It's those few whom you have to worry about.

Departing Workers

Another version of this threat is employees who are leaving the company. These folks are sometimes tempted to curry favor with their new employers by snatching sensitive information on their way out. They've either already secured a position or they anticipate securing one, and they want to demonstrate their worth and knowledge to the new boss. Because they are trusted insiders, they can provide your competitor with a variety of sensitive trade secrets.

Sometimes the employees believe that they created the work and that they're entitled to it. They have no comprehension of the concept of work for hire. Former Secretary of the Treasury, Paul O'Neill, created a political controversy when he used documents that he took from his government position and used them to write a book. There were significant questions as to whether the documents were classified and if he should have taken them with him in the first place.

Former Employees

Former employees can pose a serious threat to your organization. They can seek to hurt you out of vindictiveness, to get a payoff, or to impress a new boss. They can hurt you unintentionally, simply because they know what they know. Although they no longer have direct access to your sensitive information, they know your layout, your procedures, your habits, and your weaknesses. Chances are, they know your operation better than many of your current employees do. Perhaps most important, they know your competitors, which means they know who would value your information enough to pay them for it.

Much of the damage caused by former employees is indirect and, from an espionage standpoint, unintentional. Good salespeople, for example, want to offer the lowest prices and the best products. If they know the prices of their former employer's products, it is inconceivable that they would fail to use that knowledge to undercut the competition and land a new client. They're not out to hurt their former employers; they just want to do a good job and make a sale.

This type of casual espionage is all too common, and companies have come to expect it. With the current state of employee turnover in this country, most competing firms have employees from many, if not all, of their competitors.

Some former employees, however, maintain contact with their old workplaces solely for the purpose of gathering information. In many cases they abuse old friendships with former coworkers. As the case in Chapter 9 demonstrates, Afshin Bavand, a laid-off Ericsson employee, used his former coworkers to provide him information at will. The damage these unscrupulous people can do to your organization is considerable.

On-Site Nonemployees

Nowadays, just about every organization employs at least a few temporary workers and consultants. In some organizations, these temps make up more than 30 percent of the staff. The growth of corporate outsourcing practices has increased the number of on-site nonemployees with physical access to many organizations.

Large companies typically outsource their security and janitorial services. They don't want to invest their resources in the training and maintenance of this group of specialized workers, so they hire others to do it. It's a good business move, but it's very bad for security.

Think about it: Janitors and security guards do the bulk of their work when everyone else has left the facilities. They have wide access and virtually free reign, and nobody questions their presence in even the most sensitive parts of the building *(somebody* has to scrub the floor in the prototype development lab). Even a 10-year-old-article, from the Winter 1994 edition of *2600: The Hacker Quarterly* (a magazine for the stereotypic hackers), gives detailed advice on getting a job as a janitor for the purpose of gaining physical access to a targeted firm. If the hackers knew this that far back, you can bet that much more organized threats know it, too.

Companies also outsource many white-collar positions. Temporary employment services provide clerical workers for short-term support. Technical vendors provide on-site support. Depending upon their assignments, these nonemployees could have access to the most valuable information in a company.

Outsourcing / Offshoring

Outsourcing and offshoring have become a major political controversy. Although many people lament the loss of jobs, the situation also causes a major loss of intellectual property. Outsourcing means that you take your computer operations, manufacturing, or other jobs and give it to another company to perform, to save money. Although some outsourcing still lets work be performed in the same country, outsourcing frequently means giving work to companies in other countries where labor is significantly cheaper. Offshoring means that a company opens or buys a company in another country for work to be performed there. Offshoring means that the company actually owns the entity performing the work in the other country.

Although the countries receiving the work do include what is normally considered modern countries such as Ireland, offshoring typically involves countries such as India and China. As you will read, these are countries where a completely different mindset from that of the United States exists with regard to the treatment and protection of intellectual property. This intellectual property can easily include personal data such as credit card numbers.

As you will see later in this chapter, the countries typically involved in outsourcing and offshoring are among the most nefarious violators of intellectual property rights. Many companies actually balance out the reduced operating costs with the potential loss of intellectual property.

Malignant Threats versus Malevolent Threats

Malignant threats are those without a malicious intent. Such threats happen via accidents or errors. They can be planned for and mitigated as appropriate. Malevolent threats are caused by malicious and intended actions. They can also be planned for and mitigated.

The problem, though, is that the mitigation for the malignant threats can actually enable the malevolent threats, and vice versa. This creates major planning considerations, and some very serious studies of risks and complications must be made before any decisions are made.

One of the most currently pressing examples is the transportation of hazardous materials. Currently, there are hazard signs on railcars and trucks that transport chemicals. The hazard signs have code numbers that tell the type of material in the vehicle. The reason is that if there is ever an accident involving the vehicle, first responders need to know immediately how to handle the materials and whether extra precautions need to be taken. For example, a problem with a railcar containing chlorine should cause an evacuation of the surrounding area. Unfortunately, this information also enables terrorist attacks. Terrorists can use the hazard signs to know which railcars to attack.

Firefighters are lobbying to maintain the use of the hazard signs, whereas the Department of Homeland Security wants the signs removed because of the terrorist implications. An example given is that terrorists can wait along railways in Washington, D.C., and wait for a railcar carrying hazardous materials to go by and then blow it up, potentially causing thousands of deaths. First responders reply that railcars derail very frequently and they need to know the contents of a chemical car immediately. There is no right answer in this case.

General Threat Categories

Up to this point, I have addressed the most common threats to individuals and businesses. The previously described threats are the most direct ones and need to be addressed by everyone and every organization. Although the chapter goes on to discuss other threats and the motives and methods involved, I believe that it is important, given the current environment of fear, to put things in perspective.

Information Warriors

Information warriors are national entities that take actions to strategically forward the needs of their countries. I should clarify that I do not just mean computer warriors but all intelligence entities trying to strategically target information in all its forms. These people are extremely good at what they do. As a matter of fact, their skills are deep and refined to the point where they are without equal.

These groups accomplish strategic goals. The have well-defined requirements and take actions to gain a long-term strategic advantage. They take their time to make plans and commit their actions.

Over the long term, what these entities do is prepare for war. They infiltrate foreign infrastructures and plan to take control of the systems or bring them down at their own discretion. This strategy involves the infiltration of both cyber and physical infrastructures. Information warriors are responsible for preparing the battle space to win a war, before it begins. To be effective, they cannot be detected.

Computer hacking has become a primary method for many countries to infiltrate infrastructures. It allows even small countries to commit asymmetric warfare. In traditional warfare, the larger, stronger military wins. The goal of asymmetric warfare is to commit acts without regard to military strength. By 2000, more than 100 countries were attempting to put together an information-warfare capability. In October 2004, South Korean officials announced that North Korea put 500 people through a five-year training program to perform computer-based warfare. This announcement came in conjunction with the disclosure that a coordinated attack against sensitive South Korean computer systems had occurred. North Korea is a relative newcomer to the field.

National Intelligence Collectors

Although these people may work in conjunction with the information warriors, they have a different motivation. They are also part of a national intelligence or military entity. Frequently, the people performing the intelligence work go back and forth into the information-warfare community, given the similar skill sets required.

Whereas the information warfare experts stop at undermining an infrastructure, intelligence collectors continue to perform secondary attacks to collect information or other actions. It is true that the information warriors need to collect information to perform their actions; however, the task is passed to the collectors to gather the information.

As previously stated, more than 100 countries are developing a capability in this field. Although most people in the United States believe that these efforts target national security information, in fact they primarily target corporations and individuals. The motivations range from software piracy to industrial espionage. Their motivation is to help their economy, not their military capability. According to Gene Spafford, the executive director of the Center for Education and Research in Information Assurance and Security at Purdue University, besides North Korea the more active countries in these efforts include China, India, Brazil, South Korea, and Cuba. As is discussed later in this chapter, we must also include Russia, France, Germany, and Israel on this list.

Other Collectors

Nations are not the only entities collecting intelligence. The initial premise of this book is that you are surrounded by people collecting information for their own purposes. This discussion, though, is limited to organized entities. Companies have created their own collection programs. Although large companies all around the world have in-house programs, non-U.S. companies tend to make business intelligence a major corporate priority.

These companies assign high priority to knowing what competitors are up to, and frequently with regard to large contracts. For example, although people may not perceive the cement business as exciting, it is highly competitive. The world doesn't have many cement companies, and large projects needing cement have few sources from which to obtain it. Think about how much cement is needed for a dam or a large building. These contracts are easily worth tens of millions of dollars, and the deciding factor is usually price. What would you expect cement companies to do?

Although there are many in-house capabilities, many third-party firms specialize in business intelligence. Typically these firms are staffed by former intelligence professionals, who now turn their years of training and decades of experience to commercial targets on behalf of the highest bidder.

Terrorists

Terrorism is the top concern of everyone; however, people do not understand terrorism beyond the fear it creates. From a strategic point of view, a terrorist is a person who is attempting to achieve political goals through the use of fear, uncertainty, or doubt. Their primary goal is not to cause damage but the emotional effects of even implied damage. It is essentially another form of asymmetric warfare. There is some overlap between this section of the book and the introduction, but more detail is warranted.

Using Al-Qaeda as an example, although it is constantly stated that they commit acts of terror just because they hate freedom, they actually have stated some clear political goals. They want the death of Israel, and they want the United States and its allies out of the Middle East. They want the entire region to turn to Muslim fundamentalism. They use terrorism to intimidate political leaders around the world by creating fear and outcries within the local populations. The Al-Qaeda goals are clearly not realistic; however, they do have successes. For example, the Madrid subway bombings possibly affected the Spanish election, and the country pulled its troops out of Iraq.

To a terrorist, a political leader's warning people about a possible attack and frightening their population is as good as an actual attack. As long as they get people to change the way they do things, they are successful. Any creation of fear is a success. The images of people running out to buy plastic sheets and duct tape encourage them to continue their actions.

An important aspect to consider is that terrorists want their attacks to be visual and imply death. They want people to perceive that something they do on a regular basis can cause death. Just mentioning Pan Am 103 brings up images of the side of a 747 lying on a field. Saying "anthrax" scares people away from checking their mail. Images of the World Trade Center collapsing are burned into people's minds for the rest of their lives.

There are two notable aspects of terrorism and its involvement with espionage tactics. First is clearly the commission of the attack. Terrorists want to execute their attacks. They need to ensure that they act on contingencies and properly modify tactics based on real-time intelligence. However, the second aspect is the most important: the planning of the attack. Terrorists use a variety of intelligence methods to collect information about their targets. They also create sophisticated methods for sharing and distributing information.

For this reason, I doubt that terrorists truly want to significantly damage the Internet. I believe that terrorists used the Internet to plan and execute the September 11 attack. They needed to choose airplanes that would be fully loaded with fuel, that is, flying across the continent. They also preferred airplanes with relatively few people on board to make controlling the passengers easier. Although more than 200 people were on board the four hijacked planes, those planes could have held approximately 800 people in total. I doubt that it is a coincidence that the terrorists chose these four planes to hijack.

WHY CYBERTERRORISM IS NOT EFFECTIVE

After the September 11 attacks, we were constantly warned that computer-based attacks would be next. They never came, and even if they did, they would not be effective. The reason is that computer attacks do not create the fear that terrorists want. The anthrax attacks are a great example of an incredibly effective terrorist attack. Although I do not want to minimize even a single death, the fact is that only five people died from anthrax over a 10-week period. More people die in a day from being overweight. On top of that, anthrax is curable when properly diagnosed. The few attacks sent people scrambling to find rubber gloves and being generally afraid to check their mail, which is a daily part of our lives.

On the other hand, a computer attack does not create that imminent fear of death. People expect their computers to crash. We already have incidents that take down pieces of the air traffic control system, telephone networks, and banks. We have hospital information systems crashing. Large portions of the United States already lose power due to nonmalicious computer failures. We expect these things and are not put into mortal fear by their occurrences.

The theoretical possibility exists that a computer attack can cause devastating damage, for example by causing a nuclear reactor to go critical or overloading a power transformer. However, Dorothy Denning, who is one of the most highly regarded information warfare experts in the world, once told me, "The stars have to align for something devastating to happen."

What I hear many government officials express fear about with regard to a cyber attack is a cyber attack being combined with a physical attack. The example scenario given is, "What would have happened if the terrorists would have taken down the emergency communications system in addition to attacking the World Trade Center?" That would certainly add to the confusion and hamper the response. It would clearly, however, be a secondary attack to amplify the effects of the primary attack.

Additionally, the terrorists used computer networks to fund the operation. The leaders communicated with each other through the Internet. Today, terrorists use the Internet to scout new targets and identify our infrastructure. In his book *Black Ice*, Dan Verton identifies a wide variety of critical infrastructure specifications that sit freely on the Internet for the taking by any malicious party.

We can also expect that terrorist sleepers, such as the September 11 hijackers, to get jobs inside potential targets to better scope them out. Terrorists do want to make spectacular attacks; however, they have proven themselves to be extremely patient in their methods.

Although terrorists want their plans to go completely undetected, they want their attacks to be noticed by as many people as possible. It should be well noted, though, that compared to all the other threats, terrorists affect few people.

Organized Crime

Dozens of major organized crime rings are thriving throughout the world today. These criminal organizations include the traditional Italian Mafia, the new Eastern Bloc mafias, and drug cartels. There is even a growing criminal phenomenon known as cyber-cartels. All these kinds of criminal organizations are exclusively profit-driven.

For the most part, organized crime presents a relatively minor direct threat to most individuals and companies. However, there have been widespread reports of the Eastern Bloc mafias acquiring the expertise of former Soviet Union operatives. Some of these operatives have probably gone to work for the more established organized crime rings, providing their employers with information about companies entering markets controlled by the criminal organization. These companies want to know what the new company could possibly provide them, and how to optimize their extortion demands. This type of information is worth billions to these crime rings, and they are willing to go to extreme measures to get what they want. When they learn about a company's strategic goals, they know what the company is after, and they use the information to leverage a deal in their favor.

Some crime rings contract their intelligence capabilities to other organizations. A business might hire a criminal group to steal information from a competitor, especially if it doesn't want its government to know or its government has refused to help.

In some instances, a criminal organization might want to expand
into a new area and use some espionage techniques to gather information about potential "customers," rivals, and law enforcement.

Organized crime rings are also developing their own computer-
hacking capabilities. Although they usually hire the computer experts
they need, they have also reportedly resorted to intimidating people
into cooperating. Through underground sources, I have learned of at
least one incident in which a hacker received an "offer he couldn't
refuse." (I should point out that he was apparently paid well for his
efforts and probably did more work for them after his fears of bodily
harm were put to rest.) Criminal organizations also have their own
experts with outstanding capabilities. Admiral William Studeman, former Deputy Director of the Central Intelligence Agency, stated that the
drug cartels have the technical capability to wage a very effective information war against the United States. They use this capability to learn
of and undermine counternarcotics efforts around the world, including
attempts to learn the identity of informants and undercover agents.

The initial purpose of computer hacking in many criminal organizations was to facilitate money laundering. They sought the help of
computer experts to enable them to make large financial transactions
that went relatively unnoticed. The drug cartels and other organized
crime rings then developed the capability to perform this money laundering themselves. Eventually, the Mafia-type organizations realized
that not only could they launder their own illegally gotten gain but
could steal it as well. Today, criminal organizations steal this money
from banks throughout the world.

In the late 1990s, General Marsh, the then-chairman of the President's Commission on Critical Infrastructure Protection, casually stated
that banks lose billions of dollars a year to fraudulent transactions, and
the loss is accepted as a cost of doing business. Acknowledged electronic bank thefts have occurred in all major countries, including
China and Russia. Headlines from the London *Sunday Times* decried
that major British banks paid large sums of money to hackers not to
take down their systems. Established organized crime gangs know that
stealing money from a bank is easy. The hard part is laundering it.

Misrouted transactions are electronic transactions made against customers' accounts supposedly without their knowledge or permission.
When a victimized customer proves that he or she did not authorize
the transaction, the targeted bank reimburses the account and tries to
recover the money from the place to which it was sent. If the receiving

bank claims that the money is no longer available, the bank usually considers the money lost due to a misrouted transaction. The investigation stops because an investigation might prove that the money had been stolen, which would require the bank to report the theft, causing what would be a flood of very negative publicity. Banks consider misrouted transactions a part of the business process and do not have to report them. As one banking official told me, "What we sell is trust. If we lose people's trust, we are out of business." This fear among bankers keeps organized crime operating in the black.

Cyber cartels are a new type of organized crime ring. These organizations don't necessarily have a physical presence but are basically organized groups of hackers with purely a profit motive. They target banks and e-commerce sites to find vulnerabilities. These people start off as stereotypic hackers, and then form groups. Someone in the group comes up with the concept of formally organizing and then focusing on criminal activities. Some of these groups focus on credit card fraud by stealing credit cards from web sites and then ordering merchandise to resell.

Other cyber cartels focus on extortion. One form of extortion is as described previously, whereby a group breaks into a bank or other company and leaves evidence that the group has full control of the system and can cause great damage. It then demands a payoff to tell the bank how to fix the system and to leave the group alone. In one case, one of these cyber cartels threatened to shut off the support systems of an Antarctica research center. Sometimes the criminals demand a "protection fee" as well.

Another form the attacks take is using a zombie network to perform a denial-of-service attack against the site. The criminals launch a denial-of-service attack and then inform the victim that they will do it again unless they are paid off. This is especially effective against Internet gambling sites, near the time of large sporting events. The gambling sites tend to pay quickly because they don't want to risk losing large bets around events such as the Super Bowl.

Sometimes the criminals steal credit cards from a web site and then tell the victim that all the victim's clients will be informed of the break-ins, and the credit cards will be posted on the Internet. If the criminals are not paid off, they go through with the actions. Depending on the trustworthiness of the criminals, which is an ironic consideration, they may still post the information on the Internet even after being paid.

The case study in Chapter 10 details the workings of a cyber cartel.

Although some of these gangs may have some relationship with a traditional organized crime gang, it is not necessary. The only requirements are some organization and the knowledge to accept payments. The hacking skills required are minimal. As published by MSNBC.com, one criminal claims that 75 percent of e-commerce sites and banks can be broken into within two hours. Clearly, most of the publicized crimes of this type originate in the former Eastern Bloc countries. That is not to say that no cyber cartels come from other countries. However, the social and economic climate facilitates this type of activity, as does the public exposure of the crimes without fear of being caught.

Although individuals are not generally targeted by organized crime, we all pay the price of the slow but steady siphoning of money that these rings commit. Unfortunately, the growth of the cyber cartels and the focus on credit card theft means that millions of people a year are directly affected by the crimes.

Hackers

I used to tell people that hackers were only a nuisance in the grand scheme of computer-related crimes. Unfortunately, they have since become a major enabler and source of tremendous damage. Don't get me wrong, though: Hackers, at least the stereotype perceived to be hackers by the general public, have minimal computer expertise. They are not the geniuses that the media portrays them to be. As I have said many times to this point, they are almost always successful because of the naïveté of their victims, and not because of the talent on their part.

The term *hacker* was originally used to refer to the computer science students at the Massachusetts Institute of Technology (MIT) who had little hardware and software documentation and were forced to hack their way through primitive computer systems to circumvent problems. When personal computers began to proliferate during the 1980s, a new breed of hacker emerged. These new hackers used their PCs to connect to corporate and university mainframe computers through modems over telephone lines without permission, which was and is illegal. However, for young people who wanted to learn about computers, there were few other resources in those pre-Internet days.

Connecting to different computers around the world by telephone was an expensive proposition (no local calls to an Internet service provider in those days), and the new criminal hackers were compelled to hack the phone system, which is actually the world's largest computer network. Combining the words *phone* and *hack*, they coined the term *phreakers* to describe their activities.

Although many computer professionals believe otherwise, I doubt that the intentions of these early hackers were criminal. They wanted to learn about computers, and this kind of experimentation was one of the few ways they could do it, even though it was criminal. There was really no point of reference for these hackers. Their parents never told them that hacking was wrong; they didn't even understand what it was. The movie *War Games* glorified the hacker community, attracting many teenagers. An underground ethic developed, which painted hackers as freedom fighters protecting the public's right to information access, as well as protecting individuals from the establishment. This sure sounds good to a teenager.

Many people don't realize this, but there are major computer networks that have better capability than the Internet. These networks currently enable much of the Internet and were put together in the 1980s to connect businesses with each other. These businesses include the world's largest banks. Hackers were able to compromise many of these systems at will. Again, most hackers were not interested in money and just used the exercise as a means to learn and gather information. It was also a major ego boost to have such power.

By the end of the 1980s, many of the first hackers had grown up and were now selling information and services. Members of one of the most notorious hacker groups, the Masters of Deception, have been accused of modifying and selling credit reports, selling wiretaps to private investigators, and stealing phone services, among other crimes. Some of their members have pleaded guilty to several of these charges, and one of them admitted his guilt on "60 Minutes." Hackers began referring to hackers that break into computer systems specifically for criminal purposes as *crackers*.

Whether a person is called a hacker, a phreaker, or a cracker, his or her (mostly his) actions are considered criminal when they involve unauthorized use of a computer. The folks from MIT are offended by the use of the word *hacker* to describe anyone who illegally uses a computer. The teenagers are offended when people lump crackers in with hackers. With all due respect to the MIT group, I use the term *hacker* to identify anyone who breaks into a computer illegally. The supposed difference between a cracker and a hacker is only one of intention; the two groups are separated only by a few key strokes. Organizations must treat every intrusion as though it were committed with criminal intent.

HOW TO HACK A COMPUTER

There are really just two fundamental ways to break into a computer and they require very little skill. Some people may contend that there are thousands of different exploitations and tactics a hacker can use. However, my two categories encompass all of them and take the supposed mystique out of the whole process.

The first way to break into a computer is to take advantage of vulnerabilities built into the system. All computers are controlled by software, a.k.a. computer programs. Although a computer generally has hardware and software, vulnerabilities found in hardware are extremely rare and even those are from the "firmware," which is basically software burned into the hardware.

An operating system, such as Windows or UNIX, is actually a large set of individual computer programs. A database system is another set of computer programs. So are web browsers and servers. Any application you buy or download is software.

As most people know, all computer programs have bugs. The bugs can cause the computer to crash. They can screw up printing. We have all experienced some type of bug. Some bugs cause information leakage or elevated privileges. These bugs are security vulnerabilities. All you have to do is figure out how to consistently trigger the bug and you have created a way to break into the computer. These vulnerabilities are specific to the software; however, if software is very commonly used, such as the Windows operating system, then you know how to break into a lot of computers.

The second way to break into a computer is by taking advantage of how an otherwise secure computer is configured and maintained by an administrator or user. Even assuming that all the software on your computer is perfect, someone can create a vulnerability in the system. For example, you can have an account with no password or an easily guessed password. You can turn off all file and directory permissions. You can accidentally place files where anyone can read them. There are many more technical methods as well.

Again, all you have to do is know the type of computer you are trying to break into and you can determine dozens of vulnerabilities likely to exist on the computer. The trick then seems to be how do you find out what type of computer you are dealing with? That is actually easy to accomplish as well. All you have to do is find a vulnerability scanning tool on the Internet. The tools can scan random computers or specific computers per your direction. The scanner should report back with the type of computer it hits as well as the vulnerabilities that exist.

From that point, all you have to do is find the tools that exploit that particular vulnerability on the Internet. With a good Google search, that should take you about a minute. The software vulnerabilities typically require a computer program that you download. Some configuration errors can be exploited with a computer program; others require manually entered commands. Those commands are, again, widely available on the Internet.

Some of the tools available don't even require any original thought on the part of the hacker. The tools scan ranges of computers and automatically execute the attacks, giving you control of the computers.

Yes, there are many different operating systems. There are many different vulnerabilities to exploit. However, all those vulnerabilities fit within one of the two categories I describe. To exploit those vulnerabilities, you merely need to know how to find the right information on the Internet. You really don't need to know anything about the computers you are breaking into. Just as you don't know the nitty-gritty of how your computer works, so you don't need to know the nitty-gritty of how the hack works.

For those interested in statistics, the Computer Emergency Response Team reported that of the two different ways to hack a computer, 70 percent of successful attacks exploit configuration errors. Also, all studies indicate that 97 percent or more of all attacks were due to widely known and preventable vulnerabilities.

As the Internet began taking shape in the early 1990s, the number of hackers wandering around in cyberspace began to increase. However, the skill and knowledge required to be a hacker decreased sharply. The original hackers had to develop their own techniques for exploiting computers; hackers today have only to look on the Internet to find a computer program that exploits the computer for them. They don't even have to know how the program works to successfully break into hundreds of computers. The first hackers wanted to learn about computer systems; the new hackers just want to break into systems without the challenge of learning about them.

Hackers exploit computers through vulnerabilities that are unknowingly built into or enabled by the operating systems or other programs running on the machines. The sidebar "How to Hack a Computer" details this situation. There are very few people walking around today capable of finding new vulnerabilities. Those few who can are the true computer geniuses (see Figure 4.1). There are probably fewer than 10,000 of them in the world. These geniuses are the ones who tell other hackers about the vulnerabilities. There are perhaps 100,000 hackers who can take that knowledge and develop a tool to exploit it. When that tool is posted on the Internet for the general hacker community, it becomes available to everyone.

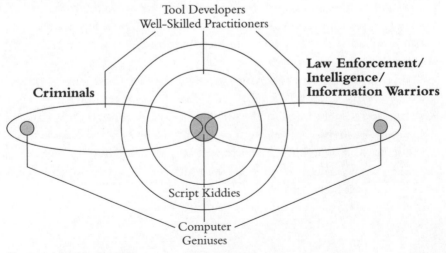

Figure 4.1 Hacker community

There are possibly up to 1,000,000 hackers around the world who fall into the "clueless" ranks, also known as *script kiddies*. These people would be lost without the knowledge and the tools, a.k.a. scripts, produced by their more competent brethren. As a matter of fact, there have been numerous cases, several of which I personally observed, involving hackers who broke into a computer system using a very sophisticated attack but then did not know basic commands to manipulate the system.

Scant rationale exists for how these hackers choose their targets. Sometimes they focus on a company that just sounds like a good target. The National Security Agency, the Computer Emergency Response Team, and other security organizations are popular targets of mischievous hackers. Hackers may devote themselves fanatically to a particular victim. Often, they target companies randomly, using the passwords captured through password sniffers (programs that capture passwords as they are sent across a computer network). Some hackers keep lists of computer systems with which they've had experience; when a new vulnerability presents itself, they check their lists for likely victims. Frequently, hackers hear about other hackers' successes and try the break-ins for themselves.

The growth of broadband access for home users has created an incredible opportunity for the script kiddies and their professional counterparts. People leave their computers turned on and always available. For this reason, hackers just perform random scans of computer networks. People with personal firewalls find they receive dozens of attempted scans per day.

This scanning can extend to dial-up networks as well. When I travel and am not protected by my home firewall, I generally receive five attempted scans per hour. In an airport lounge, I once received three scans in the first two minutes.

The threat presented by script kiddies is twofold. First, unskilled hackers can cause a lot of damage, often simply because they can't think of anything else to do after they're inside a system. Even when hackers don't intentionally cause damage, they can ravage a system accidentally. Well-trained computer professionals cause major, but accidental, damage all the time; just think about what hundreds of thousands of inept hackers can do.

Second, most hackers divulge their information out of a desire to prove themselves and to publicize their successes. They want to be "Elite" or, as they spell it, "3l33t." When a typical, immature hacker manages to break into a system, the main thing on his mind is bragging rights, and he's on the Internet, IRC, and other bulletin board systems with his story almost immediately. His story is often challenged by his peers, and he must give out the details of his activities to prove himself. That's how the word gets out about system vulnerabilities. Foreign intelligence agencies and criminals will sometimes dupe these naive hackers into finding vulnerable systems for them. Hackers so indiscriminately spread this information that they could be considered accomplices to many crimes.

Thus, the primary problem with typical hackers is not that they commit crimes but that they facilitate and mask other crimes. They make the work of law enforcement and systems administrators much more difficult, allowing other crimes to flourish in places that it should not. Foreign intelligence agencies and criminal elements rely on the hacker community to hide many of their crimes.

As previously stated, these activities can easily lead to more profit-motivated crimes. The script kiddie community has turned into a major criminal breeding ground. Criminal professionals watch the hacker stomping grounds for signs of hackers who are particularly effective. They are then anonymously approached and given a small task. If they accomplish the task, they are sent a relatively untraceable money order for payment. They are then tasked with more difficult assignments. Of course, they can decide to move on to the extortion or credit card schemes I previously described, especially when a hacker gets into his twenties and decides that he doesn't want a real job. This scenario will almost definitely be the case if he has a computer and a hacking addiction.

Probably less than 1 percent of computer hacking is actually perpetrated for criminal purposes. Just think of the effort required by law enforcement and system administrators to figure out whether a computer break-in is caused by a hacker or a master criminal. If the script kiddies were not committing so many break-ins, it would be much easier to track down the real bad guys. Criminals also use the knowledge and tools developed and publicized by hackers for their own purposes. Unfortunately, hackers don't seem to care who else uses their information.

Notable Countries and Their Espionage Efforts

The United States government is relatively unique in its espionage efforts in that it generally does not assist U.S. companies with intelligence from and about their competitors. The only exceptions involve when the intelligence agencies have information that indicates that a company or individual is being specifically targeted. I know that conspiracy theorists abound. I know when I meet with executives of foreign companies or foreign leaders, they believe it's a fact that the U.S. intelligence agencies actively target foreign companies. They might do so, but only for national purposes.

For example, if a company is potentially supplying nuclear technology to adversarial countries, the United States has a clear obligation to get details. The government will not, however, take any of the collected information and give it to a U.S. company. However, people and organizations have delusions of grandeur if they believe that they are being actively targeted by the U.S. government and are not doing anything wrong or are not involved with people who are a potential threat to national interests.

Most other governments, though, do not have the same thought processes; as Pierre Marion, the former head of the DGSE, the French foreign intelligence agency, says, "There is no such thing as an economic ally." This is the attitude of most of the world. Because of longstanding policies of the U.S. government, national security is the focus. Almost all foreign governments put economics as the main focus of their intelligence efforts. It is just a different mindset. The belief that what is good for a local company is good for their country summarizes it all.

It is easy for many Americans to show disdain for that attitude; however, you cannot change it, nor fault foreign countries for forwarding their interests in the ways that they believe are most effective. Almost all other countries actually believe that the United States is naïve in this regard. What follows are the countries that were consistently cited in my research as countries with deep skills that are capable of committing advanced espionage attacks without getting caught.

Russia

Russia is the largest and strongest country emerging from the former Soviet Union and has acquired most of the Soviet Union's wealth and resources. It has also acquired most of the Soviet Union's debts. Despite the tremendous availability of natural resources and intellectual talent, the Russian economy is in turmoil. And despite the appearance that Russia is now a friendly country, it still remains America's greatest adversary.

Although plenty of U.S. leaders state that Russian intelligence is more active than even during the Cold War, the best indication comes from General Valentin Korabelnikov, the chief of the General Staff's Main Intelligence Directorate, better known as the GRU. Although much of the country's espionage activity involves military intelligence, most of the Russian focus has moved to industrial espionage. As a matter of fact, prior to his departure Boris Yeltsin declared that the main priority of the Russian intelligence services was economic intelligence. It is unlikely that this has changed under President Vladimir Putin, a former KGB officer who was close to Yeltsin during his presidency.

Virtually all American businesses are potential targets of the Russian intelligence agencies. Although the KGB has been broken up into many separate intelligence agencies with different functions, Russian intelligence is still alive and well. Most of the KGB activities familiar to Americans were assigned to an organization known as the SVR. This organization continues to use KGB resources and spy networks that have been developed over decades. The GRU, which is considered even more diabolical than the KGB, has remained intact despite many political upheavals and is as strong as ever. Few U.S. businesses escape Russian scrutiny.

What should be of major concern to most midsize and large U.S. firms is the fact that the Russian government has been thoroughly infiltrated by organized crime. During the first free elections in Russia in the late 1980s, the only people with the money to campaign for office were successful criminals, and many secured key political positions. Other organized crime figures bought the newly privatized Russian companies previously owned by the State. Representatives from these companies sometimes sit in on meetings of the Ministry of Defense and the Ministry of Defense Industry, in which they can request and fund intelligence operations to profit their companies. In the post–Cold War world, these agencies have evolved into purely profit-driven organizations and are widely considered to be extremely ruthless.

These new Russian capitalists realize that stealing technology is much cheaper than developing it themselves. They also have the distribution mechanisms to sell goods made with stolen or pirated technologies. Because they also have significant control of the Russian government, they are extremely unlikely to suffer any punishments for their actions.

Russian intelligence agencies have tremendous assets at their disposal. They have well-established networks of moles and operatives throughout the world. Each agency strives to have at least one mole in every important American company, and indications suggest that they have accomplished their goal. A former Russian intelligence operative boasted to me that with at least one person inside, the Russians can get anything out of a company. They train these moles and provide them with any resources they need to be successful. Chapter 9 details a typical Russian collection process as it actually occurred in that case.

Today, despite its previous focus on military activities, modern Russian intelligence agencies utilize a decidedly capitalistic model for intelligence gathering. Through the auspices of the Ministry of Defense, Russian intelligence generates a very large document that lists and identifies every requirement of its intelligence agencies. This vital intelligence document is divided into four major parts: Political Structure, Military Structure, Industry Structure, and Collection Requirements.

The Political Structure section focuses on the U.S. and world political infrastructures. It identifies governmental structures and includes the names of individuals in key positions, from very low levels of the hierarchy to top officials.

The Military Structure section of the document closely parallels the Political Structure section, except that it focuses on military personnel and organization. This section describes the purpose and capabilities of each military unit and lists unit leaders. Depending on the strategic importance of the units highlighted, it may also list personnel all the way down to the platoon or squad levels (basically, units of 10 to 40 people).

The Industry Structure section identifies all businesses that could be of military or political importance to the Russian government. Russian intelligence agencies keep lists of American businesses by market sector, type of information each company might have, and key company personnel. Companies of all sizes have something to offer the Russian intelligence agencies, whether or not they appear to have anything to do with the military or politics.

No business functions in a vacuum; every business has suppliers and customers. Although one business might not have anything of importance to the Russians, it might have customers and suppliers that do. In turn, the customers and suppliers also might not have anything of importance, but *they* might have suppliers or customers that do. Intelligence agencies know that many of their primary targets protect themselves against possible attacks. To bypass the protection mechanisms and obtain access to their primary target, these intelligence agencies frequently compromise third- or fourth-party organizations that have weak or no security. Although the third parties might not suffer a direct loss, they will eventually be affected, perhaps by paying more for the services received or by losing a customer.

All organizations are potential targets. Consider the pizza delivery services example I gave in Chapter 1. A small mom-and-pop grocery store in the middle of Wyoming might sell to a frequent customer who happens to be a friend of Vice President Cheney. A gasoline station thought to be in the middle of nowhere could be a regular stop for a member of Congress. A small literary agency may represent dozens of people, some of whom (such as myself) have access to sensitive information. The possibilities are endless, and the Russian intelligence establishment prepares for this.

The Collection Requirements section of the document lists every piece of technology the Russian government and its agencies want. It is essentially a buyer's guide for intelligence operatives. The items the document lists could be anything from information about the production output of a given piece of machinery to the schematics of the machine itself. They might want to acquire a specific computer chip or the manufacturing instructions for that chip. Every listing in the Collection Requirements section includes a tracking number, a description of the item listed, possible sources for the item desired, and the maximum price the agency is willing to pay for that item. If an operative acquires the item for less, he or she earns a percentage of the money saved and everyone in the operative's chain of command is rewarded. Flash updates to this section of the document are sent out whenever the intelligence committees get together to address any new and critical needs.

In the modern Russian intelligence community, there is open competition among agencies for both financial gain and prestige. If the GRU consistently beats the SVR to the targeted information, that agency is rewarded with increased annual budget allocations. This performance-driven approach is the source of much conflict among the agencies.

Besides the traditional human espionage methods, the Russians employ many other more technical means of collecting information. They tap telephones, monitor truck lines, bug buildings, and use spy satellites, special airplanes, and naval vessels. Some Aeroflot jets are configured with communications collection devices. Every foreign firm with offices in Russia just assumes that all their offices are bugged and all their telephones are monitored.

Another way Russian companies collect industrial information is by pursuing joint ventures with foreign firms. Russian enterprises do employ many brilliant scientists and businesspeople, making them very promising business partners. However, countless intelligence reports warn that many of these joint ventures are fronts for industrial espionage. The Russians frequently exploit these business relationships to gather information well beyond the scope of the agreement. Additionally, they will use a relationship with one firm to develop a relationship with another firm, expanding the scope of their collection efforts.

The Russian industrial espionage process is very effective and highly profit driven. These people are very good at getting exactly what they want from U.S. companies. Although the U.S. economy will not crumble from these attacks, certain businesses and industries might suffer drastically.

It is extremely important to note that the GRU has one of the most advanced computer hacking abilities in the world. They are likely rivaled only by the U.S. information-warfare centers. This fact is especially important because the GRU is responsible for strategically preparing for war. Although Chechen terrorists acts are clearly a high priority, the U.S. is still the top military adversary. To prepare for a possible war, the GRU has probably compromised the control systems of the U.S. critical infrastructures. The GRU likely has laid the groundwork to cause those systems to crash or to otherwise cause those systems to create immense damage. I am not a believer of an inevitable "Electronic Pearl Harbor," but if any group is capable of accomplishing a massive computer attack, it is the GRU. As a matter of fact, although they might not have the proverbial finger on the button, they have the button.

China

China has one of the largest economies in the world. Despite the apparent widespread lack of technology throughout the country, China is focusing on the acquisition of new technologies to bring its economy into the twenty-first century. China has a population exceeding one billion, and businesses throughout the world are battling to break into China's growing consumer market. The Chinese government is pursuing a series of economic reforms to allow for this foreign expansion into the country. However, in contrast to Russia, China is not simultaneously pursuing political reforms. This allows for highly planned and controlled economic growth that will not be ruined by a weak central government.

Industrial espionage has always played an important role in Chinese economic development. For many years, China has used its military intelligence capability and tactics for economic purposes. However, the Chinese tactics are somewhat different from those of the Russians. Russian expatriates often do not maintain strong ties with the country they fought so hard to escape; many despise the Russian past and the government and want nothing to do with it. Despite their government's repressive, totalitarian society, people of Chinese descent frequently feel an ethnic devotion to their ancestors and their homeland. Chinese intelligence agencies know this and exploit this devotion at every opportunity.

Chinese methods are primarily based on opportunities. Although they have some very high-tech capabilities and well-established, trained people, they primarily focus on exploiting targets of opportunities as they arise, as opposed to specific targeting of people and technologies. This is a very important distinction. There are likely some standing targets such as space and satellite technologies; however, they mostly see what opportunities present themselves and take advantage of them. Their goal is therefore to create as many opportunities as possible.

Chinese intelligence agencies focus their recruitment efforts on Chinese nationals traveling and living abroad, as well as people of Chinese descent who are citizens of other countries. They find these people mainly through social clubs, which they join. They cultivate friendships with potential agents and try to recruit them for espionage activities.

Chinese intelligence also relies heavily on university students studying abroad. Every Chinese student who wants to study abroad must be approved by the government, and most of the students' financial support is provided to them. Because China places such a high priority on technology, the vast majority of Chinese nationals studying in the United States and around the world major in science and technology. In many cases, these students work on state-of-the-art research projects and gain access to cutting-edge technologies. After their education is completed, some of these students return to China and become teachers; others may work in Chinese research facilities.

Some Chinese students, however, are encouraged to stay in the United States and get jobs in U.S. companies after they graduate. Over time, they may be approached by intelligence operatives who ask them to provide China with sensitive information on different technologies or businesses. Other Chinese nationals are required to return home after graduation, where they might be trained as intelligence operatives and sent back overseas to obtain jobs in strategic companies.

Not all Chinese nationals traveling, studying, or working overseas are intelligence operatives or agents. But China herself does consider them to be a primary industrial espionage resource, and with so many Chinese citizens traveling abroad, the intelligence agencies need exploit only a small percentage of them to pose a considerable threat to U.S. companies.

As do the Russians, the Chinese also use satellites, spy ships, airplanes, embassy collection, wiretaps, and telephone monitoring in their intelligence-gathering activities. China has the largest military in the world, with an intelligence capability to match.

China also takes full advantage of the size of its economy. Every industrialized country in the world wants to sell its products to the Chinese people, and the Chinese government knows it. Accordingly, as part of normal trade negotiations, China forces foreign companies that want to establish businesses in China to train Chinese citizens in their U.S. factories, build factories in China, and place Chinese citizens in key management positions. Because of the immense Chinese market, many companies are willing to agree to these conditions even though they constitute a major security threat.

Chinese nationals specifically placed inside American firms are bound to engage in espionage activity. The Chinese don't even seem particularly interested in covering the tracks of their operatives. In many instances, these placed workers simply "disappear" after several months of employment. The assumption among intelligence professionals is that after the operatives collect everything they need, they simply have no reason to return. All technology inside U.S. factories built in China must be considered totally compromised.

Companies from throughout the world have been placing factories in China and will continue to do so. I already described the concept of offshoring. Given the low wages paid in China, it is one of the top places for companies to place their factories and other facilities. Although some of the workers and managers at these factories will be from their corporate headquarters, an overwhelming majority of the employees and executives are from the host country. You can guarantee that several moles will be planted inside the company, as well as many other employees "recruited" as necessary.

A Chinese Incident

I was once called in by a large oil company that wanted some advice. Basically, the company had recently been involved in an "incident." The security office received a call from an employee who said that she didn't want to sound like a racist, but one of her Chinese coworkers was spending a great deal of time speaking Chinese on the telephone. The problem was that none of their legitimate business contacts were Chinese. The security manager pulled the telephone records and found a lot of calls to a specific telephone number.

The security manager contacted the company's FBI liaison, who, after looking into it, informed the security manager that the telephone number belonged to the local Chinese Consulate. The number was actually a direct line to a person known to be a Chinese operative.

You would expect that the company would just fire this person. Unfortunately, the solution was not that simple. The security manager soon learned that the company had been seeking drilling rights in China for years. Sometime during the negotiation process, the Chinese negotiators told the company something to the effect, "Well, it appears we are close to agreement. We have a list of 30 students graduating from some of your fine U.S. academic institutions. We would look at it as a sign of good will if you would provide these students with jobs upon graduation."

So the planted agent had to be treated very carefully, and there was a very quiet separation. One of the biggest problems, though, was determining which of the other 29 student hires were spies and what the company could do to minimize the damage they could cause.

In the past year, I have met with several companies around the world, all telling me the same story. They claim that they opened a factory in China and within several months a Chinese competitor started offering a nearly identical product to the ones that they were manufacturing in their own Chinese factories, and for a cheaper price. This appears to be inevitable given the socioeconomic environment of China.

Much as does Russia, China makes heavy use of front companies. Sometimes foreign companies are steered to these front companies inside China through which to funnel their Chinese activities. Therefore, the Chinese government has full knowledge of everything going on. The people I spoke to generally believe that the People's Liberation Army owns or has direct involvement with 99 percent of all Chinese companies, both inside and outside their country.

With regard to Chinese companies outside China, many of them are front companies. U.S. intelligence agencies report that more than 3,000 Chinese front companies are operating in the U.S. alone. Not all of them are high-tech companies as people would believe. Many are restaurants, social clubs, and other places where people gather in general. Chapter 6 demonstrates the use of these "companies."

The Chinese also use a bait-and-switch technique to get into facilities to which their operatives normally do not have access. Creating a "scene" is another common tactic. Chinese government operatives infiltrate Chinese social clubs and exploit relationships there. They urge members to do all they can to provide new knowledge and job opportunities for other members. They then convince their compatriots to arrange for tours of company facilities where they are employed. In case the companies check the identities and backgrounds of visitors, Chinese operatives use the names of other people; then, at the time of the visit, the intelligence operatives show up in the others' place, and unwitting companies allow the unapproved guests through. If a company rejects the new visitors, the operatives create a scene, trying to portray it as a racial or international incident in the hopes of intimidating the company into letting them in. They also use this ploy to get into restricted areas, saying that the company is trying to hide something. I personally know of such instances in three companies. Not surprisingly, in 1996 the Defense Investigative Service put out an alert about these practices.

The Chinese infiltration efforts have been very successful around the world. They have cut significantly into the international market share of U.S. businesses in several high-technology areas, including weapons sales. This is a multibillion-dollar loss to U.S. firms. It also involves national security interests because China has been willing to sell weapons and restricted technologies to nations and organizations that are openly hostile to the United States, including Iran. The ease of acquiring technology and cheap labor, and the fact that Chinese companies don't have to invest millions of dollars in innovation, makes Chinese companies extremely competitive in the international market. It might also become competitive inside the U.S. market, depending on the results of the latest trade negotiations.

France

France has twice been publicly identified by the CIA as one of two U.S. allies that commit acts of corporate espionage against American companies as frequently as do U.S. adversaries. Perhaps no U.S. ally has been more flagrant in its intelligence-gathering activities than France. To a great extent, the French are proud of this distinction.

The French government has been using its intelligence capabilities to support its domestic businesses since the reign of Louis XIV. French companies regularly approach the DGSE (the French foreign intelligence agency) and request intelligence support. Each company must justify its request with specific financial criteria. If the DGSE considers the request valid, it uses its resources to get the desired information.

One of the most important tools of the DGSE is French hotels. It is widely reported that the agency has recruited many domestic hotel employees to facilitate its intelligence-collection activities. These employees let DGSE operatives into hotel rooms while the occupants are out. They also bug the telephones of visiting U.S. businesspeople during their stay. The U.S. National Counterintelligence Center (NCIC) reported at least one case in which hotel telephone taps resulted in a French company's beating out a U.S. competitor on a multimillion-dollar contract. Many of the major American companies warn their employees traveling to France that their rooms must be considered bugged and videotaped.

France's espionage activities are by no means limited to domestic operations. Pierre Marion has said that France has successfully placed moles inside many U.S. companies, including IBM and Texas Instruments. These are long-term operatives, expected to advance through the ranks of the company and to obtain access to the newer developments over time. France has probably targeted non-U.S. companies as well. The United States is not singled out by France, which believes that "there is no such thing as an economic ally."

CASE STUDY OF FRENCH ESPIONAGE

I was once called into a U.S. high-tech company that wanted advice on dealing with a problem. They were informed by one of their European subcontractors that a French competitor had approached them about buying all the U.S. company's technology. Although the U.S. company appreciated the information, it was left with a bigger problem. It actually had 24 European subcontractors, and only one of them reported being approached. The company had no idea what to do about the other 23 subcontracting companies.

The U.S. company performed a complete comparison of its product and the competing product from the French company. The U.S. company determined that the French company still lacked a couple of key components. It tried to sue the French company, in France. The courts laughed the case out of court, basically saying that the U.S. company should expect these things to happen.

Peter Schweizer reports in his book, *Friendly Spies*, that France bugged the first-class cabins of some Air France jets. This invasion of privacy, while considered outrageous by Americans, is looked upon by the French people as a normal part of business (the French justifiably think that high-paid executives on business trips are the only people who regularly fly first class).

U.S. companies should keep in mind that many French corporations are actually owned by the French government. French government-owned businesses are often used as collection tools. The U.S. Government Accountability Office (GAO) released a report to Congress accusing foreign-owned firms of abusing their ownership of U.S. government contractors. These companies, including the French company Loral, bought out American firms with classified government contracts. The United States allowed the companies to acquire the U.S. firms with the stipulation that the foreign owners maintain a complete separation of information. The GAO reviewed the implementation of the requirements and found them severely lacking. France, among other countries, uses these companies to gain access to very sensitive technology. To France, spying for industry is the same as spying for the government.

It is very important to note that many French companies have been notorious for their nuclear proliferation activities. France has been cited as helping Middle Eastern countries develop their nuclear capabilities. Their activities also extend to helping companies and countries in developing other military and weapons capabilities. Stories of French officials being bribed to help Saddam Hussein overcome United Nations sanctions provide indications of other uses of pilfered information.

Some French companies issued requests for proposals, and companies provided a great amount of proprietary information in an attempt to win the contract. Inevitably, the French company informed the bidders that they decided not to go ahead with the effort. Soon thereafter, the company opened a new line of business, specifically using the information provided in the proposals received.

France also bears the distinction of actively supporting the computer hacker community. France has long recognized the importance of computer hacking in the collection of information. It has developed and trained a world-class group of its own computer hackers. It also supports the underground hackers, mainly to help hide its own activities and gather information. Dr. Spafford (of Purdue University, cited earlier in this chapter) stated that France also finds new computer vulnerabilities and releases them directly to the hacker community. This allows hackers to use very advanced techniques while inadvertently masking the illegal activities of the DGSE. If the average hacker can compromise a computer system with a very advanced attack, then the companies hacked by France likely assume that the attack came from a teenage hacker rather than a well-trained DGSE operative.

The French operate one of the most capable intelligence agencies in the world. Although they do gather military intelligence information, there is little doubt that their primary goal is economic intelligence. The military information they do gather is usually collected for sale to other parties. They use the information they collect to give French companies an advantage. If your firm has ever competed against a French company, you have been a target. If you have ever produced the same product as a French company, you have been a target. If you've ever been a target of the French, your whole company was threatened.

Israel

Israel shares with France the distinction of being named by the CIA as one of the two leading allied perpetrators of industrial espionage. In contrast to France, the Israelis very strongly prefer to keep their espionage activities under wraps. They are very dependent on the U.S. for military and political support, and they don't want to antagonize their ally. However, the Israelis also believe that the very existence of their country is at stake, and they will do everything possible to protect themselves.

According to many intelligence sources, Israel has the world's best intelligence capability, person for person and dollar for dollar. Knowledgeable sources believe the Israelis to have the third best intelligence agency in the world, trailing only the United States and Russia. Although they lack the worldwide presence and many of the assets of the larger nations, the devotion of Israeli operatives and agents to their country and their cause make their intelligence organizations one of the best in the world.

Israel's primary espionage target is military technology. Israel wants advanced weapons to improve its ability to defend itself and to sell to its allies. Israel always seeks to strengthen its economy and trade balance so that it is less reliant on foreign aid.

To obtain information, Israel uses many of the same techniques that are often associated with more hostile countries. For example, Israel places people inside companies through contractual negotiations, just as China does. It recruits spies and moles. It taps the telephones of companies and individuals who are likely to have knowledge that it needs.

On this point, a concern developed when an Israeli telecommunications acquired a U.S. domestic carrier. The Israeli company now has control and access to the telephone lines of many companies.

As have its French counterparts, Israeli intelligence has had significant success in recruiting computer hackers. The Mossad and probably the LAKAM (both Israeli intelligence agencies) support hacker activities much like those of the DGSE, and occasionally try to recruit the more talented hackers. Israel has an incredibly talented base of computer-literate people. Israel is also home to some of the top computer security vendors in the world.

Similarly to the Chinese, the Israelis also utilize ethnic targeting to recruit many of their agents. Many Jews have a strong devotion to Israel even though they may never have been there. To many, supporting the country means supporting the Jewish faith. Some U.S. citizens volunteer to serve in the Israeli army. If a person is willing to give his or her life for Israel, then stealing a little information is a small thing. Although the number of American Jews who actually commit espionage for Israel is extremely small, they do exist. Jonathan Pollard, for instance, was a Naval Intelligence analyst who sold top-secret military information to Israeli agents. There are also the recent charges of a Pentagon official who passed classified documents to Israel through a political lobbying group.

Although relatively few Israeli espionage cases hit the media, it is extremely likely that Israel is every bit as active in this arena as are the French and the Chinese. They probably have agents and moles inside many U.S. and other foreign high-technology firms. They probably bug hotel rooms and tap telephone lines. Their agents are very bright and very motivated, and they usually get what they want. These are people who have infiltrated the very closed ranks of Arab terrorist organizations; to them, breaching a multibillion-dollar U.S. corporation is a walk in the park.

Many American Jews justify Israeli industrial espionage actions with the argument that Israel has always been America's strongest military ally. What they don't recognize is the economic impact of these actions.

Germany

Although the U.S. government does not typically name it, Germany is widely known to be among the most active intelligence collectors in the world. Germany maintains a very large intelligence organization, called the Bundesnachrichtendienst (BND). Although its primary focus was the Eastern Bloc, the BND has always engaged in a significant amount of industrial activity. After the breakup of the Eastern Bloc, it shifted most of its Cold War resources to industrial efforts.

The BND continues to monitor international communications and tries very actively to obtain information that can help German companies. The agency has supported Siemens, one of Germany's largest companies, by infiltrating high-technology companies around the world.

The BND's most notable public success was infiltrating the Nixon White House, and it continues to target other people and organizations that have access to sensitive trade information. There is little doubt that the BND has enjoyed many major industrial espionage successes.

Much the same as the French DGSE, the BND has a strong computer-hacking component. Project Rahab is a BND effort to hack into computer networks and compromise systems in the Global Information Infrastructure. It began in the early 1990s and continues to this point. It hoped to develop the capability to break into corporate and government computer systems at will to ensure its political, military, and economic survival.

One of Project Rahab's major reported successes includes infiltration of the SWIFT system, which is one of the world's major financial networks. SWIFT facilitates the transfer of trillions of dollars a day among financial institutions around the world. If the reports are true, Germany can monitor most of the world's financial transactions. The value of this intelligence is tremendous, and Germany is no doubt using this information to its advantage. The BND likely is using its capability to steal information from private companies as well.

Perhaps of greatest concern to U.S. citizens is the apparent willingness of German businesses to funnel sensitive information and technology to nations that are hostile to the United States. German companies have been accused of providing technological help to Iran, for example.

Alarmingly, a great deal of this technology involves nuclear and chemical technologies. Some of that technology was reportedly stolen from U.S. firms.

Honorable Mentions

All countries have an espionage capability in one form or another. For some countries, it consists primarily of computer hacking. Some countries have more robust capabilities than others, though. Some of these countries also have more access and motivation than the rest.

Japan

Perhaps no country has integrated industrial espionage into its culture to a greater extent than Japan. Japanese businesses watch their competitors, both foreign and domestic, almost as well as they watch themselves. The larger companies have entire units devoted to competitive intelligence. They're responsible for learning what their competitors are up to, what their capabilities are, how much profit they're making, how much product they're producing, what new directions they are going in, and what unique processes they've come up with. They study every publicly available document containing information about their competitors, including newspapers, magazines, annual reports, and government filings. They regularly check new filings at patent and trademark offices around the world, looking for anything of interest. Japanese companies want to know everything about their competitors.

As industrial espionage becomes embedded into the way the government functions, cases arise that demonstrate how non-Japanese companies are affected. For example, Pillsbury discovered that after submitting a patent application, the Japanese Ministry of Economy, Trade, and Industry (METI) passed the patent application to a Japanese industry trade association. The Pillsbury proprietary information was basically distributed to its competitors before the company was actually afforded the protections it was trying to obtain by filing the application with Japanese Patent Office.

Although Japanese companies usually rely on straightforward collection methods, such as reviewing open-source information, they can be extremely creative in their collection methods. One interesting tactic involved a questionnaire sent to several U.S. firms by a Japanese company. In each cover letter, the company claimed to be considering using the U.S. firm as a supplier, but before the firm could be seriously considered, it would have to complete the enclosed questionnaire. The questionnaire called for a detailed summary of all corporate locations, the names of the key people at each facility, the types of products developed, the volume of the products produced, and a variety of other sensitive information.

Japanese executives take an active role in the information-gathering process. They will covertly visit their competitors. If they can't find the time to do this on a regular basis themselves, they send their subordinates. They also pay people to monitor other companies. They even pay delivery people to report on the packages they deliver and pick up from certain companies.

A great example of the depth of Japanese competitive intelligence collection is the CEO of a Japanese coffee firm who wanted to prepare to compete against Starbucks. He traveled to the United States to visit as many Starbucks as possible to study what made his competition successful.

The Japanese government has no intelligence capability of its own. According to John Quinn, a former CIA operative and expert on Japanese business and intelligence practices, the Japanese government relies on the country's businesses to supply it with intelligence on other countries. The government has set up the Japanese External Trade Relations Office (JETRO), which is reportedly staffed by visiting corporate intelligence professionals. Although JETRO was supposedly established to improve Japanese business relations with other countries, most U.S. counterintelligence professionals consider its primary purpose to be intelligence collection.

Even though Japan is an important American ally, it represents a significant threat to U.S. companies. What international business has not been affected by a Japanese competitor? What domestic manufacturer has not had its market share cut by a Japanese company? Most Americans assume that the Japanese succeed because they are more creative. The truth is, Americans generate many times more new technologies and technological breakthroughs than Japan. The Japanese just "acquire" the technology and develop new ways of using it. The fact that they don't have to put as much money into research and development allows them to spend their money on more competitive issues and to offer their products at lower prices.

India

India may be a surprising name to many people. It is a third-world country by any account. Although it clearly contains centers of technological excellence, the majority of the country is extremely poor. By all accounts, there are more than 1,000,000,000 people in the country. I recently traveled to India and met with many high-level government officials. I don't know whether I was actually surprised when I was told that the government has no capability of actually measuring the population, given the remote areas of the country.

India does, however, have a lot in its favor. The fact that it was formerly a British colony means that many people in the country speak English. Although only a small percentage of the population may have a college education, that still represents a large number of people. The fact that the standard of living in the country is generally low means that it can offer labor at very cheap rates. For these combined reasons, India is one of the primary beneficiaries of offshoring and outsourcing.

India also has a major espionage effort. For a variety of political reasons, its intelligence agencies have been supported by both the British and Russian intelligence services. It has developed a mindset that is most similar to that of the French: What is best for native business is best for the country. Economic espionage is an integral, but hidden, part of doing business.

Many Indians are living and attending school in the United States who have as much, if not more, devotion to the country of India than the Chinese have to their country. As a matter of fact, there are immense benefits for such a person to take technologies from their U.S. employers and bring them to India to start a new company.

The growth of the offshoring and outsourcing industries in India have been a boon to their espionage efforts. Companies from all over the world are bringing their technologies and their information to them. India companies are now on the networks of U.S. companies with little or no oversight. As you will see in the case study in Chapter 7, these arrangements have extremely serious implications.

Iran

Iran has jumped to a high position in current events. If there was not so much focus on Iraq, Iran would likely be the top news story. There is little doubt that they are trying to develop a nuclear weapons capability. Indications are strong that the government has some interaction with Al-Qaeda. Although some major changes in the openness of the country have occurred, the hardliners seem to still have ultimate control.

At first thought, Iran is a backward nation with a single modern industry: oil production. The Iranians may seem medieval with their beards and veils—merely Muslim fundamentalists who despise technology, people who want to return to the old ways and shun the modern world.

The Iranian government is happy to foster this impression. Doing so hides what it's really up to. Iran is an extremely rich country that does want to modernize—not necessarily its society, but its military. Iran is actively attempting to manipulate events in Iraq and has an incredibly large and talented set of intelligence operatives acting toward that goal. It spends its oil money in a relentless pursuit of advanced weapons technology, including nuclear, chemical, and biological weapons. Iran has one of the best-financed intelligence capabilities in the world.

Russia continues to train Iranian intelligence operatives and provide them with the necessary collection equipment. Using the standard intelligence collection methods, such as theft, wiretaps, and bribes, Iran collects information from high-technology firms throughout the world. It also exchanges information with other hostile intelligence agencies, such as the Russian GRU. It also hires former Eastern Bloc experts in the nuclear, chemical, and espionage fields.

To obtain certain technologies, Iran secures the cooperation of the companies of U.S. allies, such as Germany and France. These companies have their own technology capabilities and are not subject to rules that limit the acquisition of "controlled" equipment. Consequently, these companies are able to use their ally status to acquire technology supposedly for themselves, and then sell it illegally to Iran. Iran uses these companies as intermediaries to front their activities. Iranian scientists specify their requirements, and when money is no object, they get what they want.

Although Iran's use of technology appears to be limited to noneconomic gain, its espionage activities pose a major threat to U.S. companies and the world in general. Should Iran develop a working arsenal of weapons of mass destruction or significantly improve its military capability, the Mideast could be thrown into turmoil and the world's oil supply could be threatened.

Cuba

Cuba is also high on the list of countries engaged in industrial espionage. In contrast to Iran, Cuba is a third-world country with a third-world economy. With the breakup of the Soviet Union, Cuba has lost its primary supplier of money and technology. Cuba even lost a major Russian military base. Compounding its problems is the U.S. economic boycott. With America taking the lead, other countries have avoided economic involvement with Cuba. Although many countries are clearly trading with Cuba, the effect is minimal on the economy, making economic growth very difficult. Necessity has caused Castro's government to shift its focus from military to economic growth, with the acquisition of technology serving as a top priority.

With few legal options, Cuba resorts to any means necessary to acquire new technology. As with Iran, Cuban intelligence operatives are trained by Russians. Using their education, they try to infiltrate companies to steal technology. They also bribe people, tap telephones, commit blackmail, and recruit communist sympathizers. They also use foreign companies to bypass the Cuban trade embargo. In several cases, the Cubans have acquired technologies to trade with their allies. Cuban thefts of American technologies likely will significantly impact the market share of U.S. firms. However, Cuba is a major supplier to the black market. The affect on the overall economy is minimal, but it can significantly hurt individual American companies, depending on the specific technologies that they acquire.

Petty Crime

Having discussed some of the most organized threats that companies face, I now turn to the threats that people and companies are more likely to face. The other threats are clearly more sensational; however they are not as common as the threat of things such as petty crimes. Petty crimes can cause major problems for individuals and corporations. When I ask my audiences how many people work in companies that have experienced thefts of computers, just about everyone raises a hand. In some cases, the entire computer is stolen; in other cases, only specific parts, such as memory chips, are removed. There has been a tremendous increase in laptop computer thefts in recent years from both individuals and companies.

The problem here isn't so much the loss of the hardware, although that certainly adds up. The computers themselves are often not nearly as valuable as the information they contain. A $2,500 laptop can hold information valued at more than $1 million.

One of the most notable cases of petty crime and laptop theft was when Irwin Jacobs, CEO of Qualcomm, had his laptop stolen when he turned his back to answer questions after a presentation that he gave. The laptop was never found, and the case made all the major newspapers.

Furthermore, these kinds of thefts leave the motives of the thieves unclear. Was the computer taken by a petty criminal interested only in the value of the hardware, or was it part of a more sophisticated intelligence operation targeting the information the computer holds? Petty crime confuses the issue of industrial espionage and personal well-being. The targets of a petty criminal and those of an industrial spy are frequently the same, as are the short-term effects of the theft on the company. Luckily, the long-term effects of petty crimes are much less devastating.

In either case, you are forced to replace the lost equipment and information. The effects and recovery costs associated with this kind of crime are still very large, and it always seems to happen at the wrong time.

Suppliers

Although your suppliers might not intend to compete directly with you, they are frequently trying to increase their profits, which ultimately decreases your resources. This relationship must be looked upon as a kind of threat, albeit an often unconscious one.

Your suppliers are selling you products, and in many ways, they behave as all salespeople do. Consider the process of buying a car: As you walk into an automobile dealership, the typical salesperson will gather intelligence about you. He or she will glance outside to see what kind of car you're currently driving and will notice the clothes you're wearing. Are you with a family or by yourself? Do you speak intelligently, or does it seem as though you're trying to sound intelligent? Car salespeople are trained to gather this type of intelligence to figure out what you can spend and how gullible you are.

While you're off on a test drive, you leave a copy of your driver's license with the dealer; the dealership could check your credit records while you're gone. The salesperson with you on the test drive gathers more information by asking questions. By the time you get back to the dealership, the people inside know you better than you know yourself.

All suppliers want to know as much about you as possible. They want to know about your future plans so that they can determine whether you will be likely to seek out other suppliers or need other products. The training of IBM salespeople is widely discussed in the computer professional community. Supposedly, IBM trains its people to scan office bookshelves to determine the technical level of the people they are dealing with. They are rumored to read upside down so that they can decipher notes on a potential customer's desk. It's said that they're encouraged to look for awards and pictures of families to find a basis for better rapport. They may even also look for information about other suppliers you may be considering. Before they even arrive at your office, they could have researched your company thoroughly to determine your needs and anticipate questions or objections. When they're with you, they may be probing with leading questions.

In many cases, all this probing leads to better service. Sometimes, though, it undercuts your own bargaining position. Even the suppliers of very small businesses often go to great lengths to improve their bargaining positions. If you own a mom-and-pop store, for example, suppliers can anticipate or manipulate your needs based on information they get from you, your competitors, or other suppliers. If a supplier knows that you are not looking for other suppliers, it might not offer you the lowest rates available. If you are known to be shopping around, you might get better rates.

Some people might say that this surreptitious intelligence gathering is just business and not espionage. Whatever you call it, you must be aware that your suppliers are constantly gathering information about your organization. What they learn can help or hurt you.

Customers

Essentially, customers collect information on their suppliers in the same way their suppliers collect information on them. Let's go back to the car-buying example, but now let's say that you represent the dealership. The potential buyer could do extensive research: read *Consumer Reports* and similar magazines to see how a particular car performed; use a variety of resources to learn your (the dealer's) invoice price; investigate the best time of the month to buy a car to get the best deal. The customer could also collect intelligence on the dealership, looking into the dealership sales record. Is business good or is the dealership going through a slow period? In addition, the customer could contact the local Better Business Bureau to see whether any complaints have been filed against the dealership, ask other customers about their experience with the dealership, even shop around and compare prices with other dealers.

Customers are seldom left without options if they do their homework. Unless a supplier has a monopoly, customers can usually gather information to improve their bargaining power. Even if the exercise improves their deal by only a few percentage points, it can easily be worth the effort. With the perception that the customer is competing for limited resources with the company, these few percentage points represent a huge loss to the company.

Competitors

One threat that should be on the minds of all companies is their competitors. Individuals must also consider that they have competition in their everyday pursuits that they should deal with. This section intends to address business concerns, but there are lessons to extract for everyone.

Aside from accidents and employees, the primary threat to an organization is its competitors. Virtually all business enterprises have competitors; they are a fact of life in capitalist countries. What many people don't realize is that smaller companies, by virtue of the markets they serve, have more competitors than do big corporations. Boeing, for example, is one of the largest aircraft manufacturers in the world; few companies around the world can compete with such a huge operation. A local office supply store, on the other hand, must coexist with dozens of competing enterprises: other office supplies stores, department stores, computer stores, and even supermarkets selling similar products. Competition is definitely livelier for smaller concerns.

Basically, a competitor is any business that seeks to increase its market share or profits at the expense of your business. Competitors need not behave maliciously nor act illegally to pose a threat to your enterprise. All they have to do is seek to improve their wealth, inevitably at your expense.

Your competitors profit in many ways from information collected about your business. A supermarket manager, for example, would love to know about a competitor's profit margins, supplier discounts, and upcoming special sales. Is the store planning to expand, extend its hours, or respond to an unforeseen market trend? The answers to these questions are worth millions.

Large companies face large competitors with great resources. Small mom-and-pop stores have more competitors to worry about. Midsized companies face the greatest threat in terms of competition: Their competitors have the resources to pursue them, and plenty of them are out there. More important, midsized companies are often less cognizant of the threat. They feel that they're not big, like defense contractors, so no one would want to spy on them. These operations often have the most to lose in a highly volatile marketplace. For example, Erol's Videos was put out of business as Blockbuster, a "megachain," crept unnoticed into its market areas. In turn, Blockbuster was blindsided by NetFlix.com.

Your competitors can ask vendors and customers about your capabilities, talk to your former employees, and even hire private investigators to find out whether you are fulfilling your contracts, all without breaking the law. Competitive intelligence firms specialize in providing information to companies about their competitors without engaging in illegal activity.

The results of the legal intelligence-gathering activities of your competitors can be devastating. When American Airlines decided to go head-to-head with People's Express, the original "no frills" airline, it monitored the smaller carrier —24 hours a day. Whatever discounts People's offered, American matched immediately. This intense monitoring resulted in the demise of People's, which had once been an extremely successful business. This is a clear example of the extreme nature of competitive intelligence. This type of situation goes on all the time with varying degrees of effects.

Of course, some of your competitors won't stop at legal intelligence-gathering methods. They'll resort to a range of attack techniques— simple breaking and entering to sophisticated computer hacking—to steal everything, from your customer lists to your expansion plans. Some will break the law without knowing it.

Some companies engage in the highly questionable practice of paying private individuals to acquire information about their competitors for them. According to a former Russian intelligence officer, many U.S. firms secure the services of private investigators through third parties. They hire people to hire people to hire people to get information on their competitors through illegal means. Their intention is to separate the illegal actions from the end user of the information. The Russian officer told me that this practice is common in many multibillion-dollar corporations, but smaller companies do it as well.

The threat from foreign competitors can be particularly troublesome for a number of often confusing reasons. Italy, for example, readily cooperates with countries such as the United States in the prosecution of industrial spies, even Italian ones. However, the Italian government provides an exemption when health concerns are involved. When acts of industrial espionage involve biotechnology or pharmaceutical products, the Italian government refuses to cooperate on the grounds that the actions are health related.

Multinational corporations know exactly what they can and can't get away with and become experts at covering their tracks. They use the same tactics and methods as your domestic competitors, but they also count on at least some protection from their homelands. Expecting this type of support, foreign business owners are often emboldened to commit more egregious acts of industrial espionage than are U.S. firms. This is on top of the fact that many foreign governments actively perform and support industrial espionage.

I certainly expect governments to support their own businesses. Americans can't impose their ethics on others. Governments and their intelligence agencies are expected to act in the best interests of their countries and not in the best interests of Americans. Although this does not have to be a "one or the other" situation, that is how countries typically perceive it.

Conclusion

This chapter obviously throws a lot at you and makes it seem as though you can't have a moment's peace. Although that is not my intent, I hope the point gets across that you have threats to deal with. Most people and companies are in complete denial that they have anything to worry about.

At the very least, you should start to realize that you have to consider implementing countermeasures specific to you and the threats you face. There is no magic solution, but at least you don't have to be a sitting duck.

5

How the Spies Really Get You

Clearly, many people and things are out to get you. But if you think about the discussion of risk in Chapter 2, you'll understand that even if everyone in the world wants to steal your information, they can do it only through your vulnerabilities. It doesn't matter whether the bad people are foreign intelligence agencies or seven-year-old kids looking for candy money; they will all attack you through the vulnerabilities you leave open. Who the spies are is irrelevant. It is your vulnerabilities that matter.

As you go through this chapter, the vulnerabilities described may seem too basic to allow for significant or even noticeable losses. You probably see these things in your own home or office every day, yet you haven't seen any losses worth noting. As I emphasized in Chapter 2, by overlooking the smaller losses that occur daily, you can suffer "death by 1,000 cuts." The case studies in Part II demonstrate how little things add up to billions of dollars of losses.

The best way to prevent attacks is to familiarize yourself with your organization's weaknesses. Some security-minded people recommend focusing on the attacks themselves, emphasizing a strategy of second-guessing the attackers. Prevent the potential attack, the thinking goes, and you have no problems. However, this approach cures the symptoms while ignoring the disease. For example, there was a World Trade Center attack in 1993 that used a car bomb. Security people strengthened the access controls to the World Trade Center garage; however, they did nothing to strengthen airline security, which was the source of the 2001 World Trade Center attack.

Another example is that many individuals try to protect their credit cards by tearing up their card receipts because they have heard stories about criminals going through garbage. However, thousands of people readily go to fake web sites to supposedly confirm their credit card numbers and give out even more comprehensive information.

You must acknowledge vulnerabilities holistically and account for all of them. The bad guys will eventually find a way.

Of course, some vulnerabilities are simply unavoidable. Businesses must exchange information with other businesses. Companies must bring new people into the corporate fold. Organizations of all kinds are using the Internet in myriad ways. Individuals must use their credit card and give out their account number over the telephone or Internet. As I explained in Chapter 2, there is no such thing as perfect security.

Your goal should be to understand the vulnerabilities in your organization and take reasonable steps to optimize your risk. The countermeasures for these vulnerabilities are the subject of Part III of this book.

A word about technology in this context: When most people consider information security, they think about technical issues. They believe that protecting information is all about protecting computers. Please remember that *information is information*. This phrase should be your mantra. Information on a computer can be quite valuable, but the same piece of information written on a crumbled-up cocktail napkin is worth just as much. It is just as important to protect that napkin as it is to protect the computer. Focusing on computer-based data can leave an organization extremely vulnerable to tried-and-true espionage techniques.

I think it's useful to look at vulnerabilities in four broad categories: operational, physical, personnel, and technical. Some vulnerabilities don't fit perfectly into any single category, but for clarity's sake, I've grouped the examples in this chapter into the most appropriate of these subdivisions.

Operational Vulnerabilities

Larry Hale was formerly responsible for the Department of Homeland Security's computer-incident response program. For many years before being appointed to that position, he ran the U.S. Federal Computer Incident Response Center, and he has probably dealt with more computer-hacking incidents than anyone else alive. When I interviewed him about the vulnerabilities that create the most serious losses, he said that operational problems were undoubtedly the underlying cause of just about all successful attacks. This is despite the fact that he focuses on technology-based attacks. The technology is not usually the problem. It is the use of the technology that causes most of the problems.

Operational vulnerabilities refer to weaknesses that result from the way organizations and people do daily business. When a company or person becomes a target, attackers look first to how the target performs its daily activities for vulnerabilities. How does this target go about giving out information? What do this target's actions reveal about its future plans?

This security concern is actually a military concept but is appropriate in the commercial and personal environments. In a military campaign, you might want to surprise an enemy with a sneak attack at an unexpected location, and you need to get your army over there without giving away your plans. Spies notice when you're gassing up the tanks. They notice when you put refueling stations on the way to borders. They can observe service personnel calling their families and canceling appointments. Remember the example of questioning the pizza-delivery person about deliveries to a military base (see Chapter 1)? Similarly, when military strategists work late in Washington, D.C., they call out for food, and spies take notice. Many of your operational activities telegraph your secrets.

Companies also just give their secrets away. I can call the mailrooms of hundreds of companies and ask them to send me the company business plan. And with a little creative lying on my part, they'll do it.

Operational security vulnerabilities are the most threatening and ominous weaknesses in any organization. They are also the most plentiful, because they result primarily from human error and weakness. By taking the time to learn about these weaknesses in your organization, you can prevent or minimize their exploitation.

> ### ACCOUNTING FOR OPERATIONAL VULNERABILITIES
> When President Bush made a surprise visit to Iraq for Thanksgiving 2003, he did not use a presidential motorcade to get to Air Force One, but a single, unmarked SUV. Air Force One was scheduled for a maintenance flight, and Bush was supposed to stay at his Texas ranch. Reporters accompanying the president were required to give up their cell phones. President Bush changed airplanes inside a closed hangar. Air Force One had all its lights turned off as it landed in Iraq, and it descended at the last minute. Nobody was allowed to transmit news stories or otherwise let anyone know the president was in Iraq until after he was off the ground. The Secret Service accounted for every operational vulnerability they could think of to ensure that the likelihood of a terrorist attack was kept to a minimum.

Poor Awareness

In my experience performing penetration tests and investigating information-related crimes, poor awareness of security issues stands out as the most common operational vulnerability. Moderately skilled criminals can get well-meaning employees to hand over just about any piece of information they want. The damage from this lack of awareness of general security issues is compounded by a lack of understanding of the value of your company's information. This lack of understanding underlies the success of the attackers in most of the case studies presented in Part II of this book.

Most people find it hard to believe that I can walk up to people and ask for their company's most sensitive secrets and they will give them to me. However, if I ask for information in the right way, those skeptics would probably give me the same sensitive data. I can ask for people's personal information, and they will give it to me just as readily.

When people do acknowledge that there is a potential problem, most think it will never happen to them. This attitude is a spy's best weapon. Victims who feel this way ignore basic security considerations and allow unusual incidents and requests to go unnoticed. They hand over information to anyone who asks for it in the right way. They leave valuable information out in the open, vulnerable to theft and compromise. Usually, they don't even notice that they've been attacked.

You might be surprised to know how frequently classified materials are lost when military and government personnel make a quick stop at a store. They leave their laptop or briefcase in their car, and it is stolen. Theft of computers out of government buildings is also common.

Although theft of classified information is common, it is relatively rare compared to commercial and private theft. Documents detailing valuable pharmaceutical formulas are stolen regularly. Laptop computers are stolen from cars and at airport security screenings. Most automobile thefts occur when the owners leave their car doors open, frequently with the keys in the car. Some of these thefts result from a complete ignorance that the information is highly targeted. However, the majority is clearly the result of the "It won't happen to me" syndrome.

Poor awareness also means that employees don't know the proper way to react to potentially compromising situations. They don't know how to deliver quality customer service while maintaining security. Security and customer service are not mutually exclusive. In most cases, they can even enhance each other.

Many people believe that strong security is the same as martial law, and they end up avoiding the issue altogether. They dismiss company protocol. Security warnings go in one ear and out the other. It isn't maliciousness that moves people to believe that company security measures are just procedural and unnecessarily restrictive, it is poor awareness.

Common Sense and Common Knowledge

Security professionals often complain that people lack common sense when it comes to information security. What the professionals forget is that *there is no common sense without common knowledge.* The general public is not aware of the security implications of the everyday items, such as passwords, secured telephone lines, and cleaned and locked desks. People don't realize the value of the documents they toss on the seat next to them. The fact that someone might want the information never occurs to them, nor do they realize the ultimate threat to the company's security that such behavior invites.

Even technical vulnerabilities, which are covered later in this chapter, exist primarily because of the administrators' and users' poor awareness of computer security. If they knew about the vulnerabilities, they would usually do something about it. Unfortunately, few administrators and even fewer users are given the common knowledge to exercise common sense. Consider that all security professionals need more knowledge as well.

Perhaps the most glaring example of lack of security common sense was perpetrated by John Deutch, the former director of the CIA. He was investigated, and it was proven that he allowed a classified computer to be used by his family. This dereliction of security included letting his children use the computer to browse the Internet.

I firmly believe that most people actually want to help protect their company's information, or they would if they understood the seriousness of the problem. Your employees do care, and they will cooperate if you let them know what's at stake with an appropriate employee awareness program.

Most of the operational vulnerabilities discussed in this chapter stem from poor awareness. In other words, people would not do these things if they were aware of the problem. That's why I've listed this vulnerability first, and why I believe it is so important.

Social Engineering

In a broad sense, *social engineering* can refer to any situation in which people are interacting with others to manipulate them. The Nazis originally coined the phrase to mean the manipulation of the general population; the Soviet Union adopted the term as well (the term remains offensive to many people because of its sinister roots). In the 1980s, hackers started to use this term to describe strategies for getting information from people through nontechnical means. The term can also refer to basic criminal confidence scams.

In fact, social engineering has also been used by law-enforcement agencies to capture criminals. To entice Alexei Ivanov, the perpetrator described in Chapter 10, to leave Russia, the FBI created a fictional security company and invited Ivanov for a job interview in the United States. As Ivanov traveled to the United States, the FBI hacked into his computer to gather evidence and arrested him shortly after his arrival.

Social engineering is a type of attack that exploits operational security vulnerabilities, specifically poor awareness. For example, a hacker might call a company randomly and ask people for their user IDs and passwords. To get people to give her this information, she might imitate technical support personnel. Hackers also use social engineering—or *pretext phone calls*, as the police refer to this method—to get people to give them computer access points and other information about their computers and software. Chapter 6 presents a very successful use of this attack method to compromise a very large company firm.

Social-engineering tactics have also become the basis for most crimes against individuals on the Internet. Consider the infamous "I Love You" virus, which was an e-mail virus that required users to open an attachment for an attack to be executed. To entice people to do this, the virus-writing scum used "I Love You" as the subject of the message, which appeared to come from someone the victim knew. Another example is the PayPal scam, which tricks people into going to a fake web site and disclosing their credit card information. Many people have PayPal accounts, and the message looks real.

Although hackers have a reputation for being expert social engineers, they are insignificant amateurs in the subject matter. The better salespeople are professional social engineers. However, the best by far are spies, or, specifically, human intelligence operatives. If you think of social engineering as the manipulation of people, then people who get people to betray their country under penalty of death are clearly at a level beyond what hackers can dream of. Spies receive years of training in the understanding of people and know how to detect and exploit the victim's need for MICE, as Chapter 1 describes. Operatives combine a natural ability with extensive psychological training and practice.

Reverse social engineering refers to an interesting variant on this attack method, in which the victim comes to the attacker instead of the attacker approaching the victim. For example, during one of my penetration tests, I took a job as a temporary employee and let other workers know that I knew a lot about computers. While I sat there supposedly doing my job and ignoring other people, they would interrupt me to ask questions about a new computer program the company just started using. All the workers let me sit down at their computer. I would show them a few things while I surreptitiously installed back-door software on their system as they watched. I could then log in to their computers at will from my own desk.

In a more traditional case of reverse social engineering, a hacker entered a company and posted flyers saying that the company's Help Desk telephone number changed. Of course, the flyers gave a new telephone number, which was controlled by the hacker. Employees of the company called the number regularly, and the hacker secured passwords and just about anything else he wanted to know from employees wanting help.

Social engineering is a very powerful tool. It can bypass millions of dollars' worth of security mechanisms, it's very cheap to perform, and it doesn't take much technical expertise. Although real spies are by far the best at social-engineering activities, all that's needed for someone to be apparently successful is to be a good liar. The supposedly superior social-engineering skills of a hacker are actually more a demonstration of his victims' poor awareness than a result of any real expertise.

Accidents and Carelessness

Accidents and carelessness, referred to by lawyers as "errors and omissions," take on many forms and are an unavoidable fact of life. People accidentally leave documents in the wrong places at the wrong times. Classified material is left on computers that are resold to the general public. In negotiations, an innocent slip of the tongue can cost you big time. People leave their wallets on store counters. Car keys are lost. Virtually everyone has caused the compromise of sensitive information at some time or other and will cause it in the future. Much of this is due to poor awareness, but just as frequently, an aware person slips up for a moment.

Just because accidents happen doesn't mean you should stop trying to prevent them. However, organizations typically deal with accidents after the fact. One problem is that people often fail to report accidents. Covering up a mistake is a natural reaction, but you can't stop what you don't know about.

Policies and Procedures

Policies and procedures are the foundation of a corporation. Sometimes the policies and procedures of your organization actually create security vulnerabilities.

Although good policies can go far in reducing risk, many policies and procedures are developed without any consideration for security issues. Mandatory internal reporting of sensitive issues, for example, can generate sources of revealing information. Some policies simply require too much documentation and allow for distribution that is too widespread. Policies that require people to give their names and departments when they answer the telephone give unknown callers essential information that social engineers can use.

Take a look at your policies and procedures, and ask yourself which policies force people to give out information that might be useful to an attacker. Is it necessary to divulge that information to do business? If security were a consideration, would you still give out that information? Is it necessary for Toys "Я" Us or Circuit City to ask for your telephone number when you buy something from them? For situations in which employees are required to reveal that information, do they give out just the required data, or do they go further than necessary? Obviously, some information must be given out from a business perspective, but you may be able to limit that information from a security perspective.

Predictability

Organizations and people are very predictable. Knowing this, criminals can figure out the best times to commit their crimes.

- Bank robbers usually stake out a place to watch its operational patterns. They notice when the bank opens and closes. They keep track of when the bank is least crowded and when it has the most money. They study the guards to see whether they are observant or lazy. Within a short period of time—a couple of days at most—they know more about the bank than most of its employees do.

- Terrorists watch their victims, observing when they leave for work, what routes they take, and whom they meet during a typical day. Chapter 8 gives an example of when predictably poor security procedures created the potential loss of thousands of lives and billions of dollars of damage.

- Thieves scope out homes to see when people will predictably be away from home. They know that people turn their backs on their valuables in the course of performing business transactions. They know many people throw away their credit card and ATM receipts without destroying them.

- Industrial spies know when people typically leave their offices, when buildings are left empty, when information is left unattended, and anything else that tells them the best time to strike.

From a business perspective, predictability contributes to most insider crimes. Accountants know how to embezzle money without being detected. People who handle cash know when money is most vulnerable. Most important, they know the security procedures that they must circumvent.

Procedures in Practice

All companies have their rules and regulations, but often a wide gap exists between the procedures they put on paper and the procedures their employees follow. For example, many companies have a rule that employees are forbidden to write down their passwords; this rule is one of the most common among companies with computer systems—and it's one of the most violated rules in the world. People are not supposed to take work home, but they do. They're supposed to log out of the computer whenever they get up and leave their desk, but they don't.

Personally, when I talk to individuals and go into companies, I ask people whether they would give out sensitive information to a stranger. The immediate reply is, "Of course not!" However, when I perform a penetration test and use social engineering techniques, those same people divulge anything I ask of them.

Look around your organization and notice what is actually going on. Walk around the facility. Stay after everyone else has left for the day. How hard is it for you to get your hands on sensitive information? Often, there's a big difference between the way things are supposed to be and the way things are. It is more important that you understand the way your business really functions.

Sales and Marketing

The job of the sales and marketing departments is to get the word out about products and services. In this highly competitive marketplace, salespeople often leak information about upcoming offerings to potential customers. They disclose key details, scheduling information, and product specifications—all in the service of making the sale. They don't do it to cause problems. For the most part, this is a matter of honest enthusiasm.

In one case, I was attending a competitive intelligence conference. My friend, also attending the conference, came over and said that there was a woman also attending the conference on a payphone saying that she was from a trade magazine. The woman was clearly a competitive intelligence professional and not a reporter. She had a checklist in front of her that included features about some emerging product. She apparently called a company's Sales and Marketing department and claimed to be writing an article for an issue that was going to be coming out in four months, so she needed the information that the company would be releasing around that time. She got just about everything on her list.

At trade shows, anyone expressing a sincere interest in a marketer's products can get just about any information from the salesperson. Salespeople are supposed to give out information, not protect it. On almost all occasions, if a sale is in jeopardy, sensitive information will be revealed. Trained industrial spies know how to pose as interested customers and drag out a purchase negotiation until they get the information they want.

Companies bring Microsoft Corporation their technologies for potential licensing or purchase. These companies divulge anything asked of them, because a deal with Microsoft can put a company in the big time. Frequently, nothing comes of the deal. Microsoft may sometimes come out with a product that is similar or nearly identical to some of the technologies pitched. The courts decide the resulting cases.

Examine how your own sales and marketing departments release information about your organization. Notice whether they seem to be ignoring the fact that some information is sensitive. They have a job to do, but you need to make sure that they're not undermining your security efforts when they do it.

Public Relations

To maintain a good corporate image and keep stock prices high, many companies maintain ongoing public relations campaigns, which are carefully crafted to minimize negative press. They release information about their people and anything else that might make the company look good. From a business perspective, this activity is very important; from a security perspective, any release of information is bad.

Your public relations (PR) department represents an unavoidable vulnerability. In large companies, the press releases gush out of the PR department month after month. Telling people about your organization is the job of the PR staff. They create publicity; security is the last thing on their minds. You can reduce your vulnerability in this area by making sure that they don't tell the world more than it should know.

Corporations are not the only people making PR gaffs. The U.S. Department of Defense had to issue an order limiting the amount of information that combat units put on their web sites. In one case, the web site of a U.S. destroyer that participated in the attacks on terrorist camps in Afghanistan disclosed personal information about the captain of the ship, including details on his family and home address.

Help Wanted Ads

Although the need for highly skilled employees varies with the economy, there are always help wanted ads. Some ads are vague about the job and the company, describing only the types of skills required of the potential employee. However, help wanted ads frequently divulge more information than necessary about a company's operations.

I have read listings that describe a bank's entire computer environment, explain how the bank supports billions of dollars of financial transactions daily, and include detailed descriptions of hardware and software. That last piece of information tells me exactly how to attack the bank, as discussed in the "Technical Vulnerabilities" section later in this chapter. Besides making the job appealing to potential employees, these ads reveal the intent of the company's projects, as well as vulnerabilities in your organization that criminals may use against you.

Sometimes when a position is advertised, it indicates that someone in that position will be fired. For example, the information security field is relatively small, especially with regard to senior positions in large companies. I am frequently contacted by professional recruiters about job openings for jobs currently held by friends of mine. In a relatively small field, the person soon to be fired will eventually find out. That person may be bitter and retaliate, perhaps while still in the position.

Internet Usage

The Internet can be a tremendous resource. It provides a wealth of information previously unimagined. However, the Internet can also expose major vulnerabilities within your company.

When people access the Internet, they leave tracks. Every time someone visits a web site or reads a newsgroup message, a log of the activity is collected. A good spy will examine your Internet usage and use your activity to figure out what you are up to.

Cookies allow you to be tracked across the Internet. (See discussion under "Technical Vulnerabilities.") Cookies are supposed to be for specific sites. However, most people are not aware that if you visit one site, it may place a cookie on your system for an advertiser. That cookie can then be retrieved by other sites with that advertiser.

Personal firewall software is supposed to protect you. Unfortunately, it also logs the web sites that you visit. Likewise, your web browser history has this information. Someone with access to your computer can see the sites you visited.

What your people say about your company and themselves online is also very important. While conducting research on an organization, I came upon a message posted to a technical newsgroup by an employee. He announced that he and everyone else in his department were just given new computers. He gave the model number, operating system version, and applications he was using. He was putting out a call for software that might be useful, but he was really just asking for trouble. He had, in effect, made his company a prime target for hackers and criminals around the world. He had told anyone who was interested exactly what type of computer he was using; all systems have known vulnerabilities that an attacker could exploit. From the message header, an attacker could easily figure out which company the poster worked for and even the exact Internet address of his computer. The fact that he also asked to be sent software left him particularly vulnerable; people could send him anything, including a virus-laden application that could damage his company's system.

The term *googling* is now part of our culture. It refers to the fact that you can research people by going to the Google web site. What with personal home pages, online publishing of public notices, church and charity groups putting their bulletins and announcements on the Internet, and so on, you can develop quite a dossier on most people.

Social Networking web sites are a growing phenomenon on the Internet. These sites, such as Orkut.com, Friendster, and Meetup.com, allow people to meet each other. They voluntarily put their personal information on the site in the hopes of making connections for business and personal purposes. The more specific and comprehensive the details, the better the connections—and the better the information a malicious party can collect.

Generally, any time people send information over the Internet, they are giving away information about themselves and their company. Even an innocent visit to a web site gives away some sensitive information. The repercussions for you and your company can be devastating.

Credit Cards and Travel Records

You will find your credit card number hidden on many forms you typically choose to discard, including draft hotel bills. Also remember the example of the "Good Morning America" credit card number I give in Chapter 1. These numbers and others are widely available on many forms people take for granted.

Additionally, credit card use telegraphs your personal habits. Credit card records can tell a savvy snoop almost everything about a person's life. Credit card receipts are crucial to divorce cases. Private investigators bribe people to get their target's credit card records. People are blackmailed based on information in credit card records. These records can also say a lot about what a company is doing, so they are especially useful for industrial espionage and are a staple of traditional espionage. Credit card use leaves an electronic trail that stays around for a very long time.

Different types of travel records also reveal much about a company's plans and future actions. You can figure out whom a company is negotiating with by finding out where its representatives travel. Find a copy of the representative's frequent flyer account report and you'll be able to discover exactly which hotels she stayed in. Business travelers usually choose hotels that are close to the companies they're working with. If you get a copy of the hotel record, you might learn that the representative was given a special rate reserved for people associated with a large company in a particular area. You can find out whom she called from her hotel room. If the person involved works on mergers or new stock offerings, you have insider trading information.

Telephone Records and Conversations

If you think that the information gleaned from your credit cards can disclose information about you, consider what your telephone records indicate. Jealous lovers go through the dialed and received call lists on their mate's cell phone. The actual cell phone bill has a record of every call to or from that phone. Your home and business telephones may also have detailed records.

No one can do business without using a telephone. It is probably the most essential device of the contemporary business environment, and it is easily the most ubiquitous. Consequently, telephone records, which are not that difficult to get, can reveal a lot about what you and your organization are doing.

Think about it this way: If you were to access the telephone records of a young woman and find that she has placed numerous calls to caterers, bridal stores, and photographers, you might rightly conclude that she is getting married, even if you know nothing else about her. Think about your own telephone calls. What could a record of your calls tell a potential attacker? As do credit card records, telephone records stay around for a very long time.

Obviously, the most sensitive information about a telephone conversation is the conversation itself, which can be compromised several ways. People can overhear what you're saying just by standing nearby or by sitting in the next cubicle. Telephones can be tapped in three ways: the telephone system can be compromised, the individual telephone can be bugged, and a radio receiver can be used to pick up cell and portable telephone conversations. Everyone knows about the first two, but many people don't realize that wireless telephone communications can be intercepted very easily.

In terms of potential operational vulnerabilities, what matters is what people talk about over the telephone. If your employees are aware that there is a vulnerability, they can minimize your risk by watching what they say and whom they call, especially when using cell and portable telephones.

Casual Conversations

Also, as noted in Chapter 1, people often talk about work in many inappropriate places without regard to who may be listening. Such conversations can represent significant vulnerabilities, depending on where the conversations take place and who is involved. A good spy can enter a conversation in progress and turn the discussion toward sensitive topics. These conversations can occur on the streets, at parties, on buses, and so on, and they involve just about every aspect of an individual's work.

Supplier Records

Even when you have gone to great lengths to make your own facility airtight, you still need to deal with other businesses. Your suppliers have a great deal of valuable information about you, and they aren't necessarily taking steps to keep it secure. They know what and how much your company orders, when it's delivered, when you ask for deliveries to be delayed, and when you cut back on your orders. Just knowing how much of a given item a company orders can reveal a great deal about what it intends to produce. Depending on your relationship, your suppliers could know more about you than your own employees do.

In Chapter 4, I described the case of a French company that attempted to purchase the design plans from my client's subcontractors. This is clearly a case of intentional leakage of information. However, most compromises of information by suppliers and subcontractors result from inadvertent security leaks.

Thefts of personal information, such as credit card numbers, can occur from poorly secured vendor web sites. Millions of credit cards have been compromised this way. Banks, universities, and government agencies have been compromised, and the customers suffer.

Personal Aggrandizement

An individual's desire to impress others has caused some of the biggest security problems in history. People regularly compromise information for fame or the adoration of others. Some men do stupid things to impress women.

As I mention in the Introduction, one of my female friends was a CIA operative who posed in *Playboy* magazine. She was extremely successful at getting men to divulge sensitive information. All she had to do was feign interest in a particular subject and the men would blabber away everything they knew about it.

Technical professionals seem to be particularly vulnerable in this area. If a male technical professional meets a woman who appears to be interested in his work, he will tell her everything about his job. I don't say this to criticize; it's only human nature, especially in a field where so many people simply don't understand the person's work.

Once, when I was traveling for NSA with two coworkers, I found myself sitting in the international terminal of Charles de Gaulle Airport in Paris, waiting for a flight. One of the people I was traveling with began conversing with a woman sitting next to him, and the conversation naturally turned to the reason for our trip. My coworker started talking about computers, and the woman seemed very interested. Although he didn't talk about anything sensitive, he did begin attracting attention from other people sitting nearby. Eventually, the woman asked a very natural question: "So, whom do you work for?" At that point, my coworker realized that saying he worked for one of the world's most secretive spy agencies to a stranger in the middle of this airport was not a good idea, and he sat there dumbfounded for an uncomfortably long time. I replied for him, saying that we worked for the Department of Defense. If a terrorist had been among the interested listeners in that French airport, that conversation could have gotten us killed.

I was once traveling on an airplane that was rerouted from the original destination because of weather conditions. Sitting several rows behind me was a salesperson who worked for a large defense contractor. He used the airphone to pick up his messages and to change appointments, and he carried on in such a loud voice that either he was trying to impress people or he was just plain stupid. I learned the name of his employer from four rows away (and I usually don't even learn anything about the person sitting next to me). At least 30 people heard the names of the people he was meeting with and when and where they were meeting. We also heard about his plans for a sales trip to Hungary; he clearly raised his voice whenever he said the country's name. It seemed to me that this man was very insecure—just the type of person industrial spies look for. If I were a competitor, I could have written down everything he said and handed it to my marketing department.

Working Outside the Office

In such a competitive age, it's no surprise that many people take work home from the office. They are working hard, filling every free moment, pursuing a work ethic that is the heart and soul of this country. They are also creating a serious vulnerability.

Look around the airplane the next time you fly. You'll see fellow passengers with open laptops and documents spread out and spilling onto the floor. Their bosses would be pleased, but the industrial spies reading company secrets over their shoulders are positively giddy. One of my friends, who specializes in competitive intelligence, was asked to ride on an airplane and specifically sit behind two businessmen to learn about a proposal that they were going to deliver.

Personally, I have seen critical secrets from Bristol-Meyer, Boeing, Diebold, the Department of Defense, the Nuclear Regulatory Agency, a variety of technical companies, venture capital firms, and countless others. The information was there for the taking. Luckily for these organizations, I did not have ill intent and had no reason to pay attention to what I was seeing. Given that these people did nothing to protect the information, I could actually legally sell this information to their competitors.

When you work outside the office, you don't know who is watching. When you're out in public, you have little control over your environment, and it's impossible to implement even the most basic security measures. If your organization's employees are taking work home every night, you've got a vulnerability, and your organization might be creating security leaks in service of the short-term bottom line. A corporate culture that lets this happen enables industrial espionage. Chapter 9 demonstrates how this vulnerability can be used incredibly well.

This vulnerability also applies to doing personal work in public. I've watched people pay their bills on airplanes. I see their credit card numbers. I see their telephone bills and the numbers they call. I see their addresses and sometimes their social security numbers. Think about that next time you take out papers in public.

Poor Incident-Reporting Procedures

If an employee in your organization does detect a possible security breach, does he or she know what to do about it? When employees do take action—and remember that they usually don't—what they do most often is tell their supervisors. Unfortunately, most of the supervisors I've interviewed over the years don't know what to do with this information.

Diligent employees are left helpless and frustrated when they don't get an adequate response to their concerns, which makes them even less likely to report similar incidents in the future. Remember that detecting espionage activity is the toughest part of combating it, and you need all the help you can get.

Basic Human Weakness

Most people are well-meaning and want to help others and especially their coworkers. They are used to cooperating, and management encourages them to be service oriented. So it's only natural to find people within an organization who will gladly bypass those pesky company rules to be helpful to others they believe are coworkers. Even poorly trained spies know how to take advantage of a person's good-will, making that helpfulness a weakness.

Sometimes attackers just confuse people into giving up information. When people feel overwhelmed with too much information, they often follow the lead of whoever appears to know what he or she is doing. No one wants to look stupid. Good industrial spies always look like they know what they're doing.

Perhaps the most dangerous human weakness is apathy. Many people want to avoid problems and tend to choose the path of least resistance. All a spy needs to do with these people is persist and they will eventually give in. Apathetic employees not only give up information more easily but also are much less likely to report questionable situations. They just want to do their job and go home. If there is a choice between reporting a questionable incident, thereby attracting attention and scrutiny, or just letting it go, chances are they will just let it go.

Too Little Information

Although this seems counterintuitive, giving out too little information can be as much of a problem as giving out too much. When companies play their cards too close to the vest, so to speak, they often keep potentially valuable information from their own employees and others. Security that is so tight that it strangles productive communication only helps the spies.

Companies often hide information about threats or losses, fearing that publicizing a breach in security will make them more vulnerable or lower their stock prices. Employees are never told that they should be on the lookout for specific suspicious activity; consequently, they can't help.

You can provide too little information to outside parties as well. In a personal situation, two companies approached me to subcontract to them in performing a penetration test. Neither company was willing to tell me who the customer was. Comically, it turned out that both companies were bidding on the same contract. Since neither company was willing to tell me who the customer was, I didn't discover the problem until the last minute, causing problems for everyone involved.

As I stated earlier in the chapter, poor awareness is the biggest vulnerability people and organizations face. Purposely keeping awareness poor is the worst thing a security program can do.

Contractual Relationships

Although contracts intend to protect parties, they can be one-sided or otherwise present opportunities for loss. As Chapter 4 describes, China required many companies to open themselves up in order to do business in China. Israel placed "on-site monitors" into a company named Recon/Optical as part of a development contract, and those on-site monitors turned out to be spies who robbed the company of its intellectual property. These countries are not alone, nor is this unique to governments. Large companies are notorious for one-sided contracts, and some small companies have overly aggressive legal departments that want to get it all.

Chapter 12 lists nondisclosure and noncompete agreements as types of countermeasures. However, if these agreements are overly restrictive or one-sided, they can stop you from doing business or otherwise hurt your operations. Tricky legal wording can limit you from recovering damages from the other party. These types of contracts can prevent you from hiring good employees or open your own company to employee and information poaching.

Physical Vulnerabilities

When most people think about physical security, they imagine burly guards standing inside fenced-in compounds, iron doors with impenetrable time locks, and a lot of searchlights. If they had their way, many security managers would establish just such a prison camp environment so that they could sleep better at night. Of course, the company wouldn't be much more secure. The most successful spies are the ones who exploit the small physical vulnerabilities. After all, if someone is already allowed inside the facility, say as a temporary worker or a janitor, what good are the searchlights? The greatest damage is done by people who are already on the inside.

Another often overlooked physical security issue is natural disasters. As I explain in Chapter 4, natural disasters cause more damage than malicious insiders ever have or will. A hard disk that crashes because of a power outage is just as great a loss as a hard disk that is stolen.

Also, physical vulnerabilities often facilitate attacks against nonphysical vulnerabilities. An attacker might be able to technically exploit a computer system only if she can gain physical access to a terminal.

Apathetic or Poorly Informed Guards

Traditionally, security guards are trained merely to limit access to company facilities. They stand at the door, ask for your ID, and check their approved lists. In some cases, they're also called on to search the belongings of exiting employees to make sure that people are not carrying out sensitive documents or property. But they are rarely trained to actually recognize sensitive material.

Companies typically train their security guards to look for key markings or indicators on documents. In the defense community, guards are trained to look for documents with classification identifiers at the top and bottom of a page. In the private sector, guards are told to look out for red binder covers or something else just as obvious. This situation creates an enormous physical vulnerability. Smart attackers can just take their stolen documents out of the red binders and stuff them into green ones, or they can tear the classifications from the tops and bottoms of the pages, and then stroll out the door unhindered.

Let's face it, a security guard's job isn't always the most stimulating activity in the world. Guards can easily fall into a rut and lose their enthusiasm for the work (or maybe they never had any enthusiasm in the first place). The guards are there to spot the isolated security problem, but because there are typically very few of these problems, they become bored and apathetic.

This lack of devotion is particularly damaging when guards are supposed to validate access requests by checking people's ID badges. People change their hairstyles, grow beards and mustaches, and gain or lose weight. This means that badge pictures frequently do not resemble the people carrying them. In addition, companies have "rush hours" when the traffic is heavy, so the guards must look at dozens of badges per minute. Combine apathy, inaccurate ID photographs, and overwhelming numbers, and you've got a recipe for a major physical vulnerability. There were stories at NSA about the Office of Security spot-checking the agency's guards by sending people through security with badges picturing people who did not resemble the people wearing them. In one case, a person is said to have walked in with a badge picture of a dog and was able to get through unchallenged.

Furthermore, employees are notoriously rude to guards, cursing the guards for making them wait or for checking their belongings. To avoid offending people, many guards begin to back off; they've endured so many annoyed looks and out-and-out insults that they effectively loosen your security net.

Although it is easy to blame the guards, the fact is that the management responsible for the guards is inevitably responsible for their performance and apathy. Whether management fosters or ignores the problem is irrelevant when compared to the end result. Some of the case studies in Part II demonstrate the potentially devastating results when guards demonstrate poor performance.

No Physical Access Controls

Although poorly trained guards can be a problem, not having any guards or locks on doors is a much bigger and more common problem. Walking into an office that is unattended is something I do with great regularity in my penetration-testing work. After I'm in an unlocked office, I can get into the computer systems or walk out with papers, even a computer. If spies can get through the doors, and if they look as though they know what they're doing, very few people will challenge them.

Garbage

Your organization's trash can reveal a lot. Most of the time, garbage is garbage, but it can contain incredibly important information. A great deal of credit card fraud results from people throwing out their credit card receipts, which criminals pick out of the garbage. Around Christmas time, local police departments advise people to be careful about their trash. Although people initially think the police worry too much about littering, the police know that smart criminals look for houses that discard boxes for expensive gifts. The paparazzi regularly go through the trash of the celebrities they stalk.

The Masters of Deception and Legion of Doom hacker groups were able to gain control of key telephone system assets by finding a list of passwords in the garbage of the New York Telephone Company. Companies throw away draft copies of many important documents that contain much or all of the information contained in the final draft. Oracle Corporation hired a third-party firm to investigate Microsoft. Microsoft cried industrial espionage when it learned that the third party went through the trash of Microsoft's lobbying office.

Trash is valuable. The U.S. Army has a unit devoted to trash intelli-gence. I've even heard about a case in which a trash-disposal company would pick up one company's trash and bring it over to a competitor.

Of course, you need to be able to throw out your garbage, but you must recognize it as a potentially dangerous vulnerability. Tossed into large dumpsters outside your building, your trash is almost certainly a target of corporate spies. Although most of the information you throw away will be useless, there is almost always enough valuable informa-tion to make it worthwhile for attackers to dig through the dumpster.

Open Storage

When competitors want to see how well your factory is doing, all they need to do is watch what goes in and comes out of your facilities. Depending on the size and nature of your products, this could be a very easy task, especially if your products are stored out in the open. If a foreign intelligence agency wants to know how many tanks the United States is producing, all it needs to do is count the tanks sitting outside the tank factory.

One of the primary jobs of "spy satellites" is to photograph military equipment in open storage areas. In this post-Cold War era, satellites are used for more than just military observation; industrial spies use the same techniques. The French SPOT satellite system has developed a reputation for being a reliable tool of industrial espionage. The quality of SPOT's satellite photographs rivals that of intelligence satellites.

I know one competitive intelligence specialist who was hired by a company to find out whether a competitor was meeting its delivery deadline. The spy chartered a small airplane for an hour, flew over the target's storage yard, and took pictures of the products sitting in the yard.

It's also likely that Aerobus, the European airplane manufacturer and Boeing's only real competitor for that market, monitors the pro-duction of Boeing airplanes to see whether it is behind or ahead on its orders. Aerobus uses this type of information to give its customers the impression that Boeing cannot deliver.

Some companies establish formal document-storage areas. Often, these storerooms are little more than closets with a lock. Frequently, the storage areas are left unlocked throughout the day and are locked only at night after everyone has left. These storage areas may or may not be attended, depending on corporate policy. Document storage rooms that are unattended are open to virtually anyone. Monitored storage areas are secured with varying degrees of effectiveness. In some cases, the attendant has an access list that specifies who can take out which documents, but such access lists are the exception. Typically, anyone in the company can walk in and ask for any document or browse freely through the files, picking up any document that looks interesting.

Copy Machines

"The copy machine," reads the message on a popular NSA awareness poster, "is a spy's best friend." The case in Chapter 9 is an excellent example of why the NSA made this statement. Copy machines allow people to steal information without removing it, reducing significantly the chances that they will be caught. Just about every major national espionage case has involved a massive document copying effort. In cases of industrial espionage, copy machines are just as widely used.

Copy machines are usually accessible in many locations throughout an organization, 24 hours a day, and there are always at least a few located in discreet nooks where no one would notice a spy at work. Unusual copy machine usage is one of the best ways to detect an industrial spy. Are your copy machines in your organization in visible locations? Is a video camera monitoring the areas? Does your copy machine use the available accounting features to track the number of copies different people in your organizations are making? The copy machine will always be important to anyone trying to go unnoticed.

Electronic Storage

Now that the world has moved to an environment in which every document is available electronically, CDs and other removable storage devices might have replaced the copy machine as a spy's best friend. I talk about these shortly, in the discussion of CDs and similar devices. These devices can each store truckloads of documents. Think of it: a truckload of documents that fits in your pocket. The implications are clear. In Chapter 9, you read about Afshin Bavand. Although he delivered only a few small packages to his Russian handlers, he gave away more information than dozens of investigators were able to review. The unofficial estimates were that he delivered the equivalent of three truckloads of documents.

Your Neighbors

While you are surveying your operation for physical vulnerabilities, don't forget to check out your neighbors. The closer the competition—literally—the greater the danger that they will be able to monitor your activities to their advantage. Surprisingly, many people don't consider the dangers of physical proximity to a competitor.

Competitors can set up shop in the office across the hall. They can share electrical or computer wiring facilities. They might be so close that all they need to do is put a drinking glass to the wall to hear what's going on in your company. Proximity makes you more susceptible to technical attacks as well (see the discussion on TEMPEST and wireless technologies in the "Technical Vulnerabilities" section later in this chapter). Your neighbors can watch who visits your facilities and target them as potential clients.

In one case, an attorney told me that he was involved in a major lawsuit. Somehow it appeared that his adversary knew everything about his strategy. This attorney later found out that the opposing attorneys had the hotel suite below his and then soon found a bug in his room.

If your neighbors actually have criminal intentions, they probably know the security measures you have in place, and they know how to get around them. Their workers could become very friendly with your organization's workers, creating more chances for information compromise.

Your Environment

Whenever you leave your corporate facilities, you are at the mercy of your environment. You should have no expectation of privacy beyond your home turf. If you leave anything in your hotel room, consider the information compromised, whether it's on a computer or on pieces of paper. As I point out in Chapter 4, in many foreign countries you can expect your facilities to be entered without your permission, bugged without legal repercussions, and infiltrated by local spies.

Even inside the United States, you are vulnerable beyond the walls of your facilities. I have already mentioned the susceptibility of working on airplanes. Hotel maids can leave doors open accidentally, making it easy for a spy claiming to be you to get inside, grab your papers, and run. Airports have become a favorite hunting ground of laptop thieves. One gambit has been particularly effective: The target puts his or her laptop on the conveyor belt, and one thief steps in front of the line, triggering the alarm and blocking the way while a guard searches for metal objects. Meanwhile, the laptop has gone on through the X-ray machine, and an accomplice on the other side snatches it and takes off. I could go on for pages describing the attacks and dangers you face away from the security of your company facility, even in your own country.

My friend Stan, the Russian defector, always goes to local restaurants when he targets a company. See Chapter 6. He knows he will overhear many conversations about the target.

Contributing to the problem is the fact that most people are not sufficiently aware of their surroundings when they are doing business away from the office. They don't recognize the many opportunities an adversary has to exploit them outside the cubicle.

Equipment Size

The fact that computer equipment is getting smaller all the time adds to your physical vulnerabilities. Simply put, smaller equipment—and the information it contains—is easier to steal. Desktop computers used to weigh almost 40 pounds; now we have PDAs, such as Palm Pilots and Pocket PCs, that weigh ounces. If you want to exert yourself, you can get a laptop that weighs six pounds. All this technology is very easy to conceal.

Data storage capacity is also increasing at the same time as the storage media get smaller. In the old days, the bulkiness of paper files made it difficult to steal very much information.

The ease of equipment theft has spawned a new breed of criminals called *office pirates*. They infiltrate a location and steal equipment, such as laptops, lying unattended. They dress like typical employees and walk around generally unnoticed in search of vulnerable computers. They grab the computers and casually walk out.

In a twist on this concept, I once attended a cybercrime conference in New York City. The hotel had a problem with people dressing like attendees and walking into the meeting rooms during conference breaks. They would then steal unattended laptops. The security guards actually caught one person sneaking in while I was there. They did not, however, catch the person who stole a laptop from an exhibitor's booth, which was coincidentally next to the U.S. Secret Service's booth. These thieves have a lot of nerve, the Secret Service was asleep at the switch, and people are ignorant of the problem.

Poor Inventory Tracking

Equipment tracking is a basic security requirement. As equipment gets smaller, it also becomes harder to track. It's no longer odd to move a computer from one location to another. It is so common, in fact, that companies often fail to keep track of which machine is where. More important, they often fail to notice when people carry computers out of the building.

From an information perspective, it is currently almost impossible to track electronic documents. People can copy a document without creating a record. There is no system that can track disks or other information, so thefts can occur at the will of the spy or petty thief.

Messy Desks

Most industrial spies never need to break into filing cabinets because they can find everything they want on people's desks. Many people tend to leave work out on their desks at the end of the day. It's only natural to leave out the components of the project you're right in the middle of. But when your employees leave sensitive documents unprotected on their desks, they make it easy for anyone walking by to see exactly what they're doing. Good spies will recognize this bad habit and exploit it. They can visit the office when the employee is gone, snatch sensitive documents, make copies, and return them to the pile on the desk. When the desk is really messy, a spy can just take a document, knowing that the employee will probably think it's lost somewhere in all the paper.

Inboxes

Although office inboxes are becoming uncommon, they are alive and well where they matter most—the desks of executives. Even among your neatest employees, inboxes represent a major vulnerability. People routinely leave extremely sensitive information in these boxes. Even very security-conscious workers can't stop someone else from dropping something very sensitive into their inbox. Papers lying in an inbox are vulnerable to the same exploitation as papers piled on a messy desk. Anyone can walk by and pick up the materials.

I have noticed that some people leave sensitive material in an inbox turned face down. I've even seen material taped to an office door this way. The assumption is that people will be less likely to read it as they walk by. However, this odd habit actually encourages the attention of good industrial spies. A face-down document is bound to draw attention.

Computers Not Logged Out

Even worse than messy desks and inboxes are computers left logged on and unattended. An attacker can use such a machine to access everything that person is working on, or, possibly, has ever worked on. More important, that person probably has access to other people's data as well. Computers that are left vulnerable in this way provide attackers with the foot in the door they're after. After attackers establish an initial access point, they can compromise your entire computer network. There have been cases of people sending out e-mail from someone's account pretending to be someone else to ruin that person's life. Even television's Judge Judy has decided cases involving people using other people's e-mail.

Computers with No Password Protection

It doesn't matter whether a computer has been turned off if it doesn't have any password protection. Many computer systems in use today require little more than pressing the on switch for instant access to information. Without effective password protection, your company is vulnerable to the least-skilled attackers out there. Anyone can sit down at a computer in your organization and access almost every piece of information your company has to offer.

Passwords Written Down

Establishing tight password protocols for all the computers on your system won't help if a computer's password is readily available. I don't know how many times I've walked into a highly sensitive environment and seen someone's password taped to the monitor. Sometimes there is a minor effort to hide the password, such as taping it under a keyboard or putting it on a paper in a desk. More frequently, it is on a sticky note stuck to a monitor.

Lack of Locks and Their Use

Equally disheartening to me is the fact that offices, filing cabinets, and other storage containers in many corporate facilities have no locks. A desk you can't lock is like a birthday present to a spy; an office you can't lock is like a personal piñata, except the spy is not blindfolded. Without locks, you have no power to protect information from physical attacks.

Unfortunately, even when locks are available, most people don't use them. Unless a company has a tough policy and its security guards check the desks at night, most employees will never lock up their materials. It seems to be just another aggravation to many people, and some actively resist lock-up policies. They don't want to carry around an extra key, which they might forget or lose. They just don't understand the risks involved, and they make the spy's job that much easier.

Electrical Systems

Although it's possible that an attacker might purposely cause your power supply to fail, it is much more likely that this physical vulnerability will manifest as an accident or result from a natural disaster. The 2003 U.S. Northeast power blackout resulted from tree limbs. Hurricane Isabelle caused blackouts for many people for long periods of time. Earthquakes frequently take down power in California for extended periods.

Although the media likes to focus on business when the power goes out, think about the effects on individuals. Food is ruined and people can't cook. Medicine goes bad. People on home respirators must be taken to hospitals. Important telephone calls cannot be made. Computers crash and people lose all their personal information. All this is in addition to the potential for riots in some areas.

The growth in computer usage in this country has resulted in overtaxed electrical circuits in buildings designed for a different age. Depending on your facilities, power failures might be commonplace. Such outages can cause serious damage to your computers, not to mention the loss of a great deal of work. Many PBX (corporate telephone) systems shut down when the power supply goes out, shutting off all communications. Additionally, frequent power outages can make you look incompetent or unreliable to your clients.

In some cases, poor electrical systems can create power spikes that can literally fry your computer circuitry. Lightning strikes can also cause power spikes that travel through the electrical lines. These power spikes travel through your power lines, ruining everything plugged into an electrical outlet. The reliability of your electrical circuits and sources is critical to the survival of your computers.

Your telephone system is also vulnerable to power spikes. If the telephone line itself suffers a power spike, the telephone system can be destroyed. People talking on the telephone have reportedly been electrocuted when a particularly powerful spike hit close to their location.

Placement of Buildings and Equipment

The very location of your corporate facilities and its equipment creates vulnerabilities. For example, if you are located on the coast of California, you are very susceptible to earthquakes. If you are located in Florida, you might have a hurricane problem. There's not much you can do to prevent an earthquake, but these vulnerability issues should not be ignored. Your security planning should include some consideration of building and equipment placement.

If your facility is located on a flood plain, you probably don't want to put your computer system in the basement (which many large companies do). When the sump pump in my home failed during Hurricane Isabelle, my basement office was nearly flooded. Had I not noticed the problem in time, my computer would have been destroyed. Luckily, I had set up my desk in an area of the basement that was slightly elevated. It still cost several thousand dollars for the resulting cleanup and replacement of carpet.

If your facility catches fire, the damage could be compounded by your sprinkler systems, which would surely ruin your computers. If your computers are located in the basement, you can count on the water from the upper floors flooding the area. For this reason, many companies install Halon or similar fire-suppression systems, which smother the fire without using water. Unfortunately, these systems are used only to protect large computer systems. Sprinkler systems are still widely used in companies with major investments in their computer systems.

Personnel Vulnerabilities

There is a fine line between personnel and operational vulnerabilities. Although operational vulnerabilities involve the way in which people and companies function, personnel vulnerabilities result from the ways in which companies hire and manage their employees. Weaknesses in this area greatly increase your risks, because they allow attackers to exploit all other vulnerabilities.

The human resources (HR) department is usually the first and only line of defense against insiders who would do your company harm. After those with criminal intentions make it through the hiring process, they are free, at least for a while, from scrutiny. After they have all the rights and access of your other employees, they are extremely difficult to detect.

Personnel security also involves how employees separate from the company. What company hasn't had a person who left the company under less than perfect circumstances?

Failure to Validate Claimed Backgrounds

Although many companies do take the time to fully investigate the backgrounds of the people they hire, many more do not. Few organizations even take the time to check references, verify previous job histories, or confirm educational claims of job candidates. Hiring managers admit that the job interview is their key filtering tool. Basically, if candidates seem as though they would be good workers, they are hired.

When a company finds a candidate with rare skills that are much in demand, or the company is facing a major worker shortage, the HR people tend to streamline the hiring process even further. For example, when the Transportation Security Administration needed to hire security screeners at airports, they hired many people with only tentative checks. They fired more than a thousand people when the checks were fully complete.

This is a foolhardy practice fraught with danger. We read in the newspapers of childcare workers with child molestation convictions, programmers with malicious hacking backgrounds, janitors on parole for grand theft, top executives with questionable qualifications, and doctors without medical degrees. I personally went to a doctor and was seen by a physician's assistant. It later turned out that this person worked at several medical practices and was not licensed. The consequences can be truly disastrous, or at the very least call your organization's credibility into question. You could literally be giving the key to your company to criminals.

One study indicated that as many as 70 percent of all résumés contained "purposeful inaccuracies." Sometimes it is an outright cover-up of a criminal past. Sometimes it is having completely fake references. Most of the time, people do not lie about major issues. However, can you really trust people who fib about their background? If they lie about their salary to get a larger salary offer from a new employer, how can the new employer trust them to be honest about other monetary issues?

MICE

Chapter 1 discussed MICE (money, ideology, coercion, ego), which are the main reasons people engage in malicious activities. This is related to the "Charney Theorem," as Scott Charney likes to call it. Scott is currently Chief Security Strategist at Microsoft and was previously in charge of the Department of Justice Intellectual Property and Computer Crime Unit. His theorem is that at any time, 3 percent of the population will commit a crime if offered the opportunity. I personally think the percentage is much lower.

However, the fact is that there are people who will just naturally take advantage of you if the opportunity arises. Other people may be pushed to the edge and over it by a spy of one form or another. This is an issue you must account for, especially when you consider that being an employee typically allows unfettered access to just about anything inside your walls.

Weak Management

Weak management is a very specific vulnerability because it grants many employees more opportunity to do things that create problems. Telecommuting and remote management exacerbates this problem.

Some employees take advantage of a weak management situation. The most common problem is a loss of productivity. A bigger problem arises when employees start using a company's resources to start their own business. When they do that, their new business frequently competes with their employer's. Even worse, poorly managed employees may use their employer's facilities for criminal activities, such as gambling and dealing drugs.

Poor Separation Procedures

Separation procedures establish what happens when employees leave a company. If there is not a carefully thought-out procedure to make sure that departing employees return all the computers, telephones, credit cards, and so on that have been issued to them, there will likely be problems getting everything back.

When I ran my own company, I found that I needed to get lawyers involved about half the time people left the company. People did not want to give back their computers or transfer critical files to the employees' replacements. Sometimes former employees tried to steal my clients. When I started my company, I had no idea this would be an issue. I have since discovered that separation procedures are critical.

Isolation of Human Resources

In most companies, the HR department acts independently of all other areas. The primary reason for this isolation is possible legal implications of exposing a personnel issue. Basically, HR tends to be something of an island. HR staff don't share information with other groups and they don't tell people when their group members are involved in bad situations. This actually allows the bad situations to continue and ultimately increases the damage. It is fundamentally the same consequence of giving out too little information.

Even when personnel actions don't require confidentiality, HR departments rarely inform other groups in a company that an action is pending. For example, when an employee resigns, HR typically does not inform many of the people who should know for security reasons. The IS department is not made aware that it should be watching for any unusual activity, or that it should deactivate the computer account after the employee leaves. Even if the employee does not come back to use the account, someone else might use it as an unnoticed foot in the door. During my penetration tests, I have found thousands of unused accounts in some organizations.

When a computer administrator leaves, special considerations must be made in advance. All accounts may need to have their passwords changed after the administrator departs. I was called in a week before one administrator was going to be fired to set traps for him because the company expected malicious activity. That might seem extreme; however, there have been cases of devastating retaliation. For example, *Time* magazine was attacked by a disgruntled temporary administrator who went in and deleted all the data on a critical file server after he left the company. He logged in over a modem connection using the super user password and then used another person's password to log in and commit his acts. The office was down for two days and the result was more than $100,000 worth of damage.

Security staff should also be made aware of the plans of a departing employee. Many former employees have returned to company facilities to collect and gather information after they have officially left. Because their faces look familiar, guards will be less likely to question their presence.

Even when people don't have malicious intentions, they may do things that are otherwise not allowed. Many employees seem to have a mistaken belief that they have the right to anything that they ever worked on in the company. They carry out sensitive documents to keep for their records. A recent and highly notable case is that of Paul O'Neill, the former Secretary of the Treasury, who participated in a tell-all book about his year in the White House. O'Neill admitted to taking thousands of documents with him when he left his position, which became the basis of the book and the cause of a federal investigation. Although you can appreciate a senior person taking private papers with him, it's difficult to believe that all those papers were his personal property and had nothing to do specifically with his position.

Personal Hardships

Personal hardships can drive people to do things they wouldn't do under normal circumstances. Divorce, bankruptcy, medical problems, and addictions can leave a troubled employee vulnerable to the influences of a generous and sympathetic spymaster. Although it is hard to tell whether Afshin Bavand would have otherwise committed espionage, he didn't apparently commit any crimes until he was laid off from Ericsson (see Chapter 9).

Company support programs can help employees with some personal troubles, but many workers simply won't avail themselves of such programs because they fear embarrassment or that their participation will become known and affect their job in some way. Managers should be on the lookout for changes in their employees' work habits or deportment. They could be signs of a potential vulnerability.

Technical Vulnerabilities

When people think of high-tech espionage and computer crime, they think of genius computer hackers, brilliant technologists, and sophisticated spy satellite networks. In truth, technical vulnerabilities are responsible for less than 20 percent of all losses or compromises of information for companies, and even less for individuals. Of course, that still makes technical vulnerabilities a more than $60 billion problem annually.

Basically, technical vulnerabilities allow attackers to exploit computer systems. Although typical spies take advantage of these vulnerabilities primarily to gather information to use later, more malevolent intruders may use them to damage your computer systems and hurt you or your organization. As IRM principles imply (see Chapter 3), when you destroy information assets, you potentially destroy everything of value. It can be done with a bomb, but doing it with computers makes it more socially acceptable. Technical vulnerabilities allow attackers to accomplish their goals without setting foot on your premises. As Scott Charney puts it, "Outsiders do outsider things: avoiding insiders and being detected."

Although nontechnical attacks can be much more efficient than technical ones, exploiting technical vulnerabilities can be extremely successful within a reasonable time period, and these exploits give spies long-term access to your company or personal information. When attackers combine the exploitation of technical vulnerabilities with social engineering, they often end up knowing more about you or your company than you know yourself.

Don't worry—the following discussion will not be heavily technical in nature. You don't need to be an engineer to understand this stuff, and you don't need to be technically adept in order to take steps to counter the weaknesses described in these sections. You do, however, need to be able to recognize them.

Software Bugs

Imagine you have discovered that a certain brand and model of dead bolt opens without a key if you twist the latch counterclockwise and give it a yank. That is a nontechnical example of a known vulnerability. Now, if you were a burglar, knowledge of this design flaw could be very useful. Every time you came across that particular brand and model, you could twist, yank, and open the door. In fact, you might spend your time looking for that kind of lock and exploiting its vulnerability. This is essentially what computer hackers do. They learn how to twist the lock and then they go looking for that brand. The technology behind the specific vulnerabilities is irrelevant because there will always be new ones. The problem is that the bad guys are always searching for them and the good guys don't even know they exist.

As Chapter 4 discusses, there are basically only two ways to break into a computer. The first way is by taking advantage of bugs built into the software.

All software has bugs of one form or another. A bug can cause the software to crash, the system to hang, funny characters to be printed on a page, and so on. A certain percentage of those bugs will create elevated privileges or information leakage. These bugs are the security vulnerabilities. So basically all software has bugs, and some of those bugs will be security vulnerabilities.

One of the clearest examples of a security vulnerability existed in early versions of Windows 95. That software stored passwords in clear text (not encrypted) in a specific file on the computer. So all a person needed to do was look at the specific file—from the user's desk when the user was absent or by viewing the file over the network—to find that user's password. If you were using that version of Windows, you were vulnerable.

Software is not limited to operating systems such as Windows or UNIX. Web browsers are software. Databases are software. Word processors are software. There is software that enables networking. Printers have software. Even hardware has software.

The infamous Blaster, Slammer, Nimda, and Code Red attacks exploited software bugs. They were of the type of vulnerabilities referred to as *buffer overflows*. These are problems resulting from programming errors and they tend to be the most common and devastating software vulnerabilities. From a user/victim perspective, the technical reason for the vulnerability is irrelevant. The effect is the same, and if you use the software there is little you can do about its existence until the vendor comes out with a fix.

Hackers and other people with criminal intentions regularly search the electronic world for news about security vulnerabilities. They go to

Internet sites and newsgroups. They go to private bulletin board systems and computer chat areas. They watch a variety of security-related mailing lists. Those who know where to look are flooded with information about computer vulnerabilities. These people are also flooded with tools and instructions for exploiting those weaknesses. The tools are so good that many hackers will launch very advanced attacks without having a clue as to how to use the computer access after they get it.

Most hackers are not technically adept. It is no more reasonable to consider a hacker a computer genius than it is to call a teenager holding a gun a master criminal. Both demonstrate the ability to find the tools of their craft and the willingness to use them. This is hardly genius. It doesn't matter whether the vulnerabilities are in a massive Cray supercomputer or a 10-year-old PC, or on the Windows 95 operating system or UNIX. Anyone with minimal training can learn about a vulnerability and find the tool to exploit it. Computer systems administrators don't know nearly enough about so-called known vulnerabilities, let alone the fixes for them. The attackers almost always know more.

When I first started administering systems early in my career, I was not trained to watch for new problem announcements. When the vendor released a new version of an operating system or a computer application, my colleagues and I would review the product primarily to determine whether its new functionality justified the effort and the system downtime required to install it. We never considered that there might be security problem fixes included in the release. We didn't realize that anyone who could connect to our system could take control of it. Unfortunately, my previous lack of awareness is currently very common.

Only a handful of people are actually talented enough to find *new* vulnerabilities. What they do with that information varies. People in intelligence agencies and crime rings might keep the knowledge to themselves so that they can exploit the vulnerability with impunity. People in universities and research facilities work with manufacturers to develop fixes for the problems. Manufacturers generally behave responsibly and turn around a fix within a reasonable period of time. They then release the fix and alert the Computer Emergency Response Team (CERT), which in turn alerts the general population. These fixes are also incorporated in later releases of the software.

There has supposedly been only one day zero attack, which is an attack that exploits a vulnerability that was not previously reported and known. So even the worst attacks, such as Blaster and Slammer, allowed people weeks, if not months, to proactively prevent their systems from being affected. Remember that more than 99 percent of the problems that allow spies of any type to exploit your computers are problems you have not taken the time to fix.

Configuration Errors

The second way to break into computers is by taking advantage of configuration errors. To hackers and anyone else interested in breaking into your computers, it is irrelevant whether they exploit configuration errors or software bugs. To vendors, they represent an entirely different legal subject. Software bugs are problems inherent in the operating system or computer programs; configuration errors are problems created by the way in which systems administrators and users set up and maintain the computers and networks. For people who like statistics, reliable studies by the U.S. government indicate that 70 percent of successful computer break ins exploit configuration errors.

Unless a configuration error is very common or widely exploited, no one is likely to bother posting an alert about it. System administrators are expected to read their documentation and find these kinds of problems on their own. For an overworked and often undertrained administrator, this is a task with a low priority.

Examples of configuration problems include having default passwords or no passwords on accounts, granting users too many permissions, running file-sharing programs such as KaZaA, not protecting critical files, and improperly sharing system files. The same things that make computers powerful make them easy to abuse.

Depending on the type of configuration problem, attackers might need a valid account to compromise the computer, or they might be able to compromise the system through the network connection alone. Attackers can check manually for configuration problems, or they can use a scanner that finds potential problems for them. These tools are readily available on the Internet.

Although vendors frequently include security tools with their systems, many administrators do not know that these very powerful tools are freely available to them. To use an analogy, these tools are like airbags and seat belts that have been hidden in the trunk of a car. If automobile owners want to use them, they first need to find them and figure out how to install them. The problem is basically a lack of awareness.

Poor or No Passwords

In the process of performing penetration tests, I guess people's passwords in seconds, see them taped to computers, get people to tell me their passwords, or see them through password-cracking tools. Many vulnerability-scanning tools test for common passwords.

The results are staggering. In one Fortune 10 firm, 70 percent of the user passwords were the same as their user ID. In another Fortune 10 company, 25 percent of the company's servers had the password of Administrator on the administrator accounts. If you know enough about computer networks, with this password, you can get control of just about every computer on the network. "Password" is a common password. People's first names, sports team names, and God are popular passwords. Many types of computers also have a default password that administrators and users frequently don't change, assuming that there is a password at all. People also use the names of the projects they are working on as passwords.

A truism among members of the security community suggests that people's passwords are on their desks 70 percent of the time. Although attackers might not find the password itself on the desk, they probably will see something that gives them a good clue. If they spot a photograph of a wife or girlfriend, they will try her nickname or birthday. If there is evidence of a pet, they will see if the password is the pet's name. If a sports team banner is nearby, the attacker might try variations on the team's name. (I'll bet a lot of you are looking around your desks right now.) Companies can exacerbate this vulnerability by imposing predictable passwords, such as the user's employee number, or by using default passwords that never change.

Some attackers simply use computer programs that try every word in the dictionary as a password. The success rate of this strategy is between 20 and 90 percent, depending on the company. To employ this strategy, the attackers must be attacking a poorly configured computer or already have access to the system. The attackers can either capture the password file from a computer system or just keep trying to log on to the system using a known or default user ID.

Other attackers employ what is called a password *sniffer*, which is a computer program that grabs passwords as they are sent across a computer network. The attackers must have found a way onto the network in order to use this tool, but once there, the tool can be very effective. In a similar type of attack, hackers modify a computer's login program to automatically capture the user's password and save it for the attackers. Password sniffing is an incredibly valuable tool. Although these specific attacks are hard to prevent, there are specific countermeasures that minimize or negate their effects.

Wireless Networks

Hackers and other spies compromise wireless networks in the same way that they compromise other computers—through exploiting software bugs and configuration errors. However, wireless technologies exponentially increase your security risk. These networks can be reasonably secure when implemented properly. Unfortunately, there are a lot of myths revolving around this technology.

I once went into a CompUSA store to buy some wired networking equipment. I had a question and found a department manager. He asked me why I didn't just buy wireless network equipment and save myself a lot of trouble. I told him I was concerned about security. He obnoxiously replied, "All you have to do is get a firewall and turn on encryption," and walked away. Sadly, this person gives this type of advice to dozens of people a week.

The problem is that encryption is only a small part of a solution. It just means that someone can break into your home network securely.

For example, in one case, a company set up an office wireless network, only to discover that half their systems were connecting to another company's network in a building across the street. In another case, a friend of mine told me about his daughter calling him from a friend's house when she had problems attaching to her wireless network. When he finally talked his daughter through the process, he figured out that she actually connected to a neighbor's home wireless network. Not only that, it turned out that her friend's family wireless network wasn't set up properly, and her whole family was using the neighbor's network. And yes, in both cases, there were firewalls and encryption was turned on.

Wireless networking devices have default passwords. They have default settings. They broadcast their presence by default. Generally, they are easy to install. This typically means they are easy to hack. Wireless networks are a time bomb when not perfectly implemented.

Wardriving is becoming a common activity. People take PCs and drive them around large commercial areas looking for wireless entry points. They find dozens of them within minutes. The result is similar in upscale neighborhoods.

A residual activity is *warmarking*. In this case, hacker wannabes wardrive an area. When they find a wireless access point, they take chalk and draw symbols on the source building indicating the type of connection. Warmarking actually caused a terrorist scare in Washington, D.C., when people noticed the marks on buildings and thought they were for terrorist targeting purposes. In other terrorist-related scenarios, people can easily access many supposedly secure airport computer networks through poorly configured wireless networks.

Although the range for accessing a wireless network is typically limited, something as simple as converting a Pringle's potato chip canister into an antenna can add significant range to wireless hacking efforts. Modem and Internet access points are a major problem, but they are single, controllable points of entry. Wireless networks make your whole facility, and areas well beyond your borders, an entry point.

Modem Access

Admittedly, after the discussion of wireless networks, modem access points seem almost insignificant. However, modems still present a major vulnerability.

People view the Internet as their primary computer vulnerability, and it is a major point of concern. They're afraid that this one connection point will give hackers and criminals around the world direct access to their computers and networks. To combat this perceived threat, they buy firewalls, which, in fact, can do a good job of protecting against Internet intrusions. A *firewall* is a device that secures one network segment (usually the Internet) from another segment (usually a company's internal network). Unfortunately, in their rush to shield themselves from the Internet, people often neglect the company's thousands of modem connections and, in the process, overlook one of the biggest vulnerabilities companies face.

Modems are standard features on all computers sold in this country today. People use them to work from home. Software developers create applications that give people easy access to their computers from

anywhere in the world. Password protection on these machines is the
exception rather than the rule. Consequently, when telecommuters
plug that telephone jack into the back of their machines, they're allowing anybody who dials the telephone number to connect to their computer. Due to the nature of computer networking, after someone
connects to that one computer, he or she can connect to just about any
computer in the company.

Even organization-sponsored modems can be extremely weak
when they rely on poor passwords or are not configured properly.
When organizations have thousands of these access points to monitor,
they often lose track of them. Modems are not just for PCs. Many
extremely powerful computers also have modems.

One of the worst examples of this vulnerability was when a
teenager from Worcester, Massachusetts, used a wardialer program
against his local telephone exchange. A *wardialer* is a computer program
that dials a range of telephone numbers searching for vulnerable
modems. So, for example, it will dial every number from 212-456-
0000 to 212-456-9999. It then stores whether the number was
answered by a voice, fax, or computer system. In the Worcester case,
the teenager found a modem that accessed a telephone switch that
was critical to the communications of Worcester International Airport.
There was no password on the modem, and the teenager had unfettered control of the entire system. The results included taking down
communications between the control tower and airplanes, and turning
off runway lights at will.

Data Transmission

Information is never more vulnerable than when it is being sent across
a computer network. Whenever you are connected to another computer, the information on your machine is exposed to all other computers on that network. When computers talk to each other, they shout
loudly enough for everyone to hear. Most people expect the other
computers to refrain from listening in, but that's not what happens
when your organization becomes a target.

Sending information over a computer network is like sending a
postcard through the U.S. mail. Anyone at the Post Office who wants
to can read it. Not only can the data in transit be compromised, it can
also be modified. People who know how can change its content in
mid-flight. Someone could change a funds transfer from $1,000 to

$10,000 or resend the same message over and over again, so that the $1,000 transaction message is sent ten times. People can also block your message and substitute their own.

Difficult-to-Detect System Modifications

When knowledgeable attackers compromise computers or networks, the first thing they do is modify the system files and logs. Typically, they replace normal system programs with their own versions, either to give them more information or to hide their actions. For example, they might modify a program that tells an administrator which processes are running on the system, so the program doesn't show their hacker processes. This kind of system modification is a major problem that often goes undetected, allowing crimes to continue unabated.

Users also modify computers in ways that open them to attack. They install potentially malicious software. Users also have the ability to change some passwords and file permissions. More important, they can add removable storage devices and attach their computer to a modem. All these can go undetected by even the most diligent administrators.

Spyware

One system modification that deserves special treatment is spyware. *Spyware* is similar to a virus (which I identify as a threat in Chapter 4). It installs itself on computer system and runs surreptitiously on a computer. It is also installed in the system startup procedure so that it always runs whenever the computer is running. Spyware is a vulnerability because if it infects your system; it does not destroy the system.

Spyware continually monitors your system use for any triggers of interest to the spyware developer. It could be a keystroke logger, capturing everything you type. It could also be placed there by spammers to better target you or create pop-up windows on your screen. Sometimes the intent is slightly more benign. Spyware may be placed on your system by a commercial web site so that it can direct you to the web site whenever you try to shop for something similar.

If you allow your web browser to download ActiveX-type programs, a web site can sneak in a spyware program without your conscious knowledge. From that point on, your system is infected until you purposefully disinfect it. Antivirus software would not accomplish this.

Data Storage

Although people fear that their information will be stolen while it is sent across the Internet, the fact is that your data is most vulnerable while it sits on a computer. Health-care records, credit card numbers, and so on are stolen by the millions from poorly protected computer servers. Any time information is stored on a computer, it is vulnerable to compromise, destruction, or modification. Although the information can be encrypted to prevent compromise and modification, it can still be destroyed by accident or through malicious actions. Even data on supposedly secure systems can be attacked.

People leave very valuable information on computer systems that are directly connected to computer networks. When information is on a network, other people on that network can get to it, which means they can do anything with it. They can even modify it without anyone else noticing. Someone with access to a missile-targeting system could instruct the missiles to attack the site that launched them. People have had their credit records modified. Some people have been declared dead.

TEMPEST

You may not realize it, but others can read your computer monitor from hundreds of feet away with no visible access to your machine. They can even see the information as the chip in your computer processes it. All they need is a special receiver, available to anyone through a number of mail-order catalogs for under $800. With the right instructions, they can even modify their TV sets to do the same thing.

Almost every electronic device gives off what is know as *Van Eck radiation*, which can be picked up and converted to readable signals. TEMPEST is the term associated with the control and exploitation of Van Eck radiation emanations. The technology was developed by the intelligence communities to pick up the signals. Equipment can be designed to contain the radiation.

Intelligence agencies recognize the threat presented by this phenomenon, and they pay almost twice the price for computer systems that are TEMPEST-protected. In some cases, it's cheaper to TEMPEST-shield an entire building complex than to buy protected computers. To protect a building from this kind of intrusion, the entire structure must be covered in copper. Because of the way Van Eck radiation travels, all pipes (such as water and sewer feeds) coming into the building must be copper as well. It is a difficult and expensive process, but necessary, especially in high-security environments.

Unfortunately, the commercial sector does not typically TEMPEST-protect its computers or facilities. This leaves a great deal of information vulnerable to compromise by anyone with the initiative to buy a kit through the mail. One news show drove up and down Wall Street and intercepted random computer signals, compromising an immense amount of business information.

Electromagnetic Pulses

Electromagnetic pulses (EMPs) were accidentally discovered during the testing of atomic bombs. Scientists noticed that all transistor circuits within a given area were literally fried after the detonation of a nuclear device. They later discovered that the explosion was causing a high-energy pulse that had this effect on the transistors.

Military scientists eventually developed the ability to generate EMPs without a nuclear explosion. The United States used EMP bombs during both wars with Iraq to knock out key Iraqi computer systems and radio transmitters, such as those involved with surface-to-air missiles. The U.S. Customs Service was reportedly testing an EMP gun that could be aimed at cars trying to run border patrol roadblocks. The gun would destroy all the computer chips in the car, stopping it dead in the road. Unfortunately, this technology can also be used to destroy information, although it is useless as an information-gathering tool. EMP technology can enable malicious attackers to ruin all your information.

Telephone Taps

The telephone systems have been compromised by hackers, criminals, intelligence agencies, and other miscellaneous spies for decades. Some modern telephone taps are very advanced and almost undetectable. Others are unsophisticated and easy to find. Either way, unless you specifically check for them, you will never know they are there. When you consider the amount and type of information you give away over the telephone on a regular basis, you can see how damaging this vulnerability can be if left unnoticed.

Telephone taps are easy to accomplish. Criminals interested in stealing calling card numbers installed transmitters in the telephones of Grand Central Station in New York City so that they could hear the tones of the numbers being depressed. Most people are not aware that the telephone wiring box outside their home allows you to plug in a handset. It is relatively easy to cross wire telephone trunks in apartment buildings to bring someone else's line into your home. This is in addition to the switches that are out in the open.

Bugs

Whenever there is a possibility of espionage, there is a strong possibility that a spy has planted bugs. When I give presentations, I sometimes ask the people in my audiences how many of them have performed bug sweeps. I then ask those people how many of them have found anything. On average, 40 percent of the people claiming to perform bug sweeps find something. This number has stayed constant for almost a decade. Organizations that specialize in performing bug sweeps tell me that they find bugs in about 15 percent of their cases.

In one case, a company that should have been very profitable went bankrupt. As a moving company crew was moving furniture out of the executive meeting room, it found a large transmitter behind a credenza. The company had no idea who put it there or how long it had gone unnoticed. Nevertheless, the damage was done.

The case of the U.S. embassy in Moscow is a well-known example of bug use. The Soviet Union embedded bugs in the building materials throughout the entire complex. Just to prove that all is fair in love and war, among Robert Hanssen's treasonous activities was his disclosure to the Russians that the United States planted its own bugs in the Washington, D.C., Soviet embassy.

The sophistication of bugs varies greatly, but for the most part the cheap ones work as well as the expensive ones. There are many sophisticated bugs costing thousands of dollars. On the other hand, you can go to your local Radio Shack store and buy an "FM Transmitter Kit" for about $11.

Conclusion

Previously, I stated that I believed that people were obsessed with technical vulnerabilities and attacks and ignored the other vulnerability categories. The irrational fear that emerged after the September 11 attacks proved me wrong. People became obsessed with physical vulnerabilities and started ignoring the other vulnerabilities. And even then, they paid attention to some obvious but rarely exploited vulnerabilities instead of the easily overlooked but commonly exploited physical vulnerabilities. Spies, no matter whether they are petty thieves or foreign intelligence operatives, will exploit any vulnerability, of any type, that they find available. You need to consider all vulnerabilities.

For the purposes of protecting your information and other resources, the attacks are irrelevant. The way you protect against compromise is by closing your vulnerabilities. Basing a security program on protecting against specific attacks may protect you from those attacks, but it leaves you vulnerable to all other attacks. If you do protect against specific attacks, you may accidentally close vulnerabilities that enable other attacks, but that is only if you are lucky. You must cure the underlying problem, not the symptoms. Chapter 12 discusses how you address vulnerabilities instead of attacks.

As you read through this chapter, you should have noted dozens of problems within your own environment and started deducing countermeasures appropriate for you. That is very good, because it starts to plant the idea in your head that many of these vulnerabilities are easy to address. Many people will still think that these vulnerabilities won't affect them in any significant way because they are too small and common. Through the use of a variety of different case studies, describing many different attack strategies, the case studies in Part II show how dangerous this attitude can be.

Part

II

CASE STUDIES

That's where the money is.
—Willie Sutton, in response to the
question as to why he robs banks.

You've read that an easily guessed password or failing to clean off a
desk can create multibillion dollar losses, but you may still be skeptical.
Now you'll see how real spies succeed at their craft. As you read the
case studies in this part, consider the underlying causes of their success
and how the losses could have been prevented. You'll realize that these
spies did not know some mystical secrets. What they did know is how
to execute a systematic process of exploiting expected vulnerabilities.
Doing this in a confident and repeatable manner, when there is no
room for error, is the mark of a true expert.

Each chapter in this part concludes with a section titled "Vulnerabilities Exploited." Given the results and the perpetrators of the incidents, it is easy to lose track of what exactly happened. For that reason,
these sections present the underlying causes of the tremendous successes. After reading the case studies, you will have a thorough appreciation for the countermeasures that follow in Part III. When I wrote my

first book, *Corporate Espionage*, which included similar case studies, there was some rare criticism that I told people how they could commit criminal actions, step by step. For the most part, that is true. The reality, though, is that the criminals already know how to do what I describe. More important, the vast majority of the general population uses the material as intended: to establish an appreciation for security countermeasures.

I did get an e-mail message from a real criminal hacker, anonymously of course, who told me that the case studies from *Corporate Espionage* helped him refine some of his tactics. A librarian from Texas told me that my book was the most stolen book from her library system. Additionally, I learned that SVR (the reincarnation of the KGB) officers, posing as reporters, ordered copies of the book. I'm sure there are other instances of people whom I would prefer not to learn from my book, getting copies of it.

More frequently, though, I receive messages from security managers telling me how they use my case studies for corporate-awareness programs to help prevent attacks. Just as the SVR analyzed my cases, the U.S. Defense Information Systems Agency has several of my case studies posted on its security awareness web site to demonstrate the importance of its security procedures.

It is my hope that the following case studies will have similar effects of providing awareness of the real importance of implementing good, cost-effective, and simple security countermeasures.

In several of the case studies, the identities of companies are disguised. I modified the names, industries, and locations of targeted organizations. In some cases, there is misleading information to protect the identity of the victim or to prevent a duplication of the crime. However, the basic vulnerabilities and nature of the cases are accurate.

6

Spy vs. Spy

Prologue

It was a dark, drizzly, Halloween night. I drove along a typical subur-
ban six-lane road, divided and lined with strip malls. All I was doing
was looking for a place to buy some bottled water. The road was
deserted and I drove slowly, looking side to side for a supermarket or
convenience store that might sell water.

I passed a Wal-Mart but didn't feel like having to find a parking
space and stand in a long checkout line. I was just tired and wanted to
get my water and get in and out quickly. After another mile of closed
strip malls and not knowing when I might see something that met my
criteria, I decided that I might as well go to Wal-Mart.

I was driving well below the 45-miles-per-hour speed limit in the
far-left lane of my three lanes and thought it would be easy to make a
U-turn back to the store. I then glanced into the rearview mirror and
saw a pair of headlights about three car lengths behind me. The car was
just keeping its distance behind me, not trying to pass me, despite the
fact I was driving slowly.

Unlike in the movies, the way to tell whether you are being followed is to drive slowly, not to weave in and out of traffic seeing who
weaves with you. You want to see who doesn't want to pass you. In this
case, instead of looking for the U-turn, I continued to drive 10 or so

miles below the speed limit and moved over to the middle lane to see
whether the car would continue following me or this was just a coincidence. The car stayed behind me. It was time to assume that I was
being followed. It had been more than a few years since I was last followed and I had to go through my mental checklist of what to do next.

Also unlike in the movies, you do not start speeding off when you
know you are being followed. You continue to drive at a safe speed and
distance until you can find a safe place to pull into. A "safe place" is one
that is well lit, with many people, ideally with a way inside a building
and a back door out. As luck would have it, a quarter mile up the road I
saw a gas station with a minimart. I waited until the last moment to cut
across the right lane and into the gas station. I then pulled my car up to
the door of the convenience store with the driver-side door immediately facing the store's door. My newfound friend followed me in.

I was slightly relieved when I saw a flashing red light go off on the
dashboard of the car. I still waited to see whether my friend wore a real
uniform. Not knowing what to expect, but with four or five other people now around, I got out of the car to confront the supposed officer.

"Can you tell me why you were following me?" I yelled.

He replied that I was driving below the speed limit.

"Since when is obeying the law now a cause for suspicion?"
I replied.

He commented that I crossed two lanes of traffic to get into the
gas station. I told him that it looked as though he was following me,
which he was, and that I wanted to get someplace where there were
other people.

Being that it was Halloween night, and that it would not be
uncommon for there to be a lot of drunk drivers, I couldn't blame him
for following the only car on the road. I showed him my hotel key and
rental car agreement, and he felt comfortable knowing that I just
arrived in town about an hour before and hadn't had time to be on a
drinking binge.

Little did I know that this would be typical of the week as a whole.

The Mission

We were in a midsized town on the East Coast of the United States,
performing an espionage simulation as part of a full-scope penetration
test of a Fortune 500 manufacturing company. I led the team that also

included Stan and Tony. We were targeting one of the major facilities of the company. The primary target of the attack was the computer facility; however, the whole facility was fair game.

You probably wouldn't notice the people on my team on the street, which is what makes us perfect for the job. Stan is the Russian defector whom I mentioned earlier in the book. He was a full colonel in the GRU, the Russian military intelligence organization frequently described as the evil twin of the KGB, prior to his defection. He was one of the GRU's most effective spymasters in its history. Tony, who looked like an innocent country boy, was previously a military counterintelligence officer. Ironically, he was responsible for following Russian spies at one point in his career. I was to perform the black bag operations. Between the three of us, we had dozens of years of intelligence and security experience.

Stan, Tony, and I met for breakfast and I briefed them on our potential targets. I told them that we were supposed to meet with the security manager in his office in about an hour. The first task was to get to his office without his assistance. This was not supposed to be easy.

I was at the facility about a month before, when I was given a mini-tour. I knew that there was a gate around the perimeter of the facility, with guards stationed at the gate entrances. There were also guards at the entrance of the building we were focusing on. Getting into facilities guarded in this manner was my area of responsibility.

The plan was to try the direct route. I decided that on the first day we should take only one car. I timed it so that we would drive through the perimeter gate during the morning rush hour. As luck would have it, there were two lanes going into the facility. The guards stood next to the right lane, so we took the left lane. We went by the first checkpoint easily.

I parked near the primary target and we walked over to the building. The guard desk was to the left and in front of it was a table with temporary badges—the typical name tags that you write your name on, peel off the back, and stick on your shirt. There was an inner set of doors that required an access card to unlock. Of course during the morning rush, there were a lot of people going through, many holding the door open for the person behind them.

Not knowing what the process was, I walked over to the guard desk and said I was there to meet with someone. He told me to write my name on a temporary badge and he would buzz me in. He noticed that I had a computer bag with me and told me I should fill out a form that logged in my computer. The idea was that someone would inspect my computer bag on the way out to see whether I was trying to steal a computer, but that inspection never happened.

I filled in the form with some fake information. I wrote my name on a badge and grabbed a couple of extra badges for Stan and Tony. I whispered to them to just tailgate behind someone else walking through the inner door. The guard told me that he would "buzz me in" when I walked over to the door, but that turned out to be unnecessary; I just walked in behind someone else.

I met Stan and Tony inside the door in a wide, long hallway. The Computer Operations Center, as well as the support staff and security manager, were in the basement of the building. I walked my partners over to a staircase that led downstairs. We arrived at the security manager's office before he did.

We met to determine the specific tasks we would perform and also to set up a containment strategy if anyone "caught" us. Our primary target was access to critical computer servers, whose names we were given, as well as any information about future manufacturing plans. We were to also find out what other information was readily available to people who use hostile intelligence tactics.

Further breaking down the test, I was responsible for physical access to critical facilities. Tony would perform the traditional social-engineering activities, such as pretext telephone calls and open-source information gathering. Stan was to do what he did best: figure out how a traditional intelligence operative might find people to steal information for him.

We suspected that the company had experienced many espionage incidents in the past, and were formally told just that. There was indication that foreign governments sponsored some of the espionage, but much of it was sponsored by well-financed competitors. Stan's experience was uniquely suited for the task.

The Black Bag Operation

We decided to explore the facilities to get a feel for the environment. The basement was your typical Dilbert-style cubicle setting. Several large rooms opened into each other, with the exception of the Computer Operations Center, which was a large complex walled off from the rest of the basement. There were a few strategically located doors with cipher locks that provided access to the computer rooms. Cipher locks are keypads that require the user to enter a code to unlock a door. The main computer room was about 75 feet by 200 feet, with long rows of computer racks loaded with equipment. Outside the main computer room were several telecommunications rooms where all the communications lines came in. There was also a control room at the far side of the computer room. That room had a large window looking into the computer room, as well as a door.

As we walked around the cubicle area, Stan commented on the fact that many desks had Chinese-American dictionaries on them.

"Have you seen the computer departments of U.S. colleges lately?" was my sarcastic reply.

"I'll look into that," was Stan's matter-of-fact reply.

As we walked around, we found many unattended desks with the computers logged in, a great deal of valuable information lying around, and the typical messy desks that you would expect to see in computer environments. There were several people scattered around, so we really couldn't look too carefully at any one desk.

When we got to a door to a computer room, we found it propped open, with cables coming out of the door. It turned out that major construction was going on, and the construction workers were using power from the computer rooms for their tools. We walked in the door and started wandering around. Nobody was working in the computer room. All the network administrators were in the control room. We had unchallenged access to everything.

To make the situation even better—for us, at least—the critical computers had their names taped to the monitors, and they were all logged in as the administrator. We had complete access to the systems we were told were our top priorities. If we had criminal intent, we would have added accounts to the systems and put in backdoors to allow us to gain remote access later.

I typed in some basic commands and quickly created a file in the administrator directory to prove we were there. We then quickly left and went back to the security manager's office to regroup. The systems compromised held all the critical manufacturing plans and new designs for the company's major product lines. Not only did we theoretically compromise all the current information, we would have been able to access these systems indefinitely to get any updates. This was about two hours into the test.

Everyone concluded that my black bag portion of the assignment was successful enough at this point. We had a feel for the environment and decided to move onto the other tasks. It was time to survey the outside environment, so we decided to leave for an early lunch.

We drove around to get a feel for the bars and restaurants in the area. Stan made comments about the Chinese restaurants that we passed. We finally chose a common chain restaurant. While eating, we took note of the types of people walking in and out and tried to determine whether they worked at the targeted company.

Returning to the facilities, we again had no problem driving in through the main gate and then following someone into the building.

Social Engineering

Tony told us that he wanted to start making some phone calls to see if he could get user IDs and passwords from people. The week before, he started examining the company web sites and other publicly available information. He had collected dozens of names of employees, along with information about their locations and job functions. As do all Fortune 500 companies, our client had many locations around the world.

Tony started his calls by phoning the Help Desk and pretending to be an employee who forgot his password. The support person told him that she wanted his social security number to verify his identity. Tony told her his boss was coming and he would call back. He had all the information he needed at this time.

At that point, Tony knew he could call employees and either get their passwords or their social security numbers. He decided to try for social security numbers first, because it can be assumed that if people would give up their social security number, they would more than likely give up something less personally sensitive such as a password. Tony decided to say he was with the Help Desk and was investigating a security incident.

He began the call by asking users whether they had recently changed their password. Of course, nobody ever said they did. Tony then told the person that there was a security incident where someone pretended to be a user and changed that user's password. He said he would set it back to what it was, but he needed to verify the user's identity due to the nature of this problem. He then asked for the social security number, and received it on all but one occasion. Having the social security number meant he could call the Help Desk at any time and have the password changed for his use. This meant that he would have unlimited access to just about any account he wanted. He compromised dozens of accounts over several hours.

Just to prove that it could be done, after going through his same spiel, he told some people that he could set the password back to what it was originally, "if you tell me what it was." This way, he wouldn't need to go through the Help Desk to access the accounts. He was always successful.

There was one woman who would not give Tony any information. She was the only person, out of almost 100, who did the right thing. Fortunately, or unfortunately depending on your perspective, it appeared that she didn't know to whom she should report the incident.

Black Bag Operations, Continued

I thought it would be a good idea to get shirts with company logos on them. Stan and I decided to try to find the Company Store, as it was called. It also provided us the opportunity to see whether the rest of the facility was as easy to get into as the areas we had already visited. Stan and I were told to find another building and given directions from the door to the store.

We arrived at the building and walked in the entrance, which was supposed to be an employees-only entrance. A guard was sitting at a generic desk to the side of the door. We just said, "Hi" and walked by him the way everyone else did. We found the Company Store, which turned out to be closed. In the process of walking over to the store, we found other things of interest to our mission.

We discovered that most of the buildings were connected to each other. We didn't need to drive to another entrance, which was fairly far away. It also meant that the lethargic guard we passed allowed access to the Computer Operations Center, as well as to many other critical areas throughout the company's research and development facilities.

After we confirmed we could make it all the way through to the Computer Operations Center, we had to go back and get the car. Along the way, we stopped at the bulletin boards where people could post advertisements. Mostly we found the names of people with their work telephone numbers. There were also several retirement announcements, which contained the names of people retiring, as well as the secretaries to call to confirm attendance at the retirement parties. We passed this information back to Tony for use in getting more passwords.

At this point, we decided that Stan should go off to focus on finding places to recruit spies. Tony needed a break, so I took him with me to get back into the Computer Operations Center. This time, we wanted to get into the side rooms where the networking closets are. The side door we went in through previously was now closed. It was time to prove that it wasn't a fluke that we got in the first time.

Tony and I stood at main entrance to the Computer Operations Center, next to the cipher lock. I had a pad of paper and drew something that looked like wiring plans. We heard someone coming from inside, so I pretended to start entering a code into the lock. As the person came through the door, I acted as if I had just finished entering the code, and Tony and I thanked the person for holding the door open.

Once inside, we saw a hallway. The door to the Computer Operations Center was on the right, and we just walked straight down the hallway. To the left and at the end of the hallway were the network and telecommunications rooms, whose doors were wide open. We didn't notice anything too unusual. We did, however, confirm that we could have tapped the telephones and networks.

Later, we did a late-night walk through the support areas outside the Computer Operations Center. There were passwords lying around, sensitive information sitting on desks, and terminals left logged on, some of them with administrator privileges. However, the most notable thing we found was a very large computer printout. This printout contained a list of all employees with a variety of their personal data, including their social security numbers.

As far as black bag operations, I was pretty much finished. There was little more of value I could prove. Tony continued to make his telephone calls, getting password after password. He ended up leaving early. Stan, on the other hand, found other things of interest, to put it mildly.

Spymaster at Work

Stan went to several bars located around the facility. He found out that there was a major competitor in the same city, which wasn't any secret.

Talks with bartenders uncovered that certain executives of our client frequently met with executives of the competitor. The bartenders said that they spoke very secretively.

At some of the seedier bars, Stan found many people who were drinking excessively at lunch. It wasn't hard to figure out that people drinking heavily during lunch were not very enthusiastic about the company. This was a spymaster's ideal hunting ground.

Stan also went to different restaurants to see the clientele that they attracted. Stan determined where the younger people who might want some excitement would go, where the older disgruntled people would go, and where spies would avoid.

Because this was in a post-September 11 world, Stan also decided to see how alert the company was to potential terrorist threats. He drove his car up to the primary building we were targeting, and then got out and left the car. It was even in a fire lane. He watched from a distance for 15 minutes and saw that no one even came out to check the car. That was more than enough time for a terrorist to get far away and have the car explode. He got back in his car and drove off.

Stan wanted to check whether the apathy with his car was due to the trusting Southern hospitality or unique to the guards at the company. He drove over to the competitor's facility to see whether he could leave the car in front of one of that company's buildings. He found that it was actually physically impossible to drive right up to a building. There were at least 50 feet from any road or parking lot to any building.

Sometime during Stan's travels, someone apparently noticed him. Much as I experienced two nights earlier, Stan detected someone following him. To confirm this, he turned on to one deserted road, then to another and another. Stan is a true master at this, because there have been many times that his life depended on surveillance detection and avoidance. When Stan reported this event to me, he made it a point to say that the people following him weren't very experienced. When I asked how he knew this, he said that there was only one car. A professional operation uses at least two cars, and even one car would have been less obvious. More important: "I made a U-turn on one of the deserted streets, and the car hit a signpost as he tried to follow me," he said with a smile.

Stan and I hypothesized about who it could have been. The options were a Russian spy who recognized Stan and wanted to see what he was up to, an FBI trainee doing counterterrorism work who thought Stan might have been a terrorist scoping out the companies, or possibly security from either our client or the competitor. Given all the valuable information that the company has, and the previous cases of espionage, we were certain that a variety of foreign intelligence services target it on a regular basis. There were definitely spies among us on this assignment.

Stan's experience as a GRU spymaster became a major factor. With the exception of his final stationing in the United States, the rest of his GRU career was focused on China. He was even stationed in Beijing for four years.

Even knowing this, I was still confused by a call I got from Stan a day later. "Ira, there are black duck eggs on the menu," was his cryptic comment.

"Stan, what the hell are we paying you for?" was my reply.

"Oh, my naive American friend," he said with I smile I could feel over the telephone, "black duck eggs are a Chinese delicacy. I can hardly find black duck eggs in San Francisco, let alone this little piece of s--- town in the middle of nowhere. And they're cheaper than they are on the streets of Beijing."

He went on to describe that because he saw all those Chinese-American dictionaries on the desks of the employees, he spent some time trying to find Chinese social clubs and other places where Chinese people may congregate. Stan knows the modus operandi of Chinese intelligence agents, which is to find people of Chinese descent and sift through them to see who would likely be susceptible to recruitment. Generally, these are people who have more allegiance to China than their employer or who can be coerced because of family in China. Setting up a gathering place, such as a Chinese restaurant that has hard-to-find Chinese delicacies, is a way to attract as many potential agents as possible. It is also a great place to exchange information and money.

Stan told me that he found several Chinese restaurants reasonably close to the company facilities. All but one had friendly staffs that welcomed him. At the other, he walked in and saw a menu on the reception table that had only Chinese writing. He picked it up and saw that there were Chinese delicacies not normally found in other Chinese restaurants in this country. When one of the workers realized that Stan could read Mandarin, he became distressed rather than gladly welcoming toward the potential new customer who could appreciate the rare menu items.

Stan's being followed was a fact. Whether or not this Chinese restaurant was actually one of the more than 3,000 Chinese front companies was a matter for the FBI. Stan was told that the FBI was busy doing counterterrorism work; the investigation of the restaurant was a low priority.

Case Summary

All the penetrations were finished within four days. However, my black bag operation could in fact have been declared successful and complete within four hours. Tony's work gathering user account access from all over the company was successful within two days. Stan's work took approximately four days and could have lasted longer.

Tony and I proved that if someone wanted to compromise the company, he or she could do so very quickly. Many people want to believe that although the vulnerabilities exist, nobody would really exploit them. Stan's work proved that it was extremely likely that there was at least one well-funded espionage operation targeting the company, and likely many more.

Even worse, Stan confirmed his own concerns that dozens of people in the computer support group were targeted. Not only that, this prime *and actively targeted* population had access to the most valuable information in the company.

Although most people appreciate that these types of results can happen at most companies, some people say it was just luck. My team has this type of luck on all our penetration tests. Espionage is about taking advantage of the opportunities that present themselves. If it hadn't been construction work that enabled us to get into the Computer Operations Center within two hours, there would have been another opportunity. Trained spies know how to be where opportunities present themselves, as well as how to recognize those opportunities. It is like the old saying, "Of course I believe in luck. It seems like the harder I work, the more luck I have." In this case, the work is training to quickly and effectively recognize and exploit vulnerabilities.

A few people question whether there would even be a Chinese intelligence operation to be found. They don't believe that these things happen in real life. Maybe a Chinese restaurant would ship in expensive items to sell at a large loss so that it can sell more of these items for more of a loss. People believe that these are things only for spy novels, not real life. The real spies love and rely on this ignorance and cynicism because it means that people will continue to ignore the vulnerabilities and the spies can continue to exploit them.

Vulnerabilities Exploited

When I tell people about this case, many swear that it is their company my team attacked. If not, they say that the same thing could have happened at their company because they have the same vulnerabilities.

The vulnerabilities exploited in this case were primarily operational ones, which makes sense because this was primarily an operational attack. There were also technical vulnerabilities discovered in the process.

At this point, I do not mention countermeasures in detail. Clearly, you should be able to infer security procedures that could have stopped the attack. As I said in the beginning of this section, the vulnerabilities exploited were small and usually obvious ones that should have been stopped by countermeasures in place. However, this case demonstrates that people take the obvious for granted.

Ineffective Perimeter Security

The fact that we were able to drive right past the guards at the perimeter gates, just by acting as though we knew where we were going, made the gates useless. Maybe they would have tried to stop a large truck, but consider that multiple cars could accomplish the same amount of damage that a truck could. At the very least, the guards could question visitors and announce their presence to the people being visited. As it was, the guard booths were just information booths.

Poorly Trained and Monitored Guards

There were clearly security procedures to be enforced. Guards should have been watching for people tailgating others into the facilities. The visitor badges shouldn't have just been sitting there for people to grab by the handful. I did fill out a form to register my PC, but no one checked my computer bag on the way out. The guards were too far away to stop me if they wanted to. The one guard we just walked by was useless except to people who needed directions. Stan's leaving his car right next to the building's entrance should have warranted a very quick reaction. The fact the guards didn't even care about a fire lane's being blocked, let alone the potential terrorist action, is the most telling sign of learned apathy.

It is easy to blame the individual guards for the lapses. However, in reality it is a management problem. The company acted as though just having a uniformed body were enough. They clearly did not go through enough effort of training the guards, or at the very least, spot-checking them to see how well they performed their job. Thousands of people go by the guards and their posts on a daily basis, and they should notice the same issues that I did. However, no one took any actions. It is not the fault of the individual guards if this seemingly apathetic behavior is accepted.

Poor Construction Procedures

Strong security countermeasures were in place at the company, such as cipher locks on doors to the Computer Operations Center. However, the construction situation allowed someone to prop a door open. I mentioned only one instance of this here, but there were many others. Any spy would jump on these types of opportunities.

Also, spies could easily get jobs on the construction teams. There were no background checks on the construction and support workers, and they pretty much had unimpeded access to the entire Computer Operations Center and surrounding support areas. They had more access than the regular employees of the company. As a result of our test, the company spent several hundred thousand dollars doing a bug sweep and searching for other network and voice eavesdropping devices. Although this would be a good idea anyway, it would not have been as necessary if they had controlled the construction team.

Lack of Escorts

One control that should have been in place is escorts for any visitors to the basement. Not only could this prevent abuse or criminal activity by the construction team, it would have cut down on other outsiders' ability to gain access to the Computer Operations Center and similar areas. For example, the escorts likely would have prevented doors from being propped open.

The construction workers would not question other people following them into controlled areas. That is not their job and they wouldn't know who belonged and who didn't belong, anyway. Escorts could have been told to question any unescorted person who was not authorized in controlled areas. This would likely have prevented our unfettered access to the Computer Operations Center. Although a trained spy or other criminal is not likely to be put out of business by the mere presence of an escort, it would discourage professionals from planting bugs or stopping at an unattended computer terminal. It might even catch the amateurs, of which there are many. The escorts should also have prevented doors from being propped open.

Easy Entrance to the Computer Support Floor

Even though the Computer Operations Center itself had cipher-locked doors, the support areas surrounding it had no protection. During our walk-throughs of these areas, we found more than enough information to be successful without getting into the Computer Operations Center. Many critical computers were left unattended and logged on to administrator accounts. Although those issues need to be addressed individually, the fact is that anyone with access to the building as a whole had complete access to the support area. Remember also that we found that several buildings were interconnected, which compounded this problem. As a result of the test, cipher locks were installed on all staircases that led to the basement.

Computer Terminals Not Locked

Computers in the Computer Operations Center and support areas were left unattended and logged on to administrator accounts. This meant that anyone with physical access to the facility had the ability to take complete technical control of all critical computers—a one-time compromise becomes an indefinite compromise. If screen-locking mechanisms were enabled, these compromises would not have occurred.

Telecommunications Closets Not Locked

Telecom closets are basically the spinal cord of a company. If you have access and the technical knowledge, only encrypted communications (which are rarely used, especially for voice communications) could stop you from accessing information through the communications lines. Anyone could have easily tapped into the communications lines for the Computer Operations Center. A password sniffer placed here gives an attacker all the account passwords for everyone involved in research and development, along with their data. These closets should be tightly controlled and always locked, unless they are attentively attended.

Use of Social Security Numbers as Employee Identifiers

Although you need unique identifiers for employees to prove their identities, social security numbers are clearly not a good choice. In the first place, it might be a violation of local privacy laws. Also, social security numbers are easy to get. If you find out that someone works at the targeted company, you can get that person's social security number off the Internet. You can then call the Help Desk and claim to be that person, without ever needing to contact the person directly.

No Knowledge of to Whom to Report Incidents

During Tony's social-engineering attacks, only one person out of almost a hundred refused to give him her password. This person knew that the request as a whole was a violation. Immediately after this incident, we alerted the security staff that the person should contact them about the incident. The call never came, and when we looked into it, we learned that the employee had no idea whom to tell about the strange call. So even when people did detect something unusual, they didn't know the appropriate steps to take about it.

Poor Security Awareness

The fact that Tony was able to get so many passwords indicates that the company as a whole had poor security awareness. When only one person out of a hundred does the right thing, poor security awareness is a management problem. The success of the black bag operations also proved the poor security awareness endemic throughout the company.

No Challenge of Strangers

Despite the fact that Stan, Tony, and I walked all over the company, past guards and hundreds of employees and into sensitive areas, nobody challenged us. We were clearly not personally known to anyone in the company except a small project team. We never put on those stick-on name tags because that would have aroused more suspicion than not wearing badges. At a minimum, we would expect to be challenged three or four times, at least by the guards that we passed. Although this is a symptom of poor security awareness, it is important to highlight because it is common in many companies.

Tailgating

As noted, tailgating is something the guards should have noticed. But the people who allowed us to tailgate them are also at fault. It's another sign of poor security awareness that we were able to follow people into a controlled facility, such as the building, without their looking to see whether we had a badge or an escort. This means that despite millions of dollars of strong physical locks, anyone can get into the facility. Office pirates use this technique to enter offices and walk out with computers.

This is important not only for information security but also personal safety. Outsiders can walk in and physically assault people. In one case, I was called in to perform a security assessment after an estranged husband walked into a facility, following behind others who held the door open for him, and shot his wife.

7

Nuclear Meltdown

S ome items have clear value to many different groups of people. One is the detailed design of a nuclear power plant. With the design plans, a terrorist knows how to better attack the plant or maximize the effect of the attack. A rogue nation can accelerate its progress to becoming a nuclear power. Companies that design nuclear reactors can improve their design plans. Companies that want to enter the market can do so without needing to invest much money in designing their own. Rogue companies who want to make black market spare parts for the finished reactor will know how to make cheap spare parts (usually having poor quality).

You would think that with the value so obvious, the protections afforded to such designs would be incredibly strong. This means that design plans for nuclear reactors should be hard to steal. Sadly, this was not the case.

Picture Perfect

I had to assume that entering a facility that designs and builds nuclear reactors would be difficult. For that reason, I decided that my team needed real badges to enter that facility. Although the obvious tactic would be to go to that facility to get the badge, I thought an indirect approach would be best.

Any company that produces billion-dollar nuclear reactors is a large conglomerate. Although people from one operating unit of a large conglomerate are not typically allowed access to the other facilities, people from the corporate office are granted such access. For that reason, I decided to get corporate ID badges for my one assistant, Dean, and me. Dean was to focus on the computer hacking while I worked on the black bag operation.

To get our ID badges, Dean and I traveled to the company headquarters, which were on a landscaped corporate campus with several buildings. A guard gate was just off the road; guards checked for ID badges to allow entry to the campus. So to get badges, we had to show some form of ID.

I went for lunch at a restaurant near the corporate campus. On the hostess' counter sat one of those baskets into which people drop their business card to win a free lunch. When the hostess went to seat someone, I fished through the basket and pulled out a business card from a person at the company. After lunch, I drove up to the campus gate and the guard asked to see my badge. I told him I forgot it but said, "Here's my business card." He replied, "Go ahead." Only I, as the driver, had to show ID.

It was clear that if we drove up to the main entrance of the headquarters building, we would need to go by a receptionist to get into the building. Instead, we drove into the employee garage and found a spot. We saw other employees walking over to a garage staircase and followed them through a door. We were then inside the headquarters building that easily.

Making sure that the receptionist knew we came from the inside of the building, I asked her where we had to go to get a badge. She pointed to a door off the lobby area. My partner and I went into the office and I told the person in the security office that we were working at the facility and needed to get ID badges. The guard handed us forms that he said we could fill out and bring back anytime. We went upstairs to an empty work area and completed the paperwork. We did, however, need a supervisor's signature. I faked the signature of the person who authorized the penetration test.

We walked back to the security office and handed the person our paperwork. He called over to another person, who took us back to take our pictures. Five minutes later, we had brand-new ID badges. They never called the supervisor's office to verify the signature.

With badges in hand, we hopped on a plane to head to the facility that makes the reactors.

Should Somebody from India Be Logged On?

This mission was clearly a high-stakes one. We had two people from the corporate audit department with us to record what we did and stop us if we started doing something that they thought would be too sensitive. As with all facilities that involve nuclear developments, our target was in the middle of the desert. This trip took a pretty long time, and we arrived about 10:00 P.M. We really could have waited until the morning, but we thought we should take a look around while nobody was there.

I was in a car with Dean; the two auditors were in their own car. They drove up to the gate of the facility in front of us. Dean and I watched from a car length back as the guard pointed to a building outside the gate to the left. They started their car and, to our surprise, looped back around, went out the exit gate, and parked at the building. I drove my car up and Dean and I showed the guard our ID badges. He asked where we were going and I gave him a building number. He gave me directions to the building. I then asked where the car in front of us went. He replied that they had corporate audit ID and they had to register to get a facility pass. The logic was baffling, but I wasn't about to argue with it.

Dean and I waited at the building entrance to laugh at our official, all-access corporate auditors who had less access than we did. Whatever the case was, it proved that Dean and I could access the corporate facilities at will. We went back to the hotel and checked in.

The next morning, we all drove up to the gate during the rush hour. It was only a slight surprise when we saw that we were just waved in by the guards along with everyone else. No need for a badge now. Even the auditors got in without a problem. We went and met our local contact, who took us to a conference room that was ours for the week. Dean connected to the network and started scanning. I spoke to the auditors and found out what they thought was valuable.

The auditors mentioned something that triggered my interest. They said that when people bid on a nuclear reactor or any power plant, they were frequently willing to win even if they didn't make a profit. The logic is that they can still take in more than one billion dollars. That keeps people employed. That is one billion dollars added to the winner's bottom line.

Also, if you get the competitor's proposal, you know what its bottom line is. You know what you have to bid to beat it. That is in addition to knowing the capabilities, strengths, and weaknesses of the project proposed by the competitor.

That got me thinking about the proposal process, and to the surprise of the auditors and local contacts, I went in search of the proposals instead of the designs of all the power-generation technologies. I called the company operator and asked which building housed the graphics department. She told me the number, and I told Dean that I would call to give him a computer name in a while. With that, I walked over to the building.

I found my way around the building just by asking people where the graphics department was located. When I found it, I asked for the person who worked on the proposals. The employee told me that was handled by a group within the business development group and he told me where in the same building the business development group was. A receptionist from that office pointed me to a small office in the corner. I walked over, not really sure what I was going to say.

I noticed that they were using Sun computers, which use the UNIX operating system and are more powerful than regular PCs. Three people were in the office, and I introduced myself as being from the corporate audit department. I told them that I just had a few questions. I asked what type of word processor they used and whether the proposals were stored on a server or on one of the local computers in the office. A woman told me that they used a server and gave me the name of the server. I asked one of the other people, whose desk I was standing next to, if I could just type in one line, and I would be out of their hair.

She got out of her chair, and I reached over to her keyboard and mouse. I opened a new window that allowed me to enter commands and typed "more /etc/hosts." Of course this meant nothing to the woman. A list of computer names and numbers popped up. I wrote down the number that corresponded to the name of the server that stored proposals. I thanked them for their time and walked out.

I got on my cell phone and gave Dean a quick call to tell him the number, which was the address of the server. It was a 10-minute walk through a large parking lot back to the building where we were based. Although there was a nice, cool breeze that I would have liked to enjoy, I rushed back to see how Dean was doing. It was worth the rush, because when I walked in, Dean just blandly said, "Got it."

Dean hacked into the computer and found the word processor files. We didn't have a copy of the program to read the files with full graphics mode. However, our local contact confirmed that Dean captured six proposals that included the designs for nuclear and conventional power plants. The details included the pricing and capabilities of the plants as well.

This was a morning's worth of work, and we decided to go to lunch and regroup. The local contact mentioned that there was a computer system that had the design specifications for all of the parts of company-built reactors currently in use. We thought we would target those later. The auditors also told us that the company developed a breakthrough technology that was to be commercialized in three years.

When we got back, I called the operator and asked for the research and development (R&D) group. She forwarded me to a secretary. I told the secretary that I was with corporate audit and wanted to talk to someone about how the new technology was protected. She forwarded me to an engineering manager, and I asked if I could come over.

This building was another 10-minute walk through parking lots. By this time, the sun was getting very hot and we were sweating. This time, one of the auditors came along. Dean stayed back and continued compromising systems. We walked in the front door and noticed a big, metal revolving door to our left, which allowed only one person through at a time. We saw a telephone on the wall, and I now knew why he told me I had to call when I got there. Given the revolving door, you couldn't just tailgate someone into the R&D area.

A fortyish, stereotypical geek came to meet us at the door. He used his badge to activate the revolving door for us to get through. As he took us through the offices, I saw engineering blueprints lining the wall. He took us into his office, which was lined with more blueprints. We sat down and made small talk for a few minutes.

I told him that I wanted to find out about where the new technology was being stored and how it was protected. He said, "I'd be happy to help. Who can I check with that I should be talking to you?"

Great question, but I couldn't give him a real answer. I gave him the name of our local contact who I knew would be busy in a meeting for the rest of the afternoon. He called the number and left a message. I knew this would be a long wait, and I didn't know what the local contact would say if he did call back. I changed the topic and said, "Since we can't talk about your new technology, can we talk about your computers?"

He replied that it depended on what I asked. I started asking him about computer backups and other inane topics. He didn't know the answer to the questions, and he called the systems administrator and had him come over. This person was more even more of a geek. I knew how to get him excited. Systems administrators do not get to talk to many people who are interested in what they do.

I started asking him about the type and number of computers that he had. He told me that they were UNIX servers and gave me other details. He then invited me over to the server room to take a look at things. I told the R&D manager that he should come and get us when he got a call back from my contact.

He took us into a very secure room where all the servers were. These are the servers that store the technical information of the new and older technologies. Even better for my purposes was that the servers were labeled with their names and addresses. I let him talk while I pretended to take notes, but I was really writing down the names and addresses of the computers. That was all I needed. I told the administrator that we had to get going and to tell the R&D manager that we would get back to him later.

When I got back to the meeting room, I handed Dean the list of systems to target. He told me that while we were gone, he hacked into the database that detailed how to make the parts for nuclear reactors. He said that he downloaded the database. He also asked me a question that silenced the rest of the room.

"Should somebody be logging in to the system from India?" he said.

Dean told me that after he broke in, he checked the audit logs and found a bunch of logins from India. He showed me the logs. I called the security manager for the business unit and asked him whether any-one should be logging in to the system from India. He thought for a second and then said that they had some Indian subcontractors.

I replied, "Let me be a little more specific. Should somebody from India be logged in as the administrator?"

At that point, he answered with a quick and dejected, "No."

Dean went on to compromise all the servers of the R&D group. We were supposed to be at this location for a week. However, none of us wanted to spend another day in the desert, especially because we had already stolen more than enough to prove our point. We compromised multibillion-dollar proposals, the designs of nuclear reactors, new technologies that were potentially worth billions more, details on the parts comprising nuclear reactors, and so on. We were there for a day. We packed everything up late that night and went back to the hotel. The next morning, we hopped on the first flight home.

Case Summary

Although we were provided a work area with network access and a telephone, anyone could have found an open room at the facility. This is especially true in an organization that downsized by 30 percent in the months before we were there. It was a notable that we were able to get ID badges, but we didn't need them to get through the gates during the morning rush hour.

The fact is that anyone inside the business unit who knew how to track down the right computer systems and how to break into them could have done the same things we did. Even worse is that anyone off the street with the same abilities could do it. Particularly when it comes to nuclear power plant compromises, there are plenty of interested, and capable, parties.

Vulnerabilities Exploited

As with the case study described in the previous chapter, when I describe this case to people, they swear it is their company—that is, until I mention nuclear reactors. The vulnerabilities are extremely common throughout the commercial world and in many government agencies. Even though many really strong security measures were in place, they were ignored or not implemented properly.

Poor Verification of Identities

When I entered the headquarters campus, the guard let me in by my showing a business card. Although it may be necessary to have ways for people to get onto the campus without ID badges, showing a business card should not be one of them. There should be a way to verify identities and issue temporary badges before letting someone on the corporate campus without restricting their movements.

No Locks on Secondary Entrances

After we were on the corporate campus, we were able to drive straight into the employee garage. The doors for the main entrance were well monitored but the doors in the employee garage were not monitored. And although we discovered that those doors did have an access card lock, an access card was required only during night hours. When we were inside, we found no access limitations, and people believed that we belonged there.

No Verification for Badge Issuance

Although there is no problem with someone giving out an ID badge application, there must be some verification that the person is actually authorized to have a badge. No formal system was in place to authorize a badge. The person who supposedly signed the document was not notified that the badge had been issued. In fact, I'm not sure they actually verified the identity and employment status of the person who supposedly signed the form.

Universal Acceptance of Corporate-Appearing Badges

It makes sense to use a standard ID badge throughout a company, but the possession of a company ID badge does not mean that the person needs unlimited access throughout the entire company. Also, badges can be lost or stolen. People can leave the company without returning badges. People can photocopy badges. These days, you can use a graphics package to make your own badge.

No Verification of ID Badges When It Gets Busy

The fact that the guards waved all the cars in when entering the facilities during rush hour is a clear and common (as you saw in the previous chapter) vulnerability. These companies state that physical access is their primary security countermeasure. When the stakes are very high, such as those involving nuclear power plant designs, this access cannot be allowed.

Poor Computer Security Administration

Dean was able to break into computer after computer by exploiting whatever vulnerabilities existed. There were problems with default passwords, no passwords, outdated software, and so on. Each computer we tried to attack had at least one vulnerability that allowed us to compromise it at will. Anyone around the world could have compromised, and in at least one case did compromise, critical systems. Without access controls, a computer attached to a network is vulnerable to any other computer on that network, or the networks attached to that network.

Limited Computer Auditing

Yes, the audit logs recorded the break-in from India, but nobody noticed the incident before we did. It was just luck that we chose that system to break into and that it is a standard practice for us to perform triage on systems that we compromise and check the logs. The internal administrators did not check their own logs. It was also unlikely that they had any intrusion-detection systems or misuse-and-abuse detection systems. No one inside the company noticed our attacks or the one from India, and we attacked the most sensitive systems in the company.

Labeling of Computers

Labeling computers can be useful; however, in this case, someone apparently went overboard with the new label maker. You don't need to put the computer addresses on the systems along with their names. That information can be quickly learned after you are on the system. The information definitely helps potential attackers.

Blueprints Displayed on Walls

Although we didn't bother to exploit the engineering diagrams on the wall, we could have easily been carrying hidden cameras or come back late at night to photograph the diagrams. These diagrams were the core of the new technologies, and they were sitting there at all hours for the taking. Engineers are not the only ones who exhibit critical information like this. Network administrators frequently have diagrams of their network up on their walls. These can be used to exploit networks.

8

Fill 'er Up!

Immediately after the events of September 11, 2001, the U.S. government performed a major overhaul of airport and airline security. Because the hijackers used box cutters and small pocketknives, those items were banned from carry-on items. The government also determined that other objects, such as butter knives, tweezers, and nail clippers, could potentially be used as weapons. Those items were banned as well.

The government also attempted to standardize security measures at all airports and formed the Transportation Security Administration (TSA). Waits at security-screening lines grew as security supposedly became tighter. Of course, many people were skeptical that these or other measures had any significant effect in preventing future terrorist acts.

Many people inside the government also questioned the overall effectiveness of the resulting security. For that reason, several security assessments were performed to address the concerns. Different government agencies put out press releases stating the success of attempts to get weapons through security. In November 2003, a college student was arrested for purposely breaching security by sneaking banned objects past security controls and placing them on airplanes over a period of several months. Clearly, people can still attempt to hijack airplanes.

Unfortunately, there is a significantly bigger risk at airports. The fuel depots represent tremendous targets. A gallon of fuel has the same explosive power as a quarter stick of dynamite. An airport fuel depot can store upwards of 40 million gallons of fuel, or the equivalent of 10 million sticks of dynamite. That is enough to take out an area with a diameter of 12 miles surrounding the blast point. That does not include the potential domino effects of resulting explosions of other objects and facilities, such as the planes on the ground and the rental car fuel depots.

To test the susceptibility of U.S. airports to such an attack, a government agency hired TeQuest, which uses former Special Operations soldiers to perform vulnerability assessments in high-security situations as well as to secure critical areas, to simulate an attack on a fuel depot. Clearly, these people are significantly more skilled than any group of terrorists. As you will see, they were very successful. For obvious reasons, the airport in question is not identified.

Initial Reconnaissance

The team consisted of four people: two operatives, a support specialist, and the team leader. The team leader and two operatives would perform the actual penetrations. The support specialist obtains all available public information regarding the target (news clips, layouts, plans, and yes, even satellite photos are still available if you know where to look) and maintains a chronological log of all activities that occur during the operation. Although all team members participate in the operational planning, the team leader manages the personnel, coordinates the work, and makes the final decision on which plan will be used.

The group members said they needed only three to five days to plan and execute the entire operation. They first reviewed publicly available information, such as airport maps. Additionally, they e-mailed the airport services manager to find out the minimum fuel level. To their surprise, they received an answer within an hour. They then scoped out the airport surroundings and drove around the facility. They chose to do this specifically during rush hours, especially those hours when airport ground workers came and left work. During this reconnaissance, they noticed where people parked and that there were stickers on the cars that were scanned by a device that raised the entry gate for the cars with those stickers. These gates were otherwise unattended.

The next step was to look at the fuel depot. The depots were generally secure, so a direct attack was out of the question. They found a parking lot, technically outside the airport grounds, where people went to watch planes land. It also had a great view of the airport gates. While people watched planes land, the team members took out their binoculars and watched the gates. They noticed which planes were being fueled and whether the fuel trucks went back to the depot immediately after fueling the jets.

Airports are usually very consistent on a day-to-day basis. The same flights pull up to the same gates every day. Those same flights need to be refueled at those same gates. This is especially true of early morning flights, when the airplanes have had little opportunity to arrive late and change schedules.

They found that the cargo and ground workers entered the same entrance, which was about 200 to 300 yards from the actual passenger gates.

At this point, they knew how to enter the facility. They knew which gates were closest to the employee entrance and were likely to have planes requiring fueling. They also knew that the trucks were likely to go directly back to the fuel depot.

The Preparation

Based on their observations, the attack-simulation team members now had a concept of how to perform the attack. First, they came up with a method to detonate the depot. As is typical for Special Operations, it is usually best to use things that are native to the environment. This way, you do not need to bring a lot of equipment with you, which besides being cumbersome attracts attention. Their plan was to create an explosive device, or more accurately a mock explosive device, and place it on one of the fuel trucks. They would then detonate the device remotely when the fuel truck got to the fuel depot. This would detonate the remaining gasoline in the fuel truck, which would create a chain reaction to wipe out the rest of the depot.

As former Special Operations soldiers, they are all familiar with the explosive C-4. The amount of C-4 required to ignite the fuel truck was minimal—much less than the size of two bricks. C-4, being extremely malleable, can be molded to fit around a person's shins. The detonator can be kept in a coat pocket until the bomb is to be activated. To simulate the explosive, they used pieces of wood that were sized to fit around shins.

Both operatives were fitted with explosives. They decided that Brett, the first operative, would be the primary bomber and the second operative would be the backup.

They did not make specific plans for how they would accomplish the mission. They had a general plan and could create some situations, but they knew they had to rely on exploiting vulnerabilities as they were presented. As Chapter 1 highlights, professionals can rapidly identify vulnerabilities and immediately exploit them. As in this case, sometimes there cannot be detailed plans, especially when an operation must be carried out quickly.

The Attack

The morning of the attack, the team drove to the airport in a single car. The operatives knew they didn't have one of the parking tags that would get them into the employee parking lot, so they contemplated tailgating someone through the gate. They first had to observe whether the gate came down fast enough to prevent tailgating.

Again it should be noted that there were no specific plans as to how to accomplish their mission.

As hoped for and expected, cars at the morning rush hour were bumper-to-bumper waiting to get into that parking lot. The gate was an inexpensive one and did not account for tailgating. The gate basically never went down between cars. The team drove into the line with everyone else, went through the gate, and found a parking space.

At that point, Brett and the other operative got out of the car and went in separate directions, but generally toward the employee entrance. The team leader positioned himself to film the penetration. They were all dressed in typical clothing for airport gate workers, with the exception of very loose pant legs. They watched employees walk past the guard and through the gate. They quickly noticed that many people were not displaying their badges as they went by the guard. The two operatives motioned to each other that it was okay to go. Each waited for a group of people passing by them toward the entrance and then crowded into the respective group. As each operative went by the guard, he made sure to make eye contact and nod hello.

If they did find that the guards were checking IDs carefully, they would have waited for another guard to come on duty. If all guards were diligent, they would have made up fake IDs and returned the next day.

Brett, as the primary operative, went toward the passenger gates first. The several-hundred-yard route was fairly heavily traveled at this time of day, so another person dressed like everyone else did not stand out. Nobody noticed that Brett did not display an ID badge. The second operative watched from a distance as Brett went toward a fuel truck that had just pulled up to one of the passenger jets.

Although there were two operatives, one of them was not really supposed to do anything. There is a logic to this. The first, or primary, operative is the one who is supposed to carry out the mission. However, if that person is caught or otherwise compromised, the mission must be able to continue. Most security measures are designed to concentrate on the bad guys. This means that if security finds someone doing something wrong, all resources converge on that person. With a backup already in place, the same mission can continue with only a slight delay. In some cases, the primary operative may actually want to get caught. The intent is to focus security away from the real attack, leaving the backup with less of a likelihood of being caught.

Back to the fuel truck: Brett walked over to the driver as he was getting out of his truck and started helping the driver as he unraveled the hoses to attach them to the plane. Of course, Brett made small talk, remarking that he was trying to make himself useful while he waited for someone to bring over some maintenance documents.

As the driver attached the hose to the plane and began fueling, Brett went around to the other side of the truck. He bent down on one knee, as if he were tying his shoelace, in such a way as to shield his legs with his body. In this position, someone off to his side would not have a good look at what he was doing. He quickly took the mock C-4 off one of his shins and then traded knees on the ground and took the mock C-4 off the other shin. After quickly attaching the detonator to the two explosives, he stuffed the device in a crevice of the truck and marked the area of the truck.

The whole process took about 20 seconds, which is not much longer than it would take to tie your shoelaces. He then told the driver that if anyone came looking for him, he was going to look for the documents himself and would be back. He then walked back toward the employee entrance as he gave the signal to the backup operative that the plant was completed successfully.

The reason that Brett marked the truck, even though there was a risk that it could be detected, was that he didn't want someone claiming that he lied about planting the device. In these types of penetration tests, it is common for victims to try to destroy any physical evidence after learning they were compromised.

Brett and the backup operative got back in the car, and the team drove off. They went to an area within range of the detonation device and then detonated the mock explosive when the fuel truck pulled into the depot.

This was a medium-sized international airport. Although there were only about 20 million gallons of fuel at this depot, that would still take out an area with a six-mile diameter around the blast point, without accounting for the corollary explosions.

Case Summary

Given the potential results of this attack, it appears that it was very simple to accomplish. There were no super-high-tech devices, no long-term infiltration operations, no skydiving into highly fortified compounds or other dramatic methods. To a certain extent, it seems as though whoever could get their hands on the explosives and detonator could easily accomplish the same attack.

People may say that I am being irresponsible by educating potential terrorists on how to commit future attacks. However, as is the case with the corporate attacks I describe in other chapters, these methods are already known. The mission described here was specifically designed to closely resemble an actual terrorist attack in Israel. That attack was not as successful as this one—assuming that it was a real attack and not a simulation—because the detonator went off too soon.

Knowing about the details of the failure of the Israeli attack, the simulation team used a detonation device with a frequency range that required the trigger person to be relatively close to the detonator. Although this would be unacceptable for a typical Special Operations mission, it was not out of the question for simulating a terrorist act. Sadly, there appears to be an unlimited supply of terrorists who would be willing to watch their compatriots drive away as they became martyrs.

Another issue is that this whole attack took less than three days to plan and execute. Terrorists supposedly plan their attacks for months, but terrorist-like events such as this incident can be carried out very quickly when the operatives are properly trained. This short time frame not only allows for significantly reduced costs of the operation but also means a lower likelihood of the mission's being compromised before it is executed.

Vulnerabilities Exploited

It is scary to realize that the vulnerabilities that exist in a company or even an apartment complex are the same ones that allow terrorists to potentially murder thousands of people and cause hundreds of millions of dollars of damage. I wish I could say that this team had to resort to some special tactics that only Special Operations troops could have used.

Only Watching the Obvious

After September 11, there is the obvious focus of security on passenger jets and making sure passengers are properly screened. The result is increased security for passenger areas. But that is just one aspect of airport security. The results described here could have been used to sneak weapons onto a plane, plant a bomb on the plane, blow up the terminal itself, and so on. There are many reports that detail the weaknesses of cargo facilities. If you can get in the tarmac of a cargo area, you can get on the tarmac of the passenger area. Cargo planes are as large as passenger jets, and you don't need to worry about dealing with a plane full of hostages.

Improper Physical Controls

The parking gate was not appropriate for the risk. Some parking gates, such as those at toll facilities, are fast enough that the gates come down immediately after a car clears it. That prevents tailgating. Given the nature of the terrorist threat and the focus on airports, the gate should be physically manned. Not only should the car have a parking sticker, but also all the people in the car should be required to show valid badges before the car is allowed to enter.

Apathetic Guards

A smile was as good as a badge for getting by the guard at the employee entrance. Although apathetic guards are common in most of the case studies in this book, even I believe that an incident at an airport is much more critical than compromising corporate secrets because there is the *immediate* potential for thousands of deaths.

As is the case with corporate guards, the individual guards should not be blamed. This is a management problem. The airport authorities must ensure that the guards are well aware of the threats they face and that a slip-up on their part can cause the loss of thousands of lives. The workers at the airport also observe the guards letting people through with a smile and a wink, and they should report this behavior. Guards must be forced to perform full ID checks, no matter how much it slows things down.

Inconsistent Security Measures Throughout the Facility

The TSA and federal government as a whole have no problem telling the general public to expect delays at the airport. This is while they admit that they serve the public and want to minimize any inconvenience. They cite the obvious security concerns, and for the most part, these concerns are valid. However, they tend to ignore the areas outside passenger access. The screening of employees at cargo areas is significantly weaker than the screening that the passengers go through, even though employees have significantly more access. Airport workers should go through stronger security procedures, including a visual ID check, as well as stronger protections, such as access cards and biometric scanning. The airport is providing employees with a job, not a service, and vigorous screening should be a condition of that job.

Employees Failing to Check IDs

Although it is a guard's job to check ID badges, that does not mean that typical airport workers are not responsible for looking for IDs. The fact is that terrorists do target airports. All workers must realize that they have a responsibility to protect themselves and others, which includes noticing when someone does not have a badge.

In particular, the driver of the refueling truck should have noticed someone just coming over and making life easy for him. If this were a real attack, he would have been the first person to die. Actually, a real terrorist would have just killed the driver on the tarmac. The terrorist could then drive the truck into the depot himself and detonate the explosives.

No Check of Trucks Before Entering the Fuel Depot

Because of the potential for such an attack, any vehicle entering a fuel depot should be searched for explosives. This could include visual searches, such as the searches used for those entering federal buildings, or with bomb-sniffing dogs. The threat is proven, and it can result in tremendous loss of life.

Availability of Observation Areas

There are observation areas around all major airports. It would be almost impossible to eliminate them. However, the recent attention given shoulder-fired missiles implies that these areas present a vulnerability. They not only are a point for a direct attack but also allow for reconnaissance of physical attacks against the entire airport, as this case demonstrates. Although stopping people from using those areas for observation is not realistic, the lack of a counterintelligence operation at these points means that bad guys can use them for surveillance and go unnoticed. In this case, the car the operatives used should have been noticed and put on a watch list.

Sensitive Information Easily Available

Airport maps were available on the Internet, as was a great deal of other critical information not discussed here. The fact that the airport services manager readily disclosed the minimum fuel on hand is beyond belief. Although it is true that much of the information can eventually be learned through other methods, this fact does not justify making the information readily available to any would-be terrorist.

9

The Entrepreneur

Prologue

I was being introduced to the executive management team by the company's security manager. The first thing he did was pick up a copy of my first book, *Corporate Espionage*, and say, "I originally met Ira back in 1999 and I had him sign my book. The comment Ira wrote at the time was, 'Do a good job so I don't have a Swedish case study for my next book.' It looks like I didn't do a good job."

The Spy of the Twenty-First Century

The information stolen detailed the inner workings of cellular telephone networks. It would allow people not only to tap into telephone calls at will but also pinpoint a person's exact location. It could also tell an attacker exactly how to take down the entire cellular network. If I tell you that a group of Iranians was the center of this case the Swedish government classified as Gross Espionage, the first thing you are likely to assume is that the case is terrorist related. If I add that the senior SVR (formerly the KGB) officer in charge of Sweden was personally involved and this case was so devastating that it went to Sweden's

Supreme Court, you start to picture super spies involved in high stakes espionage.

Instead picture Newman from the TV show *Seinfeld* as the spy in the center of the action. In this case, his name is Afshin Bavand. His features are slightly darker and his hair is straight. Then consider that he was a laid-off, low-level telecommunications test engineer who couldn't figure out how to work a pager. This is the super spy of the twenty-first century.

When I first contacted Afshin Bavand to see whether he would let me interview him, he wanted to make sure that I knew that this was not a cloak-and-dagger type of story. As do most criminals, he claimed that he was guilty only of something everyone else does but doesn't get caught or charged with. This 2 minutes of information took him about 10 minutes to get out.

I finally met Afshin Bavand in a visiting room in a Stockholm prison. Judging by the children's toys in the corner, and the bright lights and comfortable furniture, it was clearly a place where prisoners were given private time to meet with their families. I had two hours to try to get details out of him for my book, information that the Swedish authorities had been unable to get out of him in more than a year. On top of that, I knew I had to win over his trust and then deal with the fact that he was extremely chatty.

Bavand is 46 years old and, again, looks more like Newman than a person responsible for Gross Espionage. I told him that I was writing a book and needed case studies to demonstrate that real espionage is more a comedy of errors than cloak and dagger. It became clear that he is the consummate entrepreneur and wanted to know what was in it for him. I was not going to pay, or basically reward a felon for his crimes. I told him that this was his opportunity to get his side of the story out, and that if he didn't want to talk to me, he could go back to his cell. I also told him that assisting in a book that was intended to help security professionals would be a benefit in the future.

He mentioned a few times that for all he knew I could be with the CIA. Although I assured him I wasn't, I also asked him if it actually made any difference anyway. He started to open up a little bit; I guess he began to believe that this was a chance to get his story out. As I listened to him talk, it became clear that he was trying to get his story out the way he wants people to see it.

I will say that although he claims not to be bitter, he is very mad at the SVR, who basically left him to rot in prison and provided no help after he was arrested. He also thinks his eight-year prison sentence is excessive, because he believes everyone in the corporate world does what he did. Probably most important to him is that he is embarrassed to be caught and lose face in the Iranian community and among his friends. He is also clearly not associated with any Moslem extremists or terrorists in any way.

The case as I describe it also draws from detailed interviews of Ericsson's security staff, who primarily discussed evidence submitted in an open court. I actually met with staff members before I met with Bavand, so I knew when he was starting to lie to me. I also discussed this case with Stan Lunev, the GRU colonel, to help fill in the pieces and determine fact from fiction with regard to SVR tactics. So although I appreciate the fact Afshin Bavand met with me, he clearly lied to me about certain things, and I have to discount much of what he says and rely on the demonstrated facts of the case.

In his defense, though, by all accounts, although Bavand does believe he is extremely intelligent, he confused dates and facts while being interrogated by SÄPO, the Swedish intelligence service, that would have helped him. Remember he is a telecom engineer who can't even work a pager. His stories were also somewhat imaginative.

A Spy in the Making

Ericsson hired Afshin Bavand in 1995 as a Test and Verification Engineer for the Transmission Systems Unit based in Stockholm. Bavand, an Iranian, attended Baguel University in the Philippines to study mechanical engineering and then went on to attend a technical school in Sweden. The fact that he is Iranian is relevant only in that it created his social circle.

Upon being hired at Ericsson, he socialized with other Iranian workers. He also was a member of a tight-knit Iranian community with ties to Iranians in other countries.

Sometime during his employment, Bavand started taking home documents from work. At first, he primarily took paper copies of documents. However, as the capacity of floppy disks and CDs grew, he started taking home electronic copies of documents. According to him, this was a common practice so that people could work at home or just study up to be better at their job. Although physical security is actually very strong at Ericsson facilities, somebody carrying out a few documents or a CD containing thousands of documents in a coat pocket would easily go unnoticed.

As the telecom industry downturn started to hit in the late 1990s, Bavand was afraid of the potential downsizing and started to take home documents at a greater pace.

The Creation of an Entrepreneur

When you listen to Afshin Bavand talk, you get the impression that he is always trying to work a deal to his benefit. Well, in August 2001, Ericsson gave him the opportunity to pursue other dreams when they laid him off, along with 10,000 other workers. Ericsson did provide what is by all accounts a very generous severance package. Bavand received one year's salary as well as limited access to Ericsson computers and other facilities to help him find a new job.

He claimed that at this point, with the massive layoffs, the job market was too crowded, so he thought he would start his own business. He thought that cellular technology was just beginning to expand in Iran, and told some friends and relatives to buy licenses for cell phone towers and cells. Using Ericsson computers, he claimed, he put together a cellular architecture that his relatives could buy and install in Iran. Due to poor execution, all his plans never came to fruition in Iran.

Bavand then tried something similar with relatives in Poland. Again, nothing came of this. He said that he offered consulting services to some German companies in the setup of cellular networks. It starts to get a little murky here. Bavand told me that he actually received some consulting revenue from some German companies; however, when I tried to probe further into that, he said he shouldn't have told me about this and wouldn't answer any more questions on the matter.

I would think, though, that he went through almost half his severance pay and was beginning to get desperate for a real income. During this time, Bavand said, he continued to take out documents from Ericsson to further his business ventures, which he said would profit Ericsson.

Bavand said that he asked two of his friends to start helping him get documents. They were also Iranian test engineers. Bavand proudly told me how he would call up his friends at work and talk them through the process of accessing a centralized document storage system to download specific documents that he needed. He said his friends gladly did this because they were afraid that they would be laid off. Bavand told them that he would get them a job if that ever happened. Bavand showed them a very lavish appearance and lifestyle, helping to convince them that he could help them in the future.

Bavand Finds a Customer

Bavand also contacted an Iranian friend living in Russia. The claim was that he wanted to see whether his friend knew of any consulting work for him in Russia. Again it get murky as Bavand claimed that he approached his friend for business purposes but later told me that he knew this friend had involvement with the KGB because of immigration problems. When I asked him his friend's name, he said that he hasn't been able to make contact with this friend and that the friend's life is in danger, so he wouldn't give me a name. It is interesting to note that Bavand always referred to the SVR as the KGB, despite the name change long before he supposedly became involved with the agency, as well as the fact that he had extensive involvement with the SVR.

However, Bavand said, at that time his friend didn't know of any opportunities. Bavand was, however, contacted out of nowhere by a Russian named Boris. He claimed that he didn't know Boris' last name but that Boris traveled from Russia to meet him. Bavand first met with Boris in January 2002. During the initial meeting they discussed a wide variety of potential business ventures in the power and telecom fields. They met again two days later.

Bavand claimed that he wanted Boris to help him set up a business in Sweden and was very specific that he wanted money from the relationship. He also claimed that he never heard from Boris after the second meeting, and that the next contact he had from a Russian was not until June of that year.

The facts presented in court show that not to be the case. Boris was actually an SVR operative based in Sweden and was apparently relatively good at what he did. SÄPO regularly follows known SVR operatives as they travel around Sweden. On many occasions after January 2002, Boris would lose the SÄPO agents following him. Bank records indicate that Bavand frequently made large bank deposits the day after Boris would lose the tails.

Ericsson computer audit logs also indicate that Bavand's friends still employed by Ericsson made large numbers of retrievals from the document storage systems after the bank deposits. Again, though, Bavand claimed that he did not see Boris again, and with Boris' being good at what he did, he was never caught in the act of meeting him.

Bavand's information must have proven to be extremely promising. In June 2002, Sergei Golovkin apparently took over the handling of Bavand. Golovkin was actually a colonel in the SVR, assigned to the post of First Secretariat at the Russian embassy in Stockholm. Diplomatically, Golovkin was the third highest member of the Russian delegation in Sweden. The potential of Bavand's information apparently justified the involvement of the senior SVR officer instead of a junior officer such as Boris.

Apparently Colonel Golovkin was not nearly as skilled as his underling, because he did not lose the SÄPO tail the first time he met with Bavand. They were photographed meeting together at a cafeteria in the Centrum (city center) of the Sollentuna section of Sweden. Golovkin gave Bavand a pager and instructions on codes he would send to the pager. He also gave Bavand Russian and Swedish telephone numbers at which to contact him, as well as an e-mail address.

SÄPO probably was able to listen in on the conversation between Golovkin and Bavand, and knew to contact Ericsson security. At this point, SÄPO and Ericsson started working together to form a strategy to handle the problem. From what they could tell, Bavand provided the SVR with bulk information about a variety of different technologies. The SVR was likely sending the information back to Moscow and slowly sifting through it. Agency members then started to refine what they wanted, and provided Boris and then Golovkin with a tasking list for Bavand at each meeting. (Remember the intelligence process defined in Chapter 1.) After receiving a packet of information, Boris and Golovkin gave Bavand his money along with the tasking list for the next meeting.

Ericsson security personnel reviewed the audit logs as far back as they could, and were able to determine exactly what Bavand's assistants downloaded for him over the previous six months. Ericsson also started to closely monitor their continued computer activities. After every meeting, Bavand called his friends with requests for more information. He even went as far as to fax them the list Golovkin gave him.

Ericsson personnel would see what the friends were searching for and then determine whether they should tell SÄPO to let the exchange take place or to intercept the exchange and arrest everyone.

Bavand met with Golovkin for a second time in mid–August 2002 and a third time in September 2002. After the September meeting, Ericsson saw that the Russians specifically wanted a new telecommunications technology, still in development. Because this was extremely valuable for proprietary reasons and for the security purposes of future cell networks, Ericsson told SÄPO to intercept the next exchange.

On November 5, 2002, Bavand and Golovkin met for the final time. During the meeting, Bavand told Golovkin about two other people inside Ericsson that he now had access to. As they sat down at another outdoor café, SÄPO closed in on the pair and arrested them. They found the documents that Bavand's conspirators downloaded from the Ericsson network, and $4,000 in cash on Golovkin.

Bavand's sources were arrested the next day. The two new people mentioned at the meeting were identified and suspended from Ericsson. It was soon discovered that they had no involvement with Bavand's espionage, and they returned to work. It appears that Bavand had been trying to portray himself as a spymaster to Golovkin.

Golovkin, having full diplomatic immunity, was released soon thereafter. He and Boris had already left Sweden by the following week when Sweden declared them persona non grata and ordered them to leave the country. Bavand did not, however, have such immunity. He has been in prison since his initial arrest and will likely be there through at least 2010.

In total, Bavand reportedly received $50,000. His co-conspirators did not receive a penny because they always believed that they were just helping Bavand in his new career as a consultant. For their trouble, they were both sentenced to three years on industrial espionage charges. One of their sentences was appealed down to one year.

In a case that demonstrated a need to change Sweden's industrial espionage laws, the other person had his conviction thrown out. There were two aspects of espionage that made it a crime: misuse and access. It turns out that although this person obviously misused the Ericsson documents by giving them to Bavand, his position actually allowed him legitimate access to the document database, which was the source of his crime. According to Swedish law at the time of the crime, the legitimate access, even if abused, meant that he could not be charged with the crime. Ericsson was allowed to sue him civilly, though, which obviously was not worth the effort.

Case Summary

Bavand is the poster child for industrial spies. He always thought he was smarter than his spymasters at the SVR, one of the most efficient espionage organizations in history. This arrogance caused him to make many critical errors that should have made a colonel of the SVR cut him off as an agent.

For example, Bavand always wanted to meet in very public places. He thought that meeting in public would demonstrate an absence of wrongdoing. Unfortunately for him, it also allowed for extremely easy surveillance by SÄPO. Given the stakes, Golovkin should have had him use dead drops. Golovkin did attempt to communicate with Bavand covertly, but he wasn't smart enough to decipher the prearranged code. These are all big red flags for an operative. Again, the fact that Bavand was detected only after Golovkin could not detect surveillance also demonstrates a flaw with Golovkin's skills.

One critical piece of evidence against Bavand was his own computer. Bavand actually created directories on his computer for each set of information that he gave to Boris and Golovkin, and he named the directories by the month of the exchange. Golovkin should have clearly instructed him to get rid of any evidence. At the very least, the reason would be so that if Bavand ever did get caught, SÄPO would not know exactly what he handed over.

All in all, SÄPO and Ericsson calculated that if all the documents Bavand handed over were printed, it would take three trucks to transport them. For his efforts, Bavand received only $50,000. Again, the information would allow Russia, and anyone else it would give or sell the information to, to tap into any telephone call, track any individual on the cellular network, and crash the cellular network. Remember that, as Chapter 4 describes, the GRU is directly tasked with the ability to bring any piece of the critical infrastructure down. At the very least, the information could have been given to Russian or Chinese competitors to compete directly against Ericsson with their own technologies. Although Bavand may not be aware of the strategic implications of his actions, the charge of Gross Espionage is more than justified for his crimes. Needless to say, the SVR provided Bavand with no support at all.

Just for the record, Bavand claimed to me that he never received money from Golovkin, and the $4,000 carried by Golovkin received on November 5, 2002, would have been the first money he received for the information. He claims that those cash deposits he made that consistently coincided with his previous meetings with Golovkin and the times that Boris lost his surveillance occurred because Iranians regularly transfer money for each other, and he was just transferring money for friends and relatives. Concerning the documents on his computer coinciding with the meetings with people, and also with the downloading of information from the Ericsson storage system, Bavand claimed that he would have never been stupid enough to store the information so obviously. Again, those are his claims, but the facts seem to contradict them.

Before I describe the vulnerabilities exploited, I must state that although there was a great deal of potential damage done, this is generally a security success story. Remember that there is no such thing as perfect security. Ericsson was able to quickly determine what was compromised and track future compromises. It worked closely with SÄPO to study the compromise and see how far the company should let it go. What is probably most important is that Ericsson and SÄPO now know what the Russians do and do not know. (Please review the importance of this knowledge in Chapter 1.) They now know what they need to protect and keep a closer eye on.

At the same time, the case was an eye opener for Ericsson. As Chapter 4 covers, the SVR has a standing target list of companies to compromise, a list on which Ericsson stands out. The SVR reviews all visa applications of people traveling to Russia to see whether they work for a targeted company and whether there is any way to exploit them. The employees at Ericsson now know that this is the real world, not a spy novel. How many companies in exactly their position can make that claim?

Vulnerabilities Exploited

Although this is somewhat of a security success story, there are definitely lessons to be learned. These lessons are, sadly, extremely common for most large companies, and I would probably say that most other companies would not fare as well.

Layoffs

When the telecommunications sector experienced a downturn, Ericsson laid off more than 10,000 people. Think of all the disgruntled workers there are. Although Ericsson created a good severance package, there are probably many malicious people out there who are likely more discreet than Bavand was. Although it is unlikely that these people would go to the extreme of selling secrets to Russia, they would likely do harm to Ericsson if given the opportunity.

Anytime a company lets people go when the people don't want to go, bad feelings will arise. Sometimes the layoffs are unavoidable. However, more frequently, jobs all over the world are being exported to places such as China and India. People affected by such layoffs will be more prone to malicious acts than normal.

Generous Severance Assistance

By all accounts, Ericsson truly regretted the layoffs it had to make. The company did everything it could to help the displaced workers. Unfortunately, it was too generous. Allowing employees access to Ericsson resources inside their facilities was intended to help the employees find new jobs, both inside and outside the company. The computer resources allowed for training for new career fields, as well as serving as a great resource in general.

Although a one-year salary severance package was a gesture of good will and much more than anyone would expect, continued access to facilities provides access to a potentially malicious group of people. There were other ways to accomplish the goal of assisting laid-off employees.

Low Morale

Bavand's greatest assets were his two friends still employed by Ericsson. Whenever you have a company lay off tens of thousands of people, all employees fear for their jobs. They learn that if there is one round of layoffs, there will likely be more. Even worse is that the longer they are employed, the more trouble they will have finding a new position because the job market is already flooded with their former coworkers. It is only human nature to try to make sure that you have a backup plan in case the worst happens. Bavand was his friends' backup plan. The morale created by the corporate layoffs helped in Bavand's efforts.

Centralized Document Storage with Unlimited Access

Centralized document storage is extremely useful in the sharing of information and facilitating new development efforts. It also allows a test engineer to know what standards to use to test new systems. It is also one-stop shopping for a spy.

The lack of access control allowed any user on the network to access any document on the system. This was clearly a problem.

Lack of Auditing

It is clear that the Ericsson document storage system logged any access. Ericsson's security staff made excellent use of those logs after the staff was contacted by SÄPO about Bavand's meeting with the SVR. Unfortunately, there had been no regular auditing of the access logs before that. The auditing could have been either manual or computer based to search for unauthorized use or an unusual number of accesses.

CD Capacity

Bavand was able to supply the SVR with thousands of documents, approximately three truckloads of information, in fewer than 10 meetings held in public. Clearly, this feat was possible only because Bavand provided the SVR with the documents in electronic format.

10

The Criminal Face of the Internet Age

I considered dozens of cases for inclusion in this book. The cases described up to this point demonstrate some compromise of computer systems, but only as part of a more coordinated attack that represents the most costly kind. Although attacks that focus on computer hacking via the Internet are clearly the most numerous, they are not the most devastating. However, there are such cases that do result in large losses and demonstrate great technical expertise.

Back in the late 1990s, news stories started reporting that banks were being extorted by computer hackers. The stories described how criminals would contact banks and provide them proof that they had administrator access to their system. The criminals then demanded money for not disclosing the attacks and for not creating damage to the systems in the future. In the new millennium, more e-commerce sites came online, and the attacks started targeting these new sites that popped up out of nowhere and thought little about security.

So, when it came time to choose a case of a computer-based attack, I wanted one that demonstrated both clear criminal activity and as many aspects of computer crime as possible. The fact that the case covered here also included the hacking of banks and the indictment of an FBI undercover agent made it all the better.

I tracked down Alexey Ivanov, who together with his partner, Vasily Gorshkov, extorted tens of thousands of dollars, if not more, from companies processing financial transactions throughout the United States. They had at least 56,000 credit card numbers in their possession at the time of their arrest. The judge determined that they caused more than $25,000,000 in damage to organizations that included at least one bank, eBay, Amazon.com, PayPal, and a wide variety of Internet service providers (ISPs) and credit card processors. Alexey accomplished a great deal in his life for a 20-year-old from Russia.

The Making of a Criminal

Alexey grew up in Chelyabinsk, Russia, which has the reputation of being one of the most polluted cities in the world. This industrial city has a population of about 1.2 million people. Alexey began playing with computers in 1993 at the age of 13. I had to admit that I was taken aback when he said that he was most interested in computer viruses because of their ability to take on a life of their own. Although he said he wrote viruses as tests, he claimed to have never released any. He started a bulletin board system in 1996 for the sharing of virus information.

By this time, he was also breaking into computers. This was at a time when UNIX was the most commonly used system on the Internet, and he became very skilled in cracking those systems. The most common and simple attack that he used was exploiting the "finger" command, which basically provided him with a list of accounts on remote systems. He just guessed passwords of the accounts and accessed the accounts. From there, he had a valid account and used other exploits to get elevated privileges. That was of course assuming that the accounts he compromised did not already include the administrator's account.

He graduated high school in Spring 1997 and moved out of his home at around that time. He did, however, need employment. After hacking the local ISP, he told that company about his break-ins and was offered a job in early 1998. He also started to attend Chelyabinsk State University and study computer science. Given all of Alexey's experience, he was learning little in his computer classes.

That was okay because by this time he was already breaking into computer systems on a regular basis. He accessed the Internet Relay Chat (IRC) channel specific to Chelyabinsk and found several people to help mentor him and expand his computer knowledge. With their help, he moved on to breaking into many Internet systems, especially online merchant systems in which credit card information was plentiful.

Going Pro

Here's some background. It was on IRC where Alexey met his future co-conspirators. Most important among them was Vasily Gorshkov, who became the local ringleader. Alexey was among the most talented with regard to finding and compromising merchant systems, and he bartered credit card numbers for a variety of purposes. Alexey's hacking and IRC activities took up four hours of his time, which was on top of going to school full time and working at the ISP.

This schedule eventually took its toll on Alexey; in June 1999 he stopped attending Chelyabinsk State University, quit the ISP, and started working for a local moving firm. As fits the stereotype of Russia, he made more money moving furniture than maintaining the computer systems of an ISP. Computer hacking and IRC still filled his spare time. The group also started to physically meet in local bars. It was at one of these meetings that Gorshkov recommended that the group become more organized and profit motivated in its activities.

The group evolved into a formal business relationship. Despite the fact that Alexey was physically well suited to moving furniture all day, it became physically taxing and he welcomed a less physical and more profitable alternative. Using Alexey's other strength of compromising credit cards, the group focused on fraud as its primary modus operandi. Specifically, it used stolen credit cards to purchase things online and then resell those goods to legitimate wholesalers and retailers in Chelyabinsk. The group created PayPal accounts with stolen credit card numbers and free e-mail accounts, using these when convenient.

The group's favorite online sources were Amazon.com and eBay. At this time, Amazon.com provided primarily DVDs, CDs, and books. eBay and a few other sites provided access to the more valuable commodities, such as computer equipment and other merchandise. Initially, the materials were ordered to locations in Chelyabinsk. However, antifraud measures soon determined that fraud was too rampant among orders going to Russia, so the group had to think of alternatives.

Chelyabinsk is approximately 150 miles from the Kazakhstan border. Although it is still a former Soviet republic, and fraud runs rampant in that country as well, the world and web merchants treat that country differently than Russia. Gorshkov took a six-hour drive to Kostunay, which is the city in Kazakhstan that is closest to Chelyabinsk, 150 miles inside Kazakhstan. There he went through the local paper and looked through the classified ads.

You have to understand the culture of the former Soviet republics to understand the group's scheme. Kazakhstan is infamous for its corruption and criminal activity. There are few jobs that pay well that are not associated with organized crime. Women are frequently solicited to enter prostitution, and consequently, there are classified ads from women offering to do any work that is legal and not involved in prostitution. Gorshkov would respond to those ads and tell the women that all they had to do was receive packages.

They were paid 50 rubles, or about $2 per package they received. To show the women that they were not part of a criminal activity, they would open the packages in front of the women to show them that there were no drugs, guns, and so on in the packages. This way the women were comfortable and not inclined to inform the police or organized criminals to claim rewards.

With the pieces in place, they could start initiating their fraud. Basically, they would create accounts on Amazon.com and eBay using stolen credit cards and free e-mail accounts, and buy things using those accounts. The merchandise was shipped to the women in Kostunay, and Alexey and Gorshkov would periodically drive to Kostunay to pick up the packages.

To make sure that the border guards didn't give them any troubles as they were crossing back into Russia, they would stop on the way to the border and drive into the woods. There they would take everything out of the boxes and just try to toss them into the car to make them appear to be nothing valuable. They would throw jackets or blankets on top of the merchandise whenever possible.

This is really the phase that created problems within the organization. Actually, the choice of merchandise ordered is what created the problems. The group had six people at this time. Alexey and Gorshkov preferred to order/steal computer and memory chips. These items were extremely valuable, given their weight and size, and not likely to be understood as valuable by border guards. Most of the other accomplices liked to order items for a more youthful consumer, such as game controllers and toys. These items stood out and were also less profitable. It was also these things that the border guards would tend to "confiscate" or take as bribes, thereby putting the rest of the merchandise at risk.

When the merchandise was in Chelyabinsk, the group would sell it to the wholesalers and retailers. Books, DVDs, and CDs, which were sold retail for approximately $30, tended to net the group $10 apiece. For the computer equipment, the group found a wholesaler in Chelyabinsk that would typically give the group $80 per chip and resell the items for $100.

Going Separate Ways

In January/February 2000, within six months of coming up with their grand vision, group members became greedy and the team began to split up. Alexey and Gorshkov went their separate ways to focus on the higher-return merchandise; the other four people went off to form their own group focused on game controllers and other toys. Alexey believes, however, that Gorshkov maintained involvement with the other group.

Also in January 2000, Gorshkov believed that they had to set up a legitimate front organization. For that reason, he put up a shingle and set up a web design company. Alexey and Gorshkov were the principals of this company, and they hired several programmers. Although they took on legitimate web design business, they used the programmers to further their own criminal endeavors. In this way, tech.net.ru was born.

Alexey decided that the fraud they were committing was inefficient. He wanted to automate the different tasks involved in fraud, allowing for more volume. He began to task the hired programmers with different pieces of the puzzle. This way, the programmers would not be able to put together what was really going on. For example, one programmer would create an e-mail program. Another would create a database access program. Alexey would integrate the different programs with one another. The programs when finished were to create many seemingly valid PayPal and eBay accounts that had great feedback and seemingly posed little risk to sellers.

As part of the effort, Alexey decided to try some phishing schemes. He basically used some eBay "power functions" and was able to pull down lists of thousands of eBay users with PayPal accounts. He created a web page that looked like a legitimate eBay page that asked for account information. He decided to test only a small sample and sent offers of a $50 bonus to 150 users. He received the account information from 120 of the solicited accounts.

Luckily for these people, and many, many other eBay users, Alexey never had time to fully implement his automated fraud scheme.

More Profitable Endeavors

Alexey realized that although there was a lot of money to be made through his and Gorshkov's fraud, there were more profitable ways for them to make money. Remember, Alexey got his first job as a result of hacking into an ISP. He was also breaking into the sites of web merchants to steal credit card numbers and enable the fraud. So, he started to offer his expertise to help some sites fix their systems.

In 1999, Alexey broke into several web-hosting companies. These companies hosted many Internet sites, including many online merchants. If he compromised one system on the network, he had access to hundreds of web sites.

One of these companies was Lightrealm, which has since been purchased by Micron Electronics. Through IRC, Alexey was able to gain access to an account. The computers were using the BSD operating system, which is basically a version of UNIX. The systems themselves were maintained securely; however, Alexey looked around the computers and found some administration programs that were written by the Lightrealm staff to automate some administration functions. Alexey was able to modify the programs to give him superuser privileges. Having the privileges, Alexey installed some backdoors, giving him access to the system even if the Lightrealm administrators found him and kicked him off.

The Lightrealm administrators did find him and tried to kick him off. At this point he started negotiations for payment. He offered to fix the vulnerabilities that he had compromised and to find other vulnerabilities. The administrators refused to pay and kept trying to kick him out. He kept breaking back in. The administrators apparently did not want to let their management know that they were compromised and couldn't keep the assailant out, no matter what they knew to try.

As was Alexey's modus operandi, he had captured many credit card numbers and threatened to expose them if he was not paid. In September 1999, the administrators let their management know what was going on, and management made a deal with Alexey. He was to be paid $80 per month, and an additional $50-$100 per vulnerability found. By January 2000, Alexey was paid approximately $1,000.

One thing that is notable is that Alexey was very open about his identity. He made little to no effort to disguise it. He also made no effort to launder any money, but had the money sent straight to his account. He even started distributing his resume and posted it to DICE.com. Alexey had no concern about U.S. law enforcement. His big concern was just to stay away from the Russian mafia.

There were several other break-ins that primarily focused on hosting companies that hosted web merchants and UNIX systems. Until January 2000, Alexey was pursuing these extortion attempts on his own, supplementing his income from the eBay and Amazon fraud endeavors. When Gorshkov and Alexey spun off tech.net.ru, Alexey introduced Gorshkov to his side job and convinced him that they should be doing more of this.

Given that Alexey previously focused on UNIX systems, it is likely that Gorshkov was the one who suggested a more efficient way of finding victims. The pair started using the Yahoo! search engine to find vulnerable sites. They searched for banks, online merchants, online casinos, and other organizations that processed financial transactions; then they did a cross search to look for signs that the sites used the Microsoft IIS web server software. The IIS web server has many known vulnerabilities that are likely to be present if the systems are not well maintained. Of course, they were very successful.

One of their first successes was casinovega.com. He was initially able to break into the site and manipulate the database to make it look as though he had won money. He then cashed out, contacted the administrators, and was quickly paid.

Alexey and Gorshkov then moved on to more stubborn companies. In January 2000, Alexey first broke into Online Information Bureau of Vernon, Connecticut, a processor of financial transaction using a widely known IIS vulnerability. He stole some credit card information and went through the typical extortion threats of releasing the information. They refused to give in, called the FBI, and hired a security consultant for $5,000 to lock him out. Alexey was still able to get in time and time again.

All told, there were claims that more than a dozen companies were hit by Gorshkov and Ivanov. It appears that Alexey would perform the break-ins and Gorshkov would typically perform the extortion.

A Legitimate Job Offer

Ironically, throughout the whole effort Alexey and Gorshkov always appeared to hope for a legitimate job. Their hopes seemed to start coming true in June 2000. Alexey received an e-mail from a company called Invita, offering him a job/partnership. Soon, Alexey told the company that he had a partner who was also interested. After a few months, and some back and forth, Invita arranged for a visa for Alexey and Gorshkov. Alexey and Gorshkov paid for their own airfare and flew to Seattle, Washington, on November 10, 2000.

After having a long but otherwise enjoyable flight over, and some alcohol, they were met at the airport by the Invita owners and driven to their offices. The Invita staff welcomed hem, and asked them to demonstrate their skills. Gorshkov used one of Invita's computers to log onto his tech.net.ru servers to download some tools. Alexey, however, felt uncomfortable with that and decided to use his own laptop to log on and give the demo.

After a successful meeting, they got back in the car to go to their hotel. During the ride, they were stopped by FBI agents and arrested. Invita was an FBI front company set up specifically for this sting.

There was a keystroke logger on the Invita computer that Gorshkov used. After Alexey and Gorshkov left, the FBI used the captured password to log on to Gorshkov's account at tech.net.ru. They searched his files and found stolen credit card numbers and a variety of other incriminating evidence. This gave them enough evidence to arrest the pair.

Following the advice of a public defender, Alexey gave the FBI the password for his laptop. Unfortunately for him, he used the same password on the tech.net.ru system, and the FBI was able to go into his account on the system and find more evidence that helped convict him.

Case Summary

Many things about this case are highly unusual. One of the more ironic events was that an FBI agent was actually indicted by the Russian government for the sting. Russia basically charges that the FBI agent destroyed data on the tech.net.ru systems while he broke into the systems to gather evidence against Gorshkov and Ivanov. Remember, tech.net.ru did take on legitimate projects. At this point, if the FBI agent sets foot in Russia, he will be arrested. So far, Russia hasn't attempted to extradite him.

Newspaper accounts of these events implied the involvement of the Russian mafia, with many independent cells all being coordinated under a central authority. There is no evidence supporting any real involvement of the mafia. Although Gorshkov probably controlled two cells, one with Alexey and one with the other members of the original group, this was likely a haphazard result of his being the leader of the original group. There are, sadly, plenty of other individuals and mafia groups who can put hacker cells together, and they won't go looking for legitimate employment.

Gorshkov's and Ivanov's major weakness was the desire to get a legitimate job. It was likely extremely easy for the FBI to tie Alexey's e-mail that he used for extortion to the résumé on DICE.com and many other sites. The pair also disclosed a great deal of personal information to their victims in their pursuit of legitimate work from those companies. The FBI was able to use this information to social-engineer the pair into a sting.

A judge decided that Gorshkov and Ivanov caused or intended to cause more than $25,000,000 in damage. United States law now says that every stolen credit card is worth $500 when calculating punishment on top of the actual damages. Gorshkov was sentenced to three years in jail and ordered to pay $700,000 in restitution. He served some time and then left the United States and went back to Chelyabinsk.

Alexey Ivanov is another story. He pleaded guilty to similar charges in August 2002. However, it took more than a year to sentence him because Alexey wanted to stay in the United States. He was also believed to be the more dangerous of the two. The judge had several psychological evaluations performed to see whether Alexey was likely to be a repeat criminal. After reviewing the assessments, the judge decided to sentence him to four years and ordered him to pay $900,000 in restitution. He was let out approximately a year later and remains in the United States, where he is starting to pay the restitution. Several of his victims have since gone out of business, through no fault of Alexey's.

One of the more upsetting things to Alexey is that part of his restitution involves paying the fees of several consultants who were hired by his victims. His issue is that many of the consultants failed to stop him and should not be paid at all.

Again, credit card fraud and cyber extortion continues at an increasing rate. Many companies are readily paying extortion. Individuals are putting up with the aggravation of having their credit cards stolen and abused, and merchants absorb the losses. Although the FBI and several other agencies have made arrests in other cases as well, the majority of similar cases go unsolved.

Vulnerabilities Exploited

There are many vulnerabilities exploited from many different perspectives in this case. The crimes committed here are so common that individuals should carefully look to see whether they do the same as the victims in this case. Sadly, many of the vulnerabilities that expose personal information are beyond the control of the individual. Even if a person is careful about whom he or she does business with, this case shows that third parties, such as credit card processing services, can expose people's personal information. So look through these vulnerabilities carefully and see what applies to your company and you personally.

Known Vulnerabilities

All the crimes committed by Alexey and Gorshkov began with known vulnerabilities, such as widely known software security vulnerabilities and poor system configurations. Vulnerabilities were found on all common operating systems, including both UNIX and Windows. A poorly maintained system is a poorly maintained system. Systems that processed financial data were not immune and continue to be vulnerable.

Errors in Custom-Written Code

As mentioned in Chapter 5, any software is subject to vulnerabilities. It is somewhat common for administrators to write their own software to assist in their daily tasks. The administrator tools in this case not only had vulnerabilities but also were written in computer languages that allow anyone to read the executable program. This means that anyone who found the programs could read, find vulnerabilities, and modify the programs. The software should have been better written or at least tested for security concerns. Additionally, software that uses administrator accesses should have been better protected.

Failure to Detect Compromises

Alexey was running rampant over hundreds of systems, and except for extremely rare occurrences, people learned of the break-ins only after he told them about it. If he just wanted credit card numbers, he stole the cards and nobody knew until people saw charges against their account. Even then, it was unlikely that the victims actually knew that a computer system was hacked to get the card. The lack of any intrusion-detection software enabled attacks to continue indefinitely.

Failure to Want to Alert Others to Compromises

In the case of Lightrealm (which is no longer in business) and several other victims, the administrators did not want to alert their management to the break-ins. The administrators did not know whether Alexey was doing other things, or had already started abusing the credit cards stolen. These administrators exposed their company to extra liability.

Many other companies, such as casinovega.com, apparently did not notify law enforcement or its customers about the compromise of information. This allowed the criminals to continue their exploits and use the credit cards at will.

Poorly Skilled Administrators

Again, the critical enabler of all the attacks was the presence of known vulnerabilities on the systems. Although even good administrators may have a vulnerability or two on their systems, the vulnerabilities encountered were rampant. Not only that, it became clear that they were not capable of properly responding to a major incident. Some of them didn't even know where to start.

Poorly Skilled Security Consultants

To me, the most heinous vulnerability encountered was poorly skilled security consultants. People who claimed to have sufficient skills to repel hacker attacks charged thousands of dollars in fees and were unable to do the job. In most other cases, such a situation not only emboldens criminals but also angers them to commit retaliatory actions. Also, it is likely that if the security people didn't actually stop the attacks and do anything productive, they wasted money that could be better spent on other security efforts. The situation also perpetuates the hacker myth that hackers have some super skills, and weakens the profession as a whole.

Incident response is one of the most difficult tasks in the security profession. It is not for people who dabble in the field or fancy themselves as security professionals. They have to be able to go in prepared to fend off skilled attackers who probably know more about the systems than the people in the organization you are working for do. They have to know how to take the systems offline and reload the software from scratch, which requires strong administration skills.

At least two compromised companies, E-money.com and Online Information Bureau, hired consultants for several thousand dollars to prevent future attacks. Both of the consultants failed miserably, especially considering that Alexey used extremely basic attacks. The consultants should have never put themselves in this position. Additionally, the victims should have looked harder at their credentials in the first place, and considered alternatives. At the very least, they should have asked for several references.

Companies Believing Security Is an Expensive Option

As is typical of all hacker cases, Alexey's victims want reimbursement not only for the damages and expenses caused by him and his team but also for the cost to implement security countermeasures that should have been there in the first place. The twisted argument is that if nobody would break in, then they would not need security. The fact is that people will attempt to compromise any organization, and Alexey specifically targeted organizations processing financial data. Security should have been a business fundamental in his victims' cases.

A corollary to this type of mind set is that of companies that give security work to the lowest bidders. For example, Online Information Bureau spent $5,000 on the security consultant. Having personally worked on many incident responses, I would put the cost for repelling a hacker who appears to be able to completely control a company's infrastructure at $50,000, to be extremely conservative.

This in no way removes the responsibility from the criminals for their actions. However, the fact that the systems were vulnerable to extremely basic attacks is completely unacceptable.

Storing Unnecessary Data

Alexey mentioned that in many of the systems he broke into, the computers unnecessarily had credit card numbers that were no longer necessary. They were remnants of previous transactions. Unnecessary storage of information, such as credit card numbers, or other personally sensitive information, such as social security numbers, presents a vulnerability that should not exist.

Poor Security Awareness

The phishing tests that Alexey performed were extremely successful. This success is a result of poor awareness of the fact that you should never send personal information to a web site that you are directed to by an e-mail. Although it could be claimed that Alexey, having performed his tests in early 2000, was an early pioneer in the phishing field, these attacks continue and are due to poor awareness.

From an alternative perspective, Alexey Ivanov himself demonstrated poor security awareness. He was committing major felonies and embarrassing his victims, and yet he gave out a great deal of his personal information. He and his accomplice bragged that they were untouchable by U.S. law enforcement and then they freely traveled to the United States for a job interview. Logical thought should have told Alexey to do otherwise.

Culture and International Relations

This case demonstrates that Russia is a breeding ground for would-be computer criminals. There are many intelligent people who make little money. They have basic computer education, and the information about hacking is widely available. They also have a large number of extremely vulnerable systems available to them, including systems that hold financial information. Again, this does not excuse criminal action but demonstrates the temptation to criminal action as a fact of life that no company can ignore.

This is compounded by the fact that an action considered criminal in the United States might not be criminal where the acts originated. That means that there is little likelihood that the local police will assist the victims, or even the U.S. government, in any way. You also have to consider that even if something is universally recognized as a criminal act, will local authorities actually care enough to take any actions against their citizens? In some cases, the criminal might be protected by the local police. Alexey's boldness was due to many of these issues. These are probably some of the reasons that the FBI decided to access the tech.net.ru computers without contacting Russian authorities first.

Password Reuse

Alexey Ivanov demonstrated a common security vulnerability in using the same password for his laptop and for his account on tech.net.ru. After he gave up the laptop password, he gave the FBI all they needed to have full access to his most sensitive data.

11

Crimes Against Individuals

When people think about computer crime, they think of the damage that hackers can cause. As Chapter 4 states, hackers do not cause as much crime as the media portrays. However, the media wants to portray anybody that commits a crime that involves the computer as a hacker.

For example, when a Brooklyn, New York, busboy, Abraham Abdallah, stole money from the bank and stock accounts of some of Fortune 100's Wealthiest People, the media wanted to brand him a computer hacker. Although Abdallah did use computers to access credit reporting agencies, it is nothing more than any person browsing the web could have done. He just had criminal intent.

More important, Abdallah knew how to commit fraud. Abdallah knew the lingo of the banking community. He knew how to "ask" to transfer money. He knew what information was needed, and he found it. He might have used the computers as a tool to find the information; however, he never "hacked into" a computer. He didn't have to.

All Abdallah basically did was look up the credit records of famous people. Then, using the information in the credit reports, which includes bank records, he contacted the banks, pretending to be those people, and asked for money to be sent to another account. The credit records contained most of the necessary information. His knowledge of banking lingo and processes filled in the rest.

I was asked to appear on several television networks, in the United States and abroad, to talk about the hacking nature of the crime. As I explained that there was no "hacking" performed, the interviewers began to get the point and state that anyone with the nerve to commit these crimes could have impersonated the wealthiest people in the world.

This single case represents the nature of the majority of computer crimes against people, and the misunderstanding of the nature of those crimes. They do not involve hacking; they involve people committing fraud while using the computer as a tool. This is just the nature of crime in general. Criminals will use whatever tools are available to facilitate their crimes.

Technical Computer Crimes

Although I want the reader to know that most crimes against individuals are not the result of computer genius but of traditional crimes moving into the computer world, there are crimes that involve technology. These crimes are almost always against companies and organizations, and not individuals. However, you should know how to tell whether they affect or involve you.

Stories of hackers such as Alexey Ivanov stealing hundreds of thousands of credit cards have become common. When the news reports these incidents you learn that the cards were stolen from web sites. Individuals appear to be the victims, but they never did anything wrong. The sites to which they gave the card numbers left them unprotected.

Surprisingly, millions of other credit card numbers and other personal information are stolen by the simple theft of a laptop. Banks, credit card processors, and other companies that process credit cards and personal information use many computers to store information for a variety of purposes. In dozens of different scenarios, companies download databases onto computers that are easily stolen.

These situations happen surprisingly often and are not limited to the theft of computers. Sometimes people steal backup tapes or disk drives. In one Canadian case, an IBM subsidiary disclosed that it could not locate a computer drive that contained sensitive information of a bank's customers. It is unknown how frequently tapes and storage devices that contain this type of information go missing.

Generally, you do not have to suffer a financial loss as a result of such a hacking incident. If your card is misused, you can request that your card be credited back the fraudulent charge. The credit card company takes the loss. Ironically, the company with the poor security does not get hit. This means that companies have little incentive to better secure themselves. This is why Visa and MasterCard have begun to issue security requirements to vendors.

The problem is that you now have to be extremely proactive in reviewing your credit card statements. Although you may not have to incur the loss in the end, you still have to be very diligent in checking your credit card statements. You should always do this, but you have to be much more aware when you hear that a vendor that you deal with has been hacked.

Until people hold companies responsible for poor computer security, there will not be accountability. Do you remember the names of companies that were recently hacked? Did you consciously avoid doing business with them? For some vendors, being put in the news was an economic windfall because it served as free publicity, whether or not it was a result of being hacked.

You are also not affected when banks are electronically robbed. For example, when Citibank experienced the infamous, and almost forgotten, $12,000,000 theft by Russian hacker Vladmir Levin, no depositor actually lost the money. The thefts were discovered by corporations who found their accounts improperly charged. They reported the improper transaction to Citibank, which credited back the money. Because of the inexperience of Levin, Citibank was able to recover almost all the money. The remaining $400,000 was charged against its profits.

Citibank is actually one of the most secure banks in the world. As discussed in Chapter 4, banks regularly lose billions of dollars a year to electronic theft. It is accounted for only in their bookkeeping processes. Borrowers end up paying higher interest rates to cover these thefts. Although you might expect that banks would attempt to drastically cut these losses, the losses are actually small compared to the other sources of loss, such as credit card theft.

The moral is that computer hacking against corporations is commonplace and goes widely unreported. Consumers cover the cost of these losses by paying higher prices, fees, taxes, and other expenses. It is up to the average Internet user to reward or punish companies that are hacked by deciding who to patronize.

However, you have to realize that in some cases, victims of crimes did nothing wrong. For example, when E★Trade.com was the victim of a denial-of-service attack, the company had done nothing wrong. Hundreds of other computers were hacked, flooding E★Trade.com and preventing E★Trade.com computers from responding to valid users. There was little that the company could have done to prevent the attacks.

Also, there is no such thing as perfect security. People will make mistakes. Systems that are supposedly secure can eventually be hacked. What you should look for is how the company handles the incident. Is it proactive? Does it claim to be learning from the situation? Or, does it attempt to blame others? Obviously, a company that learns from its mistakes is more likely to be secure in the future.

The Crimes You Are Likely to Face

Bob Sullivan, a reporter from MSNBC.com, solicited Internet criminals to keep a diary and anonymously send it to him. One criminal took the reporter up on his offer. The criminal kept the diary for about two days. What was described was a person with no remorse, pushing the limits of credit card companies, free e-mail services, free web sites, and people's stupidity. This criminal basically spammed people to get them to go to a web site, where they were asked for their credit card numbers to buy something. Although this type of fraud does trigger a relatively rapid response from free e-mail and web site services, by the time the relevant accounts were killed in this case, the criminal was able to get a dozen or so credit cards. He then used those credit cards to order supplies and other merchandise that he sold, traded, or gave away.

To me, this was not a "computer crime." It was a fraud that happened to use a computer as a tool of the crime. If you can call this a computer crime, you would also have to call crimes in which someone uses a telephone a computer crime because the whole phone network is built on computers. Admittedly though, investigating these crimes does take a special expertise.

People try to defraud or con you every day. The Federal Trade Commission recently reported that most spam contained false information. Spammers are really trying to get your credit card information.

Another of the FTC's studies found that most computer crimes were actually fraud related. What follows is a description of the 10 most common frauds that the FTC is asked to investigate, as well as a couple of other crimes that emerged since the FTC released its original list.

Internet Auctions

eBay created a revolution on the Internet. It is one of the few dot-com companies that justified its stock valuation. There are many other web sites on the Internet offering auction services. For example, even Amazon.com has an incredibly robust auction capability.

The benefits of online auctions are clear. People who would have never before been able to sell a possession at a fair value now have an outlet that gives them a worldwide market. Buyers can sit in their homes and get items that they never knew existed. There are even people who make a living from online auctions alone.

Before I discuss the problems of the auctions, I just want to mention that most auctions go perfectly fine. Again, it just requires the application of a little common sense to make sure that you are safe.

The major risk is that as a buyer, you may pay and the seller may not send you the item as billed. It is also possible that the quality of the item is not what is expected, or a rare item is a forgery. For example, the seller might put a picture of an item on the Internet, but the item is not as pictured. Also, that Cal Ripken autograph may not be real.

It is also important to keep track of having received the item. Keep copies of all screen shots or e-mails involved in the transactions. This way you have a trail of proof that you purchased the item, the described quality of the item, and the expected date of shipment. People frequently forget that they ordered an item and may not notice if they do not receive it.

Problems also exist for sellers. The buyer's credit card number may not be good. The check may bounce. On the minor side, the buyer might complain that the quality of your item is not as described, even though you as the seller believe otherwise.

Many auction services also allow for the opportunity for buyers and sellers to provide feedback about each other. Before making any bids, you have the opportunity to review the seller's reputation. If you see that the person generally has a good rating and appears legitimate, there will likely be few problems with the person. It is likely that even with the best buyer or seller, there will be a few negative comments.

Be aware that creating a new auction site identity is very easy. Doing so allows a seller with very poor feedback to just create a new online persona and start fresh. Although little or no feedback may not be a problem at all, you should be aware of the possibility that it may also indicate a poor track record.

The easiest auction crime to get sucked into is the hijacking of a valid account of a seller with good feedback. Using phishing techniques, discussed later, the criminal gets the password to the seller's account. The criminal then modifies the account information slightly so that it is harder for the real account holder to detect the compromise and then puts a mythical item up for auction. When the time comes, the buyer is told to send his money through a criminal escrow service, and he never sees his money again. The actual seller account holder's reputation is then ruined and the criminal goes on to the next account.

Buyers should also be aware of a frequent scam in which a seller basically bids the price up for and ends up buying the item herself. Although this may sound counterintuitive, the scam causes the price to artificially inflate. The seller then contacts all the bidders and tells them that she has an identical item available. The seller offers the item to the bidder at a specific price, reflecting the inflated price of the auction. This transaction occurs off the auction site, and the auction site cannot intervene on your behalf.

Before closing this section, I want to again remind the reader that most auctions take place without any problems.

Internet Access Services

Many Internet companies also provide telephone services and use the same marketing strategies. One of the most questionable strategies is sending people unsolicited checks. By cashing the checks, people unknowingly agree to switch their phone or Internet access service. Unfortunately, most people do not realize that by cashing a check, they agreed to the switch. Nor do they realize that the services typically charge higher rates.

When you sign the checks, you are also signing an agreement on the check that authorizes the carrier switch. This is clearly a case demonstrating that there is no such thing as money for nothing. You have to read the fine print on the check, and the attached forms, to see what you are really getting.

Web Cramming

In this scam, a company or individual is called and offered a low-cost web site. You are given 30 days free and then told that if you decide to keep the service after the 30 days, there will be a small monthly charged billed directly to your account. The scammers then give you a web site that is slightly more than worthless, and bill your credit card or telephone account automatically.

Unfortunately, the charge is small and may go unnoticed for a long period of time. Also, many small businesses and individuals may not realize that what they get is not very valuable. You have to take quick actions to get the billing to stop, and with any luck get a refund.

Travel and Vacation Scams

Before the Internet became popular, there was a common travel scam in which people would call you up or send you mail and tell you that you can get a luxurious trip for a very low cost. You were to pay the fee up front.

As the day of your trip drew closer, you would find that you had to pay for many extras. There also were limitations on the date of your trip, the airfare to get to your accommodations was not included, and so forth. Obviously, you would likely find that your accommodations were not as luxurious as described.

The Internet has greatly reduced the costs for the travel scammers. They can now take advantage of the spam abilities of the Internet and reach a larger pool of victims for no cost. This means that the average Internet user is likely to receive dozens of these offers a year.

This is another case proving that if something sounds too good to be true, it probably is. However, some travel offers may be legitimate, and you might want an inexpensive trip.

Investments

I receive "Hot Stock Tips" via e-mail on almost a regular basis. I also get them via fax. Of course, they are from an investment firm that I have never heard of. There are also the chat rooms and bulletin boards that have many anonymous experts offering their hot tips as well.

I am sure that it won't surprise you to learn that these self-proclaimed experts and advisors are not independent. They either own the stock described or they are paid to help drive the price up. Although you may be able to find legitimate information about a company on the Internet, you must be extremely skeptical about all anonymous and unsolicited investment advice.

Modem Hijacking

This scam takes advantage of people's interest in pornography. Special browsers or tools are offered that access "free" pornography. People download the tools from the Internet and install them on their computer.

What happens is when you start the browser or tool, it dials a "pay per call" telephone number, usually international, much the same as a 900 number. You view the pornography while racking up hundreds of dollars in bills. The charges are added to your telephone bill. Although you can challenge a domestic telephone charge, it is extremely difficult to challenge an international pay-per-call charge. The domestic telephone companies must honor the charges of international telephone companies so that their charges can be honored overseas. International telephone companies do not have to adhere to U.S. laws.

Some of the tools are designed to hide the fact that they are dialing other numbers. They deactivate the modem speaker and then disconnect the current Internet session. They then dial the toll number. Because the speaker is not working, this calling is hard to detect.

Compounding this scam is the fact that many people may be embarrassed to challenge the charges. There is a stigma to paying for pornography. Many people would prefer to be taken rather than admit that they spent all that time looking at adult material.

Credit Card Fraud

The story of the criminal at the beginning of this chapter is a classic example of credit card fraud. When people refer to credit card fraud over the Internet, they most commonly mean the theft of credit card numbers over the Internet via fraud. It is easy to set up a web site that offers just about anything in the world. The offer of free pornography is a criminal's favorite.

Whenever you go to an Internet site that wants your credit card number, you must seriously think about it. First and foremost, do you trust the site? Do you know who runs it? Is the site on a free web page

server (that is, it does not have its own domain name)? If it offers anything free, you should be very concerned.

I always double-check the web address that I go to. Even if the
web site appears to be legitimate, many criminals are smart enough to
copy the real web pages onto a different address. For example, a criminal might register easy misspellings or alterations of well-known stores.
The criminal might get the use of "bestbuys.com," which looks like
"bestbuy.com."

Another trick is to put a "redirect" command in a web address. No
matter what the beginning of the web address is, if the address contains
the redirect command, you go to the site referred to by the redirect. Be
especially careful of this when you are being referred to buy something
by an e-mail message or a stranger's web site.

Multilevel Marketing and Pyramid Schemes

Multilevel marketing schemes and pyramid schemes can be related.
A pyramid scheme is essentially a chain letter that has you send money
to the top person on the chain. The scheme goes that you receive the
e-mail, send some amount such as $10 to the person at the top of the
list, and then take their name off the top and add your name to the
bottom. Then you forward the e-mail to 10 of your friends. Supposedly, if everyone in your chain then sends $10, by the time you rise to
the top of the list you will be sent millions of dollars. The more the
chain expands, the more you make.

These schemes are illegal and impossible. By the time you get to
the top of the list, there need to be millions of people involved. Only
the people on the top of the list have a chance of a return. And again, it
is illegal anyway.

Concerning multilevel marketing, I must first state that many of
these plans are legitimate. Many people have become very rich from
them. However, many more have not. That fact holds true for all business
opportunities. However, if you receive word of a multilevel marketing
opportunity via the Internet, chances are much higher that it is a scam.

All multilevel marketing relies upon people to recruit other people
into their chain, by definition. The indications of fraud, though, are
usually obvious. The biggest red flag is a high buy-in fee. Almost all
plans have fees associated with their program; however, if you have to
"invest" hundreds of dollars for the opportunity, it demonstrates that
the company does not plan to see profits from you for the long term.

Another indication of fraud is that you can sell your products and services only to other people in the multilevel marketing plan. Even as a standard business practice, you want to be able to sell to as many people as possible.

Probably one of the biggest red flags is when the only thing you are selling is membership in the marketing chain. That is a straight-out pyramid scheme and is, again, illegal. A common scheme involves ads that tell how to make money stuffing envelopes or sending e-mails. You are asked to send a dollar for basic information. You receive the information in the mail, which refers to valuable information that you provide to consumers who need it. To get the full package, you send in $30. What you receive are templates for the ads that you responded to. So essentially, you are selling a pyramid scheme.

Remember that when you choose to participate in a plan, you are responsible for all representations that you make. For example, if you say that pills you are selling are more healthful than eating food, then they had better be. It doesn't matter if you are only repeating what you have been told; you are responsible.

Business Opportunities

The ads for business opportunities are very similar to the ads for pyramid schemes. Anything that says, "Make money fast," "$100,000 per year guaranteed," "Start your own company with no money down," and the like is certain to be a fraud. Ads such as these on the Internet are usually for Internet-related products or services.

Some ads, and I mean very few, may be legitimate. They may sell legitimate opportunities. However, you must look into these things very carefully. A common scam was to offer territories for Internet kiosks. Although everything was delivered as offered, you had to buy the equipment, put in the telecom lines, pay for all maintenance, and cover other fees. The company providing you the opportunity made its money selling you all the equipment and your territory.

Now that you have spent all that money, how many people will turn out to be willing to pay money to access the Internet at a pizza parlor, when the library and Internet cafés offer the access for free? The payback just isn't there.

Work-at-home opportunities are extremely tempting for people. Besides the envelope stuffing I previously mentioned, another common scheme is to make crafts at home. You buy the materials and equipment,

make the products, and then send them back to the company for payment. The problem is that almost always, your products "Are not up to
quality standards," and the company refuses to pay you. So the scam is
that you buy the supplies and the company has no intention of paying
you for your efforts.

Healthcare Products and Services

Lose weight fast. Miracle drug cures cancer. New scientific breakthrough not known to the public. When you see these claims, ignore
them. They come in the form of e-mail spam, or sometimes rogue web
sites, offering the cure to everything.

By this point, you should realize the trend in these scams. When
something sounds too good to be true, it usually is. Do you actually
think that if a product existed that added 3 inches to penis size it
wouldn't be on the front pages of newspapers and more publicized
than Viagra?

Phishing

Phishing has become one of the most insidious types of computer-
related crimes, resulting in fraud-related losses in excess of
$2,400,000,000 annually. Phishing is basically a type of spam attack
that combines several of the previously mentioned attacks. Someone
first hacks into an Internet web server and then creates a web site
that looks like a page from a legitimate and respected company, such
as eBay, PayPal, Citibank, or U.S. Bank. The web page requires people
to enter their personal information, such as account numbers, PIN
numbers, mother's maiden name, or credit card code.

The criminal then creates a spam message that apparently comes
from the company being spoofed. The message claims that your
account at the company has been the subject of fraud and requires that
you verify your personal information for your account to be unlocked.
Less frequently, the criminal uses the method of Alexey Ivanov and
claims to offer a prize.

The message itself is actually a random spam, which relies on the
fact that there are millions of people with accounts at the organization
that the criminal claims to be part of. Send enough out of these messages and you will hit someone who is both a client of the spoofed
company and naïve enough to fall for it.

The message contains a link to click that sends you to the supposed page to confirm your information. If your e-mail allows HTML display, you will see a web address that seems to go to the actual site. If you can see the source code of the message, you will see that it displays what appears to be the valid address, but the commands actually send you to the attacker's page.

Again, the web page you go to actually looks like the right page from eBay or whatever. The attacker recreated the look and feel of the actual page being simulated, and the page frequently has links that go directly to the vendor being faked. After garnering all your account information, the criminal can create fraudulent transactions or sell your information to other criminals.

Future Crimes

Although predicting the future is impossible, the new crimes we have seen will not be significantly different than the current crimes we see. Look at all the previous crimes I mention. Most of them are a variation of crimes previously committed via telephone or direct mail. Although Internet attacks are much more random, the volume of potential victims that a criminal reaches means that the criminal can be significantly more successful with significantly less effort.

Any new crimes will just be different versions of the old ones. The more advanced ones will likely combine several attacks, such as the phishing attack. There will likely be increased use of spyware and Trojan horses. Some attacks will likely be automated to the point that the victim will not have to take any actions except open an e-mail message without touching an attachment.

Malicious Software

Spyware has become a plague on individuals. Initially, spyware started out as small software programs that advertisers put on your computer when you browsed their web site. From that point on, it would forward you to their site if you went to a competing site. Spyware has since evolved to include keystroke loggers and other software that intentionally captures your personal information and sends it on to the attacker. The attackers also moved to distributing spyware via spam, viruses, worms, and similar methods. Although some spyware is not necessarily malicious, most of it is, and the U.S. Congress and many localities are in the process of passing laws against it.

Another type of malicious software is "zombie" software. The moniker sounds ominous; the effects are even more ominous. After the software is surreptitiously loaded on your system through methods similar to spyware, your computer can be remotely controlled by the attacker. For example, a recent virus opened computers to spyware and then identified the system. After the system is known to be compromised, it sits there waiting to receive a command from its new master.

The first wide-scale use of zombie computers occurred during the massive denial-of-service attacks against E*Trade, Yahoo!, and other large web sites in 2000. In that case, the attacks essentially blew the sites off the Internet for an extended period of time. Unfortunately, the use of zombie computers has become more organized. Zombie computers are shared on the Internet through a variety of methods and are available for random use. Spammers are the most sophisticated users of zombie computer networks and use them to send spam through thousands of random computers around the world, bypassing several spam controls.

Zombie computers are also being used for extortion purposes. A growing crime is the use of denial-of-service attacks to extort legitimate web-based businesses for money. Criminals contact the businesses and say that they will continue to initiate denial-of-service attacks against them unless they are paid money. The computers used in the extortions are those random zombies.

The actual owners of the compromised computers do not know that they are the source of thousands of spam messages or a massive attack against a huge web site. It is not until their ISP stops all their access privileges that they realize they have a problem.

Vulnerabilities Exploited

Despite the variety of the attacks this section describes, the underlying vulnerabilities are the same. Crimes against people typically involve the use of basic technology and rely on people's naïveté. This does not include those crimes in which people attack corporate computers to capture personal informational. Although people pay the price for these attacks, these are not technically attacks against them.

Poor Awareness and Greed

Clearly, most of the attacks rely on people's unawareness of basic operational security principles. Some of the attacks scare people into believing they have to take action quickly. If people are unaware that, gulp, people lie on the Internet, they will be victims on the Internet and in the real world.

One aspect of awareness includes the technical aspect of how computers work. For example, few people realize that an e-mail message can display a web link but actually directly you to a completely different site. It is also important to know that a redirect command or an @ symbol in a web address is a very bad thing. Many basic technical issues that the general public is not aware of are easily manipulated by a criminal with even minimal technical knowledge.

I also mention greed in the section heading because I believe that most people are generally aware that people lie on the Internet. The potential for profit or something for nothing causes people to do things they wouldn't otherwise do. When money is involved, people become more naïve.

No or Improperly Maintained Antivirus Software

Any attacks that involve malicious software are almost always preventable. Antivirus product vendors do include checks for malicious software in e-mail messages. Although some worms do spread throughout the world in mere hours, all the attacks described here have circulated for months, if not years. There is little excuse to be hit by such a virus.

At the same time, you should have your e-mail reader configured to warn you against running programs, frequently called executables, from your e-mail. I am in the computer field and can tell you that I have sent executables only twice in the last five years via e-mail. Unless he or she is pirating software, the average person will never have to receive a software program via e-mail.

Conclusion

The most important thing to take away from this chapter is that almost all crimes that involve computers *and* affect you are traditional crimes that now have been modified to use the computer as a tool of the crime. That means that the perpetrator does not have to be a computer genius; it also means that the perpetrator can be stopped—and caught.

Even the crimes that do require "computer skills," such as computer hacking, are primarily enabled by preventable problems. The following chapters discuss the recommended countermeasures.

If it sounds too good to be true, it probably is. This sentence should be your mantra on the Internet. People who are taken by Internet scams are embarrassed when they realize they are a victim. They usually find that all signs of fraud were there and they ignored them. I will also take this opportunity to remind you to always review your credit card and telephone bills. Although this is a reactive countermeasure, it is a fail-safe way to avoid being a long-term victim of crime.

Part

III

STOPPING THE SPIES

The mark of an outstanding pilot is one who does not get into a position where they have to use their outstanding skills.
—Anonymous, posted by the doorway of the Ft. Meade Flying Activity

Part I introduced the way spies think, what they target, who they are, and how they get you. From my experience, few people believe that the best spies don't use super-advanced methods but instead go after the simple things. Few people believe that the simple things create devastating losses, so Part II presents some examples of extremely sophisticated espionage attacks. I hope that Part II reveals that the sophistication was primarily in the organization of the attacks, not in the individual tactics used.

Now that you see that big losses result from small vulnerabilities, you are ready to accept, and most important, implement the "Optimal" countermeasures. As you read through Chapter 12, make notes as to which countermeasures are possibly applicable to you and your organization. Chapter 13 provides guidance for finalizing your choice and implementation of the specific countermeasures most relevant to your circumstances.

12

Taking Control

The case studies in Part II described a wide range of incidents and perpetrators, from the most diabolical intelligence agencies to callow hackers. They all illustrate typical, modern, foreign, and corporate espionage methods and tactics. As I have pointed out, in all instances the crimes should have been prevented with simple, low-cost countermeasures.

As you have probably ascertained by now, you have a great deal of what you need already at your disposal. However, this doesn't mean that your current security plan is sufficient, especially because you are probably not making the best use of your resources. All too frequently, the security countermeasures available are poorly applied or not being applied at all. So it is important to consider not only what you need but also what you have that you are not using.

The biggest problem you'll face in your efforts to implement further countermeasures in your organization is simple ignorance. Most people and organizations tend to be unaware of the most common threats to their security. When they think about these matters at all, they imagine superspies and high-tech wunderkind. They buy into the hype of the information warfare bogeyman and industrial espionage spooks. They feel helpless and do nothing. It is my fervent hope that the preceding case studies have at least begun to dispel these misconceptions. An individual can do a great deal to prevent attacks by even the most well-equipped intelligence operation.

Remember, too, that countermeasures are not in place just to prevent attacks but also to detect them. Because attacks will never be
completely preventable, your goal is to reduce the damage they cause,
or preferably to detect the signs of an attack in progress so that it is
never completed. Even if you do not detect an attack until after it is
complete, at least you know how to mitigate the effects of the loss.
Examining a successful attack can also tell you how to stop similar
attacks in the future.

There are signs of espionage and computer crime all around, yet
they are ignored as glitches. Spam filling up e-mail inboxes, your network connection being very active while you're not doing anything,
computer log-ins in the middle of the night, desks left in subtle disarray,
strange telephone calls—all are possible indications of an attack. If you
and your company would just look for signs of intrusion and report
them, you'd increase your security a thousand-fold. The countermeasures proposed in this chapter will help tremendously with the task of
detection, which can be even more critical than just stopping an attack.

No security strategy can prevent every loss, but that fact shouldn't
stop organizations from taking action. Countermeasures are never perfect; accidents and mistakes are unavoidable, but their effect on an
organization can be greatly minimized.

As you read through this chapter, consider carefully which tactics
best suit you, your organization, and your specific security needs. It is
unwise to put a countermeasure into place just because everyone else
is doing it. Take a look at the following recommendations and consider
carefully how they will affect you and your situation. You don't want to
end up spending more on countermeasures than your information is
worth. The goal is an effective strategy that addresses your particular
threats and vulnerabilities appropriately. Chapter 13 assists in a final
determination of the countermeasures to implement.

However, you can start now to consider countermeasures and do a
quick read as to the potential applicability of each. Look at it from a risk
perspective, determining whether the countermeasure cost-effectively
addresses a relevant vulnerability. Consider each of the following countermeasures and ask yourself these questions:

- Do I already have and use this countermeasure?
- Does my organization have vulnerabilities that the countermeasure addresses?

- Is the countermeasure relevant to my industry?
- Can I easily implement it?
- Is the countermeasure worth the cost?
- Is the countermeasure in conflict with my organization's culture?

If any answer to the preceding questions causes you trouble, this doesn't necessarily mean that you should not implement the countermeasure. For example, one of the most problematic questions has to do with organizational culture. Many research organizations rely on a collegial spirit of openness. This doesn't necessarily mean that this is the way things should stay. It does, however, mean that you likely must approach the implementation of certain countermeasures very carefully from an organizational and political perspective.

All the countermeasures discussed in this chapter—both basic and sophisticated—are widely available. I've broken them down into the same categories I use to define vulnerabilities: operational, physical, personnel, and technical. However, you won't necessarily be using them to counter weaknesses in identical categories.

For example, poor awareness is an operational vulnerability. However, a technical countermeasure, such as token-based authentication (discussed later in this chapter), is extremely effective at countering attacks that rely on poor awareness, such as social engineering to get users' passwords. Similarly, good administrator training is an operational countermeasure that addresses technical vulnerabilities incredibly well. So remember to keep an open mind about the far-reaching effects that countermeasures can have.

As I stated before, most of the countermeasures seem basic—even too basic—to be effective against real criminals with even basic skills. However, I originally learned most of these countermeasures while working for the U.S. intelligence community. When there is an espionage case against it, the case sounds incredible when played out in the media. When a complete investigation of the incident is conducted, 99 percent of the time it comes to light that although there was something slightly new, the crimes were enabled by a breakdown of the simplest security procedures. That is on top of the fact that given the immense size of the intelligence community and the immense resources targeting it, there are relatively few successful cases of espionage.

What I present here is clearly not an exhaustive list of countermeasures. These measures are, however, some of the most useful and comprehensive available. I fully encourage you as the reader to seek out other sources of countermeasures and the areas most relevant to you. In the meantime, though, if you implement the countermeasures from this chapter that are relevant to you, you will significantly reduce your risk, even against the most diabolical and malevolent spies of all forms.

Countermeasures for Everyone

The case studies in Part II ended with a discussion of crimes against individuals, and it is appropriate to begin the discussion of countermeasures for those crimes. The reason is that crimes against individuals are not only the most devastating but also that the countermeasures against those crimes are universal to good security programs.

Common Sense

I already stated that there is no common sense without common knowledge, and that there is no common knowledge with regard to general computer concepts. However, there is common knowledge with regard to general fraud. As Chapter 11 demonstrates, most computer crimes are just traditional crimes moving to a new media.

Do you think a stranger is going to contact you from Africa and offer you millions of dollars to help him launder money? Do you really think that you won millions of dollars in an overseas lottery that you never entered? Do you really want to buy pharmaceutical products from people who can't spell the names correctly or have no standards of quality control? Scams are scams. Common sense tells the average person that this is not right, but some people just want to give it a try.

Limit Internet Postings

For some reason, people open themselves up on the Internet. They create web logs (a.k.a. blogs), put their profiles on Friendster.com, create very descriptive IM profiles, and so on. These activities not only increase their exposure to spam but also open them up to a variety of Internet crimes. Although the Internet does create tremendous social potential, you cannot stand in the middle of Times Square, yell, "Be my friend!" and expect the best from everyone.

Clear Cookies, History, Temp, and Log Files

Chapter 5 discussed how you leave tracks all over the Internet and especially your own computer. To protect your privacy and potential security breaches, you must make it a habit to clear your computer of tell-tale traces. The first place to start is with your web browser. Open the browser and find the delete cookies and history functions.

If you use Internet Explorer, you can just go to the Tools menu and click the Internet Options feature. There you will find the ability to delete history, cookies, and temporary files. I recommend that you definitely delete the history and files on a regular basis. As opposed to deleting cookies outright, I recommend that you go into the Settings option and click View Files. The files that will be named will be primarily cookie files. Go through those filenames and delete any files intended for a web site that you don't want tracking you. If you don't want to delete the cookies one by one, you can delete all of them on the previous screen. However, some of the cookies may actually be useful on sites that you want to visit frequently. It is your choice.

You must also look into the other applications on your system that track your activities. I strongly recommend a personal firewall, but some firewalls log the web address of all the sites you visit. Other applications may have a similar effect. For example, deleted e-mails on your PC can also be retrieved for a period of time, depending on how your e-mail is configured. You may also want to take the opportunity to go through your applications and search through the menus to see what else might be available.

There are also some file erasure utilities available in stores. The primary purpose of these tools is to completely delete file remnants that typically remain when you delete files. However, many of them also search your entire system to find temporary files, cookies, and a variety of other privacy threats. This is clearly invaluable in protecting your privacy.

IRA'S FOUR GOLDEN RULES

Although you may be exposed to a variety of crimes on the Internet, there are things you can do that can save you when everything else goes wrong. These things are generally simple, inexpensive, but invaluable when the worst happens.

- *Install anti-virus software and keep it updated:* Viruses and worms are the most likely and common attacks you will encounter. One virus can destroy your computer and everything you have on it, or do even worse. Anti-virus software prevents just about all known virus attacks. It can also help prevent Trojan horses and other sleepers abusing your system. Because dozens of new viruses appear every week, vendors update the software weekly or sometimes more often for rapidly spreading attacks. To help this process along, all common anti-virus software has a feature that allows for automatic updates. Make sure that you enable this feature when you install your software. This is some of the best money you will ever spend.

- *Install a personal firewall and keep it updated:* Sadly, hacking and malicious attacks that were previously reserved for powerful computer servers are now being developed for PCs. As can be expected, the marketplace kept up with this and personal firewall software was created. This is essentially a strong protection for PCs that does stop many attacks that are not virus related. This type of computer software should now be considered a "must" for all PCs that you own. Also, just as anti-virus products need updating for the latest viruses, so does personal firewall software for the latest attacks. Enabling the automatic update feature is as necessary as the software itself.

- *Install anti-spyware software and keep it updated:* Spyware is just slightly less despicable than viruses. Not only does it spy on you and steal your information, it causes many other negative effects on your system. Although Congress has banned spyware, the ban will obviously not make the problem disappear. In addition to the other software mentioned previously, you must install at least one anti-spyware product and maybe two. So far there is no standard for anti-spyware and these programs are inconsistent as to what they block. I recommend that you get at least one package that specifically stops spyware, and another one that describes itself as a "pop-up" or ad blocker. Luckily, many vendors are now beginning to bundle anti-spyware with firewalls and anti-virus software. As with the similar software, you must make sure that your software updates itself on a regular basis to account for new types of spyware.

- *Make regular backups:* No matter how well you protect yourself, something will happen. It can be a virus or malicious hack attack that was too new to be stopped by the most recent updates, or it can be as simple as a disk crash caused by accidentally pressing the power button. Whatever the case, if you have backups, you can at least recover your information. Make sure that you back up all critical files at least on a weekly, if not daily, basis. If you configure your system well and are even slightly disciplined about keeping all your files in something like the "My Documents" directory, you can just copy that directory onto a CD or one of the higher-capacity USB thumb drives. If you have a lot of downloaded music or home pictures on your computer, you may want to create a separate directory and backup system for them.

System Utilities

If you want to be proactive about your own security, one of the best things you can do is prepare for a disaster. Although regular backups can help you significantly if there is ever a crash, there are some things you might never be able to recover. Additionally, it can be expected that not everyone will perform these backups. For this reason, I recommend that people proactively purchase Norton SystemWorks. It contains a variety of tools that perform many of the features I describe. It also includes the Utilities set, which contains utilities that can help you recover from what would otherwise be complete disasters. I learned the usefulness of these utilities the hard way when I had a complete disk crash. The entire system was otherwise ruined. Norton Utilities allowed me to recover 95 percent of what I needed. I would have been completely devastated without the product. I did not take my own advice to perform regular backups. Learn from my mistakes and do things proactively.

Operational Countermeasures

Operations countermeasures are nontechnical procedures or processes integrated into an organization's day-to-day operations. The idea here is to create a corporate culture in which security is subtle but second nature. Most of the countermeasures described in this section are easy to implement and inexpensive. They won't work, though, unless the employees are well informed about the procedures, the purpose of the procedures, and the consequences of ignoring them.

For the most part, these countermeasures are nonintrusive. No company should have to place itself under martial law to keep its information safe. However, when the stakes are high, more intrusive measures may be necessary.

The problem with operational countermeasures is that they must become second nature to employees or they easily may be taken for granted even by security professionals. Security professionals tend to focus on computers or facilities, ignoring operational solutions. The types of countermeasures discussed here provide an incredibly high payback. It's usually worth taking a small amount of resources from the other security disciplines to help create an organizational culture that supports security as a whole.

Awareness Training

There is probably no more effective countermeasure, dollar for dollar, than a good security awareness program. In all the case studies presented in Part II, better user awareness could have significantly minimized or prevented the attacks. In every case, someone should have noticed the unusual behavior of coworkers, the irregular access to computer accounts, physical access by strangers, or the social engineering tactics employed. If the victims had just been more aware, the attackers could have been stopped dead in their tracks.

Many security awareness programs are considered to be worthless by security professionals, and I'm inclined to agree with that assessment. In researching the problem, I've discovered that far too many so-called awareness programs are nothing more than speeches informing employees of the consequences of illegal activities. The focus is on employees' misbehavior and on penalties.

IT'S HOW YOU SAY IT, NOT WHAT YOU SAY

Over the years, I have seen too many books and security professionals describe a problem and then, for the solution, state that you should tell people either what to do or what not to do. This approach is completely worthless. It is like telling someone that automobile accidents happen, so they should drive safely. People already believe that they drive safely.

Although it is important for an awareness program to ensure that the right things are covered, the critical success factor for an awareness program is the delivery methods. The advice must be simple. It must be made personal. The awareness program must be ongoing and almost ubiquitous to the day-to-day operations.

Advice is generally plentiful and useless. Advice that is realistic, understandable, actionable, and repeated is useful.

Threatening to fire people caught stealing secrets is not only a waste of time, it's counterproductive. It's no wonder that "security" has such a negative connotation for so many. People learn to fear the word, and they report incidents to the department only as a last resort—and sometimes only when they believe they are being set up. Some security people believe that threatening workers acts as a deterrent; I believe such threats destroy morale and reduce overall cooperation. The fact of the matter is that most criminals never believe they will get caught anyway. You want your people to start perceiving your security department as a resource they can turn to when they have or see a problem. Don't present it as an oppressive force that they have to avoid at all costs.

Programs that focus on penalties do nothing to educate, and that should be the primary purpose of any awareness program. You should work to inform your people of the threat their organization faces. Obviously, you have to tell them about your policies, and people should be made aware that criminal actions are dealt with harshly. Keep things in proportion; most of your employees have no criminal intentions. People should be made aware of the penalties, but they must not be taught to dwell on them.

One of the most effective ways to educate your people about security issues is to tell them about real cases. That's why case studies comprise a substantial part of this book. All too often, organizations try to hide the truth about previous attacks against them in the misguided belief that knowledge of a breach will make them more vulnerable. It is only when people hear about real cases, however, that they believe the threat is real. Organizations can filter out sensitive details of a case and still use it to get the point across. If a company does not have a case of its own to talk about—which is extremely rare—company officials can use a case from a similar organization. Stories of corporate espionage affecting organizations of all sizes fill newspapers and business magazines and can be found easily on the Internet.

One of the most satisfying aspects of having written my original book, *Corporate Espionage*, is that security managers from all over the world, including intelligence agencies, requested permission to use some of the case studies from the book for their internal awareness programs. They place the case studies on internal web sites or send them around in their company newsletters for quick distribution and awareness.

Remember that you have to tell employees exactly what they should be doing, and what you tell them should be clear and simple. You have to let people know about the threats, but you must also tell them what to do about it. They should know exactly what their actions should be in different circumstances and what you expect of them. The other countermeasures discussed here should be clearly understood by all employees.

Your people must also be made aware of the value of information itself. Employees honestly don't know that a list of customers is critical to both your company and others. They don't realize that a competitor can ruin your entire software development efforts if it gains access to certain phone numbers. They don't know about the cascading effect of small compromises of the data they handle each day. Show them how the information they control affects your organization. And don't forget to mention the countermeasures your organization uses.

An effective awareness program stresses the usefulness of simple and basic countermeasures. You'll want to give examples of how the little things stopped, or could have stopped, major corporate espionage cases. Show your people how their seemingly small contributions can make a major difference. Let them know that *they* can be the ones to stop those mythical (hopefully you now see them as mythical) James Bonds and evil computer geniuses.

Remember that you have to tell employees exactly what they should be doing, and what you tell them should be clear and simple. You have to let people know about the threats, but you must also tell them what to do about it. They should know exactly what their actions should be in different circumstances and what you expect of them. The other countermeasures discussed here should be clearly understood by all employees.

Classifying Information

It's a simple and unavoidable fact of life: businesses must exchange information, both within their own organization and among their customers and suppliers. However, all information is not created equal, nor should it be equally available. It is perfectly reasonable and even advisable to categorize some of your company's information for the purposes of controlling its distribution among different groups. You can restrict access to certain customers, different levels of employees, various project teams, senior management, and specific individuals. You get to decide which information is available to which groups.

Most organizations already classify their information. Usually, however, they have few if any formal processes in place, which means that lots of data slips through the cracks.

Also, companies rarely utilize fine distinctions for sensitive materials. They don't often stop to think about the relative value of information. For example, in general, only employees should have access to a company's telephone directories. The same may be said about the organization's business plan. However, the business plan is easily much more sensitive than the telephone directory—the compromise of the former could certainly hurt your organization; the compromise of the latter could destroy your organization. If both are classified merely as "sensitive," your employees are going to treat the documents as equally valuable.

For this reason, I recommend utilizing an extra level of control for certain types of information. For example, some information could be restricted to employees only, but it may also be designated as controlled in a library and protected by limited removal procedures.

You must also decide who in your organization will actually be doing the categorizing. In many companies, the people creating the information are responsible for categorizing it. Although this is probably the only realistic way of implementing this countermeasure, I strongly advise establishing clear organizational guidelines. Also ensure that these guidelines are widely available and enforced. Most employees will take the path of least resistance, if unchecked, and classify information in a way that will minimize their aggravation in the present and future.

Examples of common data classification used in companies include:

- Any document containing the name of an employee is restricted to company employees.

- Information concerning product development is restricted to people working specifically on the development.

- Corporate financial information is restricted to senior officials and others responsible for compiling the information.

Special measures should be put in place to regulate the flow of information that is classified as especially sensitive. At the very least, access to such data should require a signature on a log sheet, and someone should be designated to check the logs on a regular basis.

Security Alert System

People have to know whom to tell when they discover potential security problems. The only thing most people think to do is tell their supervisor. If they have a bad relationship with the boss, they might be disinclined to bring up a problem. If they do tell their supervisor, then the supervisor must know what to do with that information. In most cases I've investigated, the supervisors have no clearer idea about what action to take than the people they supervise.

Not wanting to seem stupid, many managers ignore critical situations. In other cases, they believe it to be their jobs to handle the situations themselves and act accordingly, never letting upper management and the security department in on the problems. Some managers believe that going to security will create problems for them and their groups. Yet managers do their employers no favors when they try to handle possible industrial espionage situations without outside help. They also let indications of more serious problems go unnoticed.

To facilitate communication within your company about potential security breaches, I strongly advise establishing simple and easy reporting procedures. The simpler and easier, the better. Company e-mail is a wonderful vehicle for this. It provides a very fast, cheap, and reliable method of contacting security. Users can type up a quick message at their desks and fire it off to the security account, best named "security." There is a small risk that an attacker who has compromised the mail server might see the message, but the resulting increase in communication throughout the company makes the risk well worth taking. To increase the confidentiality of your company e-mail, you might enable the use of encryption (described later in this chapter).

Rewards

One of the best ways to encourage employees to cooperate with security is to show them that you appreciate their efforts. A useful way to express this appreciation is by offering rewards for employee cooperation. Make certain, however, that you are rewarding people for awareness and proper action, not snitching on coworkers. You don't want to give the people in your organization the impression that you pass out rewards for eavesdropping.

Cash rewards work best, but when money is tight, a small gift might suffice. Gift certificates are always good. If no money at all is available, then you can use a graphics package to create a certificate of recognition. When possible, you'll want the company president or other senior official to sign the certificate. The cash value of the reward is not as important as the act of recognition. In this case at least, it really is the thought that counts.

Call Backs Before Disclosing Sensitive Information

In the ideal world, information would be given out on a face-to-face basis only. However, the reality of the modern organization is that people work closely with other people whom they may never meet. They exchange e-mails and telephone calls. However, they generally have a well-established relationship with one another through internal mechanisms. Sometimes, though, employees have no choice but to release information to anonymous strangers, but when an unknown caller asks for any sensitive data, his or her identity should be verified before even the most seemingly innocuous information is handed over.

If an employee is asked for information that is clearly sensitive, and he or she doesn't know who the person is but thinks that the reason seems valid, then the employee should ask for the person's name and telephone number. The employee should then hang up, confirm the telephone number with a company telephone directory, and then call the person back at that number. Or, if the person says that he or she is not at the listed directory number, then the employee should check with someone (such as a secretary) to verify that the person is indeed at the location he or she claims to be at. This whole process normally takes about 15 seconds. Large corporations even have online telephone directories to facilitate the process.

Anyone can claim to be someone else, and a quick telephone check can prevent major compromises. This process should be part of normal company procedures. If a caller balks, then he or she just might be an attacker. If the complainer claims to be the CEO, for example, then the employee can say, "If you are who you claim to be, I might be fired for doing my job. If you are not who you claim to be and I give you the information, then I will definitely be fired." This will usually quell any resistance.

This countermeasure is a no-cost solution that is simple to implement. Although not perfect, it sets up a tremendous hurdle that every anonymous attacker must clear. It can be used for any release of sensitive information, but it can also be used in response to requests for sensitive services, such as the changing of passwords. In all organizations, people forget their passwords from time to time and call the company help desk to reset it. Before giving out any password information, the help desk personnel should either personally recognize the callers or take the time to call them back at their assigned numbers. If it were implemented properly at banks and credit companies, this strategy could also decrease a tremendous amount of identity theft. Individuals should also do this with their own affairs. If you will be giving out your credit card number or other sensitive information, make sure that you initiate the phone call (after all, you should be calling your credit card company, and not the other way around).

Verifying the Need for Information Access

Almost as important as establishing a procedure for verifying the identity of persons seeking information from your organization is verifying that that person actually needs access. In most organizations, there are really very few people who need access to very sensitive information. In most cases, verification will take no more than a few minutes and require little more than a single telephone call, but even a few hours' delay should not be considered a major problem. The inconvenience is minor when compared with the potential for loss. The attack described in Chapter 7 would have been significantly hampered, and I would have actually been caught, if any of the people I met with had sought to verify, through my supervisor, my need for the information before meeting with me. Failure to ask a few simple questions could have resulted in a multibillion-dollar loss.

When it comes to very valuable information, consider designating a member of the security team as the project security officer (PSO). The job of the PSO is to keep track of who is authorized to access information about a particular project. The PSO also acts as the primary point of contact between security and the project team. The PSO position does not have to be especially time-consuming. Essentially, the PSO is contacted only when someone new wants access to the data for which the PSO is responsible. The PSO also typically attends project meetings to keep abreast of project status and pending security issues.

You must allow for exceptions in your security plan, but they should not go unchallenged. When exceptions arise, the need for the exception should be verified.

Verifying Identities and Purposes

Unfortunately, putting a name on a list just isn't enough. That personable gentleman standing in your office doorway, asking so winningly for access to sensitive information, may or may not actually be who he says he is. (He might even be me.) In organizations in which the employees don't know each other personally—a common situation in most large companies—your people must fall back on identity-verifying procedures. These procedures need not necessarily be complex. Something as simple as looking at the person's access badge or calling his or her boss can make all the difference.

Your identification procedures should even apply to your security personnel. In the course of my work as a penetration tester, I've had occasion to venture into restricted territory at the client companies, often after regular working hours. Whenever people stopped me and asked what I was doing, I'd just tell them I was with security. Invariably, they'd say okay and be on their way.

Industrial spies come up with very creative stories to facilitate their larceny. Professional liars are supposed to sound and look good. It's their job. Some of them claim to be security consultants. Whether they claim to be a security officer, the president's personal assistant, or God Almighty, make them prove it!

Removing Personal Identifiers from Access Badges

Most companies that utilize access badges put their employees' names and ID numbers on them. Then, there they are, on hundreds of shirt pockets for the entire world to see, providing any observer with enough information to perpetrate a simple impersonation or a key transaction. After all, employee numbers are inevitably used for other purposes throughout the company. In some cases, would-be spies get this information by hanging out in local bars at quitting time.

In some situations, it may be desirable to display ID numbers but not names. Police in some countries display only numbers on their badges to prevent invaders from identifying and killing the local police to suppress resistance. (Prior to countries being invaded during World War II, Nazi sympathizers collected the names of policemen from their name tags and handed lists over to the Nazis after the invasion.) Although you are unlikely to find yourself in situations quite this extreme, the point is to keep the names and numbers apart; the combination causes the problems. Similarly, all paperwork that combines this information should be protected.

Nondisclosure/Noncompete Agreements

It is virtually impossible to prevent your employees, vendors, and customers from taking information and using it for other purposes; however, you can minimize your losses and put other people on notice. By requiring your employees to sign nondisclosure/noncompete agreements, you create a legal recourse should that person use your information against you. These agreements vary in content and extent, but their basic purpose is to keep your organization from becoming a training ground for competitors. The nondisclosure aspect of the agreement binds your employee contractually against disclosing your company's information to a competitor (usually, a new employer). The noncompete component ensures that an employee cannot take your information to start a business that competes directly against yours.

Employers must place reasonable limitations in these agreements. For example, you cannot prevent an employee from ever competing against you; you may state only that he or she cannot compete against you for a period of time, usually months. The agreement can further restrict a former employee's ability to actively market products or services to your established client base for a specific time period. Most people will sign a reasonable agreement without complaint.

Nondisclosure/noncompete clauses should also be a part of contracts with vendors and customers whenever possible. In the situation I describe in Chapter 4, in which a French company approached my client's suppliers to buy all its technology, the only legal recourse my client had against its suppliers was the nondisclosure clause of its contract. Clearly, you have more leverage with suppliers than customers; however, it should be a consideration where applicable.

Review of Corporate Releases

Although employees release potentially sensitive company information through speeches and articles, the organizations themselves release much more information than any employee ever will. Companies are required by law to publish detailed financial data as well as a wide variety of other information, but most organizations go well beyond these requirements. John Quinn, a former CIA operative and vice president of the Operations Security Professional Society, studied Securities and Exchange Commission (SEC) filings. He found that companies produce much more revealing documentation than is legally required. Besides creating a major vulnerability, this overcompensation probably doubles the cost of producing the documents.

This phenomenon is true not only of legally required information disbursements but also of corporate releases in general. Companies discuss an immense amount of information in their press releases and marketing materials.

Companies must take special care to monitor the tendency of PR departments to give out more information than is necessary or even advisable. The content of press releases, brochures, and advertising must pass a test of reasonableness. Most organizations can get their message across by putting out much less information. The security department should definitely be in the information release cycle. You'll want to require security people to offer their input in a timely manner, and you'll also want to take into account the promotional needs of your company, but a judicious application of moderation in this area could yield a big security payoff.

Ultimately, your PR and security departments should work together to protect the sensitive information in your organization.

A spirit of cooperation between these two departments can be invaluable to a company.

Strict Guidelines for Marketers and Salespeople

Marketers and salespeople exist for one purpose: to sell products or services. Their companies judge them, reward them, and penalize them on their sales records. When they make their quotas, they're heroes; when they fail to hit their targets, they're in the unemployment line.

In the heat of battle, salespeople can lose perspective. When facing a sale that can go either way, they will naturally be very tempted to say whatever it takes—and release whatever information they think is necessary—to close the transaction. Marketing people are always searching for the right words and pictures to promote your company, even if those words and pictures reveal sensitive data.

You can't really blame these hardworking folks for their voluble natures, but you must implement policies that effectively contain overzealousness. They represent a potentially dangerous information leak that you can plug with strictly enforced information-dispersal guidelines. These guidelines should specify the types of information they can release and especially the types of information that they *cannot* release. Companies should also find ways to spot-check their sales and marketing staffers to ensure that they are following the rules.

Reporting Unusual or Frequent Contact with Competitors and Others Especially Interested in Your Work

Most companies want to stay out of their employees' personal lives for a wide variety of reasons. Not only is employee surveillance difficult and time-consuming, it lowers morale; no one wants to work for Big Brother. Yet, industrial spies often contact employees outside work to collect information and set up penetrations. They show up at company social functions, attend conferences, and hang out at the local watering hole. This sort of thing happens more frequently than businesses want to admit.

Although most casual contact with competitors is innocent, at some point extended contact can be the sign of an unhealthy or unlawful interest. Employees, and even your vendors, should be instructed to report any unusual interest in your business.

As Chapter 4 describes, Chinese operatives look for people of Chinese descent and find out where they work and what their job is. They do it in restaurants and social clubs. The Chinese are one group among many that are active in targeting companies. Again, your employees are your best resource to notice an unhealthy interest in your business.

Although you will encounter clear problems, you should also look for patterns. More frequently, employees report circumstances that in and of themselves are not problems; the trends they indicate show that there is a concerted ongoing effort. Again, it is not unusual for foreign countries and competitors to use extreme efforts to compromise a company.

Monitoring Internet Activity

Internet usage has become ubiquitous to business operations, with Internet connections to everybody's desk. People use instant messaging, e-mail, mailing lists, and so on. They keep web logs and maintain personal web pages. All this exposes those people and your company to tremendous problems, as Chapter 5 discusses in detail.

At a basic level, monitoring Internet activity allows you to see who spends too much time in nonbusiness-related pursuits. There are valid reasons to use the Internet, but employees requiring a great deal of time online should be given personal accounts they can use to gather information without indicating that they are from your organization. Employees who are apparently wasting time should, of course, be told to stop.

At a more fundamental level, monitoring allows you to see your exposure on the Internet with regard to technical and competitive intelligence exposure. You want to ensure that your marketing staff adheres to security policies and that your technical staff does not place too much information about your technical environment in the public domain. You should periodically check the EDGAR database to see whether your company files too much information with the SEC.

Occasionally, you may find hacker discussion lists revealing information about your technical vulnerabilities. Previously, I found a list of credit card numbers issued by specific banks. Sometimes there are passwords for corporate accounts listed on web sites.

Large corporations and celebrities have hate sites providing negative and unfactual information about them. Because of this, many public relations firms offer services to track Internet exposure. From a technical perspective, your security department can do a Google search on its company's domain names and other trademarks. This search should also include newsgroup and mailing lists so that you get a complete picture of your exposure.

Minimize Data Storage

In many of the case studies, and especially that of Chapter 10, too much information is stored on computer systems. The more data that is stored, the higher the damage will be if there ever is a compromise of the computer system, database, or other sensitive area. For that reason, there should be an operational process in place to regularly review data storage and move old and unused data to an offline storage device, and prevent its availability to anyone. This way, you still have access to information, albeit a little more time consuming, while removing an unnecessary risk.

Monitoring Technical Vulnerabilities

Although many people find this hard to believe, technical vulnerabilities are best countered with operational countermeasures. The fact that a technical vulnerability exists is an operational problem. Security is a process. If a technical vulnerability exists, it is because something is deficient in that process that allows the vulnerability to exist.

Hackers and other criminals attack your computer systems by exploiting known vulnerabilities and poor configurations. New vulnerabilities appear with annoying regularity about all types of computer systems. As some holes are plugged, new holes appear. Barriers are erected; routes around them are plotted. It's the nature of the beast.

Known technical vulnerabilities allow attackers to steal billions of dollars' worth of information annually from banks and other organizations around the world. Fortunately, almost anything you know about, you can fix. Updating for known vulnerabilities and poor system configurations would have prevented or minimized the penetrations described in Chapters 6, 7, 9, and 10. Ferreting out these weaknesses could prevent at least 98 percent of all computer hacking-related crimes.

The only effective way to cope with the ebb and flow of system vulnerabilities is to establish regular monitoring procedures for weak spots and the fixes for them. The mailing lists of legitimate security organizations, such as CERT and Infraguard, can provide invaluable resources in your search efforts. These resources list the most recently uncovered vulnerabilities and the latest fixes. Computer vendors and software companies also issue alerts concerning their specific software. Unfortunately, fixes are typically published only after they have proven themselves, which means that the vulnerabilities may be known for months before the CERT and vendors issue an advisory. Joining industry-specific Infraguard and industry specific Information Sharing and Advisory Capabilities (ISACs) can provide you with advanced warning information. There are also commercial services, such as SecurityFocus and TruSecure, that provide similar information.

You can also acquire commercial tools to regularly scan your own systems. These tools, known as vulnerability scanners, scan your systems for known vulnerabilities. Although they don't proactively alert you to new vulnerabilities, if the software is properly maintained via automatic updates, they will let you know that they exist in your network. These tools are available from Internet Security Systems, Foundstone, and Symantec among other companies. A comprehensive service that provides automatic updates and regular scans is available from Qualys (www.qualys.com). Typically these scanners will check for both software- and configuration-based vulnerabilities that can be exploited over the Internet and internal network connections.

Technical Training

I have already mentioned Awareness Training as the most critical countermeasure for you and your organization. Security training for your technical staff is also critical. Your administration staff is your front line in protecting your computers. Although administrators may have received some basic training in how to administer their systems in general, most of these classes are extremely weak from a security perspective.

Too many administrators learn about security concerns after they have been compromised. You need to ensure that these people take proactive security training. Security conferences typically provide seminars on securing specific operating systems. SANS Institute (www.sans.org) is one of the most well-established organizations providing training for administrators on securing specific operating systems.

Organizations cannot skimp on technical security training. If administrators are not already trained in proper security procedures, this should be a company's top priority.

HACKER TRAINING

There is a growing trend of companies offering "Hacker Training" or "Ethical Hacker Training." These courses intend to show students how to break into systems. It is assumed that the students are legitimate computer professionals who want to improve their skills. The logic assumes that you can better secure systems by knowing how to break them.

As Chapter 4 discusses, it is much more difficult to secure systems than break into them. At the same time, training budgets and opportunities are limited, so when there is an opportunity for security training, people must opt for training to secure systems and not break them. If people are already thoroughly familiar with securing their systems and they want to round out their skill set, maybe then they can be considered good candidates for hacker training.

Also, although the need exists for some security professionals to perform penetration tests, this need is relatively rare. A penetration test is much more complicated than a course can teach. A penetration test can create devastating technical damage. As Chapters 6 and 7 demonstrate, you may encounter actual security breaches and must know how to respond and switch into an incident-investigation mode. On top of that, there are a wide variety of legal and political issues to be aware of. To be qualified to perform a penetration test, training must be accompanied by experience under the mentorship of experienced penetration testers. Basically, Ethical Hacker Training by itself merely trains people to become dangerous.

Join Infraguard and Other Professional Organizations

Infraguard is an FBI-sponsored organization that allows for the exchange of information. For practical purposes, it functions like a professional organization. It also allows for advanced warnings of vulnerabilities, on top of the sharing of knowledge and experience among other members. One important facet of Infraguard is that it allows you direct communication with law enforcement officers. This is invaluable in that you are personally acquainted with an individual that you can contact should you actually have a situation that requires law enforcement.

There are many national-level security organizations that provide information. However, I believe that you get the most out of those organizations that have regional-level meetings. These local meetings provide for a good exchange of information and learning at a personal level. Security people are generally few within an organization, and the local meetings allow for a peer group. Recommended organizations include the Information Systems Security Association (www.issa.org) and the American Society of Industrial Security (www.asisonline.org).

Separate Telephone Lines

Telephone records can divulge a tremendous amount of information about an organization and its operations. For this reason, I recommend that companies install at least a few separate telephone lines outside the existing company telephone exchanges. These numbers should be reserved for sensitive business and their use should be limited. Adversaries know your typical telephone exchanges and will search their records. Special numbers that are not typically allocated to your organization are much harder for adversaries to find. This minimizes the likelihood that they will see your telephone patterns and pick up on highly sensitive conversations and projects.

I also strongly recommend that the security staff get cell phones that are not identified to the company. A well-organized penetration effort will attempt to compromise the communications system of the security staff so that perpetrators can monitor the staff to see whether their activities have been detected, and to check the status of any active investigations. Lines that are independent of the company and the known security staff help to stop any counterintelligence efforts against you.

Limiting Telephone Conversation Topics

No matter what telephone lines you and your people use, you should try to limit the sensitivity of the topics discussed over the phone. Phones are relatively easy to bug and could provide a lot of information to eavesdroppers.

If you are traveling overseas, especially in hotels, assume that your top competitor is listening to your phone conversations. It's probably true! Choose your words wisely, because multimillion-dollar business deals have been and will be compromised. The National Counterintelligence

Center has reported that a multimillion–dollar deal was compromised because the French government tapped a hotel telephone call and used the information against the target. The threat is very real, and you must act accordingly.

Limiting Cellular and Cordless Telephone Topics

Cellular and cordless telephones are ubiquitous. If a regular telephone is a vulnerable medium of communication, cell phones and cordless phones are an open line to your competitors. Everything you say on a cellular or cordless telephone can be heard by anyone with the right equipment. I have friends who sell this type of eavesdropping equipment. You can find it on the Internet. Whenever you use one of these types of telephones, never talk about sensitive issues. If you must talk about sensitive issues, try to use code words or, better yet, hang up these types of phones and go to a landline.

From a personal nature, make sure that you never use these types of phones when you give out your credit card or social security numbers, nor for that matter whenever you give out anything that you personally consider sensitive. People are listening.

Limiting Conversations Away from Work

It's natural for people to discuss their work outside the office. Work dominates our lives, takes up most of our time, and, if we're lucky, engages us in satisfying ways we want to share with others. If you're getting together with coworkers, the tendency is even stronger.

However, for security's sake, people should avoid discussing work-related topics away from the office. Companies should help their employees to understand the potential damage they can do with these kinds of conversations. They should establish strict policies and work to gain their employees' cooperation by explaining why the policies are in place. Even spouses should be reminded that what they hear can be very sensitive, and they should avoid repeating casual comments about their spouse's work.

In some companies, you find signs posted in the elevators reminding people not to discuss work outside the facilities. Employees must be made especially aware to be aware of who is around them while discussing work at airports, restaurants, and elsewhere. This of course includes cell phone conversations.

Change Patterns When Conducting Sensitive Business

One of the biggest operations vulnerabilities is predictability. When potential attackers know the patterns of your life, they can exploit them. If you regularly call your customers at a specific time, the bad guys will know when to tap your telephone. If you leave your office at the same time every day, the spies will know when to begin following you. If you eat breakfast at the same pancake house every morning, the spooks can be in the next booth, listening.

I worked with one client whose competitors simply hired private investigators to follow their salespeople around, compiling a list of sales calls. The next day, the competing company sent out its own sales people to call on the very same people. I know that this case is not unique.

If you are at some risk, it is important to vary your patterns deliberately. Take a different route to work every so often. Make your calls in the morning instead of the afternoon this week.

Also, consider your paper trail. Companies might want to issue multiple corporate credit cards and advise their people to use them only for sensitive projects. Never put down your frequent flyer number when you are traveling on a sensitive trip. When possible, use cash. Competitors and foreign intelligence agencies have compromised many computer, and especially credit card, records in an effort to put together profiles of the activities of targeted organizations. Many companies hire private investigators to do this. Seems a little like we've entered the world of James Bond here, but when the stakes are high and the vulnerabilities are many, these are reasonable precautions that can help enormously to minimize certain exposures.

Security Interaction with Other Departments

The security department tends to be an island, interacting with other departments only when necessary, after the fact of some incident. Sometimes security allows problems to continue during an investigation while not notifying stakeholders, which allows the situation to get worse before it gets better.

When security people work with others in an organization, especially managers, human resources personnel, and the information technology (IT) departments, they simply do a better job of circumventing problems. They have an opportunity to study the extent of the problems more thoroughly while minimizing potential losses. Others can bring additional skills to an investigation, allowing for earlier detection of other problems. To address their privacy concerns, extremely safety-conscious security people can require those assisting their investigations to sign confidentiality statements, in which they promise to not disclose anything they learn to others.

Disaster-Recovery and Incident-Handling Procedures

The only guarantee a qualified security professional can ever give his or her company or client is that there will be a problem. Again, there is no such thing as perfect security. For this reason, there must be disaster-recovery and incident-handling procedures. Equally important, these procedures must be tested on a regular basis.

Disaster-recovery procedures are emergency plans that help overcome service outages. These outages can be caused by hackers but are usually the result of equipment failures, natural disasters, programming errors, and power crashes. You should consider the different types of system outages and decide on strategies for recovery from each of them. For example, you could hire a company with a computer system that resembles yours so that you could switch over to its facilities in the event of a major equipment problem; this way, you may suffer a temporary outage, but the other company lets you use its computers to get you back up and running.

From a disaster-recovery perspective, the World Trade Center attacks represent a tremendous success. Companies that lost their complete facilities and thousands of computers were able to get up and running within a week. The New York Stock Exchange suffered a devastating loss of its communications capabilities, yet it was up and running within a week. Although this was a very obvious case of a disaster, there are disasters that occur frequently on a much smaller scale.

Incidents are security breaches that do not necessarily cause outages but nevertheless represent a danger to the organization. These could include hacker incidents, computer viruses, thefts of computers, and information thefts, among other things. Your organization should categorize the different types of incidents and decide exactly how you want to respond to each of them. You should consult with your company's general counsel on your prosecution policies and also to determine whether the security department may sometimes let the problems continue as a means of catching the attackers. You must assess the potential liability from such action. You'll also want to consult with your PR department on how to deal with the press should the news get out that you have a problem.

One of the most critical decisions organizations have to make is whether to let the incident continue. Although some people contend that you must intervene immediately, there are several factors to consider. If you close up the holes, the attackers will know that you have spotted them and close up shop. You've stopped their information-collection activities, but you've also impeded the collection of evidence against them. You may never learn their identity or the extent of the breach. Letting the incident continue allows for the compromise of more information or additional thefts, but it also allows you to track down the attackers and see how far they are entrenched in your organization (they might have installed a few back doors into your organization).

Organizations should also acquire the resources necessary to fully investigate potential incidents and correct them. This involves an investment in hardware, software, and personnel. It can also involve contracting with consulting firms that offer an emergency response service.

The most critical success factor in dealing with incidents is preparation. Part of that preparation should include testing your security procedures to see whether they actually work. You should hold drills to simulate all kinds of problems, including disasters. You have to find your weaknesses before they materialize to haunt you.

Perform Periodic Vulnerability Assessments with Penetration Testing

Despite your best efforts, some vulnerabilities are bound to go unnoticed. It's almost inevitable. However, you need to discover all your weaknesses to accurately assess your risk and to know which countermeasures to put into place and where to put them. Even a small nick in your armor can be exploited by wily attackers, and any attackers worth their salt will try to get at you from more than one angle. The key is to find as many of your vulnerabilities as possible before the attackers do.

An assessment is a free-form test that is generally overt and attempts to find as many vulnerabilities as possible. A penetration test takes an attacker's perspective in targeting an organization. This test is covert and not as comprehensive. It can, however, find vulnerabilities that cannot be found through other methods.

WHY NOT TO HIRE OR CONTRACT A HACKER

When people think about technical penetration testing, they think about hackers. They also tend to ask themselves the question, "Who better to protect yourself from a hacker than a hacker?" At face value, this makes sense to many people. The problem is that this is an extremely bad practice.

I should specify that in this section, when I say *hacker,* I mean a computer criminal who has either been convicted or just basically admits to committing crimes.

In the first place, the logic just is not right. Although I don't want to get too technical in this discussion, I will provide an analogy. If a person stabs someone, does that mean that she is qualified as a surgeon and can fix the damage she causes? If he is a serial killer, would that make him an even more qualified surgeon? Just because you know how to damage something doesn't mean that you know how to fix it. Computers are extremely complicated. Breaking something this complicated is easy. As Chapter 4 outlines, almost all hackers just know a few tricks that the average person does not.

There is also the concept of performing a penetration test responsibly. As I mentioned, a great deal of damage can be done during a penetration test. Whoever performs the work must know not just how to break into a computer, but the pitfalls that will be encountered. The tester must also know how to present his or her results from a business perspective so that recommended actions actually get performed.

Many people then say, well, what if I find a hacker I think is really talented? A really talented expert in penetration testing will have a thick résumé, not a rap sheet. As you can see by case studies in Chapter 6 and 7, I access some very valuable and sensitive information. Frankly, I have accessed information that I do not speak about that can cause extremely serious damage to a company should it be revealed.

When you know that someone is a criminal, rarely do you know the full extent of that person's crimes or the maliciousness of his or her actions. How can you justify to your executive management or board of directors that you knowingly hired a criminal and gave that person potential access to the most sensitive information in your company? The question to you is, "Do you want to put your job and your company on the line to hire a criminal?"

As I also mentioned, much of the time that I perform penetration tests, I find evidence of criminal activities and have to turn the effort into an incident response. Can you trust a criminal to investigate another criminal? You never know whether they are friends. Also, one of the consistent hacker ethics (if you can call it that) within the hacker community is, "Never 'narc' on another hacker." Can you trust a hacker in that regard? And if you ever catch the criminal targeting you, he will likely challenge any charges against him, saying that the other criminal you let into your midst is framing him.

For every hacker you show me, I can provide you with 30 résumés of skilled professionals who not only have a clean record but also are more talented. Many of these people fit into the elite ranks of the information warriors I describe in Chapter 4. Hiring known and admitted criminals is not just stupid, it is dangerous.

This is not to completely blackball a teenager who has run-ins. If she can keep her nose clean for a period of time and get a legitimate education and legitimate job experience, that could be a sign that she has reformed. Such people are talented enough that they develop other skills besides hacking. On the other hand, someone who is convicted after becoming an adult or after multiple crimes is clearly a criminal whom you cannot justify hiring or contracting for a trusted role.

That's why many organizations perform penetration tests, similar to those conducted in Chapters 6, 7, and 8. During such a penetration test, a trusted team of espionage or technical experts simulates an attack for the purposes of exposing weak spots. The results of such a test tell you not only where you need to spend the greatest effort bolstering your security but also where to place detection mechanisms.

Deciding who should perform a penetration test can be a tricky matter. Many people within an organization like the idea of performing a penetration test because it sounds like it might be fun, but poorly trained testers can leave behind more holes than were there before they started. Many amateurs just don't know how to clean up after themselves, and they can ruffle a lot of feathers in the process. A good penetration test doesn't point fingers or take down individual names, but it does provide a summary finding that companies can use to accurately assess their risk and prioritize countermeasures. A good tester can also spot-check specific countermeasures and evaluate their efficacy.

Companies are well advised to consider hiring outside consultants to perform this kind of work. A qualified outsider is less likely to have political agendas than are people with stakes in the organization. It should be noted, though, that you need to understand the skill of outside parties. The case studies in this book detail penetration tests that take an espionage-based approach of targeting information. Unfortunately, most consultants in the field target computer access. Sometimes that is acceptable, if you want only to know the weaknesses in your computers. If you want espionage-type assessments, you must find people who have that specific experience.

With accurate vulnerability assessments combined with penetration test results, you can tailor your security program to the specific needs of your organization.

Personnel Countermeasures

Personnel countermeasures address vulnerabilities in the many ways that companies hire, maintain, and terminate employees. Most of these countermeasures involve the human resources (HR) department. HR is the company gatekeeper, so to speak, responsible for hiring competent and trustworthy people. That department is also responsible for your workers at the time of their termination. HR is there at the beginning and the end, and that's where most of these countermeasures are most frequently implemented. (After a person enters the workplace, the local manager becomes the responsible party and operations countermeasures are more applicable.)

Some of these countermeasures should be implemented with or by the security department. There is a great deal of crossover between responsibilities here, and both security and HR should work together for the betterment of the entire organization.

I should say that personnel countermeasures are the only way that you potentially have to stop the threat. Generally, countermeasures counter vulnerabilities and not threats. You really cannot stop a hurricane, earthquake, or a person from hating you. We have not been able to hunt terrorists down to extinction. A corporation is not able to legally take active preventive measures against a person. However, if you can keep someone with ill intent from becoming an insider, you have prevented such a person from doing you harm, at least for now as an insider.

Background Checks

Perhaps the most effective thing an organization can do to increase security is require background checks of employees. In many market sectors, this is a common requirement. Background checks should include a criminal records check, verification of previous employment, and validation of educational claims. Recent surveys indicate that more than 80 percent of employment candidates lie about their backgrounds on job applications. In most cases, the lies are inconsequential, but some people who are not qualified for the jobs they apply for talk their way through interviews and into positions of responsibility. Other studies show that concerns about background checks deter many people from lying on their applications.

Depending on the types of positions applied for, companies might also want to conduct psychological testing on prospective employees. This kind of screening procedure is usually reserved for very sensitive positions and senior managers. Some companies hire an organizational psychologist to assess the suitability of certain candidates for key positions. Some organizations perform psychological tests on all their employees to try to get desirable behavioral traits.

Most companies cite the cost of background checks as a reason for not performing them. A basic background check costs between $30 and $50. The total cost of hiring a new employee almost always exceeds $3,000. In some cases, the cost of a new hire exceeds $10,000. When the cost of the background check is compared with total hiring costs, it is inconsequential. For more senior employees and people in sensitive positions, you might want to consider more extensive background checks. These are more costly but they're worth the expense because the stakes are high.

Background checks do not guarantee that employees will never commit illegal acts against your organization, but they do weed out many undesirables. One company that recently started performing background checks found that the organization was rejecting 5 to 10 percent of applicants based on the checks; upper management believes its new policy will save the company a tremendous amount in future legal and regulatory problems.

Checks on Spouses

Although most organizations don't extend their background checks beyond the employment candidate, some companies do perform background checks on immediate family members as well. Spouses in particular have come under the scrutiny of some HR departments.

Usually, the extent of this background check depends on the position for which the candidate is applying. Besides a standard background check, you could ask spouses to sign nondisclosure agreements. Spouses are privileged to pillow talk, informal gatherings, overhearing telephone calls, and so on. They likely have as much knowledge of company happenings as many people inside the company.

If the resources are available, this deeper level of inquiry can sometimes yield important information. Simply because a husband or wife happens to work for your competitor doesn't mean that he or she will necessarily use his or her insider connection to gather information, but such a connection must be considered a vulnerability. Spouses have been known to influence their better halves to commit industrial espionage. As demonstrated in Chapter 6, Chinese intelligence agencies use family bonds to achieve their successes. Do not think that they will target only people directly employed by their victims.

Employee Hotlines

HR and security departments should establish a hotline that allows people to report problems that are not necessarily security related. A hotline could allow workers to point out disgruntled coworkers or to request assistance with personal problems. The idea is to facilitate the exchange of information outside the security loop. People are sometimes hesitant to go to security because of the stigma attached to it, but they might call up someone in HR.

In two cases I know about first hand, coworkers reported people who were acting unusual, and it turned out that the people were spying on behalf of a foreign government. More frequently, people might be saving their own lives when their coworkers are mentally unstable.

Coordination Between HR and Information Systems Department

One of the most pervasive problems among companies and organizations is that people who leave the company often have accounts on the system long after their termination. When I perform my penetration tests, I almost always gain extremely valuable information from accounts of terminated employees. When I investigate incidents, I find that they frequently involve compromises of these orphaned accounts. On several occasions, I found that the criminals were former and extremely disgruntled employees who still had access to their accounts. In one of the more extreme cases, a former salesman walked in to a client's office to which a current company salesperson was to deliver a proposal the following day. The former employee handed the potential client his former employer's proposal and said, "Here is the proposal my former company is going to give you tomorrow. Here is mine, and here is why it is better." I soon discovered that the former salesman had access not only to his own account but also to another account containing the company's master proposal database. This was a Fortune 50 company, but the problem is far from unique to such companies.

The root of this problem lies in a lack of communication between the human resources people and the technical departments. HR should contact IS *before* anyone is fired. It should deliver as much advanced warning as possible when it knows that people are scheduled to leave the organization. The quicker, the better. This gives IS a chance to remove accounts the day the person leaves the building.

IS should also be contacted when there is trouble with employees. It should know which accounts might need special attention. That way, it can increase auditing of the specific accounts and watch for suspicious activities. The IS department people can't do this if they don't know about it. This countermeasure hinges on HR's willingness to take a minor extra step.

Coordinating HR and the Security Department

IS is not the only department that needs to know when personnel actions occur. Someone who attracted the attention of HR is significantly more likely to be disgruntled even if he or she has not yet been fired.

HR should also inform the security department whenever someone leaves the company. Security should always monitor employees when they are about to leave an organization. The department will want to be prepared to remove an employee's physical accesses the minute he or she leaves the company.

One of the problems with former employees is that the security guards are familiar with their faces. In large organizations, former employees often find that they can walk right through the gate. After an employee has departed the company for good, security can distribute photographs to the guards, which will let the guards know which one of those familiar faces should no longer be welcomed.

Many organizations have employees escorted out after they are terminated, giving them minimal time to clear their desks. Some companies even immediately escort someone out of a building right after they resign under good terms. Although I personally do not like this type of behavior and believe that it can create bad feelings where none previously existed, I can understand this behavior given all the horror stories I learn about.

The exchange of information between the HR and security departments should be a two-way street. Security people tend to perform their work in a vacuum, keeping their investigations secret. This exponentially increases the potential danger to a company. When security people discover an employee problem, they should contact someone in HR. Security should resist the urge to act in a vacuum, which only hinders investigations and exacerbates problems.

Tracking Information Access

Often, after an employee has left a company, no one knows for certain which information that person had access to. Someone inside the organization should know, definitely, which facilities and projects are available to which people. Although it is impossible to know everything a person ever saw or accessed, keeping a high-level record of assignments is helpful. This knowledge allows for damage assessment and control when people are involved in security incidents or when they leave the company. With a formal access policy in place for sensitive information (as I recommended previously), tracking information access should be a simple matter.

Reviewing Visitors

While you're scrutinizing your employees, don't forget to take a long look at your visitors. Anyone who comes into your company is a potential threat. A person's physical presence gives him or her a certain amount of access, which real pros can often exploit and turn into greater access.

Foreign operatives have been known to wear shoes with glue on them to pick up traces of unique chemicals on a factory floor. Stan, the GRU defector who assisted in performing the penetration test described in Chapter 6, was once given special gloves that looked like real skin to run across a stealth fighter to pick up traces of stealth materials when it was known that he would have access to the plane. Employees of a Japanese company once wore ties whose points were lined with sponges to absorb chemicals from a competitor.

Make sure that your organization has a way to let security know about pending visits, and the earlier, the better. This countermeasure won't work without this advance notice. Security will probably want to make a few phone calls to verify the reasons for the visit and the identities of the visitors. You can call the FBI ANSIR office to see whether anything is amiss.

After your visitors have come onsite, limit what they see. Even if the visitors are customers you are trying to impress, be careful where you take them and what you reveal. There's usually no need to go overboard.

If the visitor is to have access to extremely sensitive information, you should perform a public records background check. Also, many firms have the capability to perform overseas background checks when dealing with foreign visitors.

Categorize Employees and Establish Roles

Employees within any given organization fall into three basic categories: regular employees, contractors, and temps. All three categories should not enjoy the same access to information in your company. Although you must place full trust in your regular employees, there's no reason to trust the others at quite the same level. Temporary and contract employees don't have the same investment in your company as regular employees do. That doesn't mean they are necessarily more criminally inclined, but spies are much more likely to assume the guise of a contractor or a temp because they go through less scrutiny.

Contract employees are usually specialists hired for specific projects, which eventually come to an end. They will need greater access than a temp because they have greater responsibilities, but they should never be allowed too deeply into the inner sanctum. Temporary employees should never be placed in positions of trust unless they have a long-standing relationship with the company and are well known to their managers.

Differentiate the different categories of your workers in all forms of company identification. Access badges for temps and contractors should be strikingly different in appearance from regular access badges. Make them a different color, or write TEMP or CONTRACTOR on them in big, bold letters. The idea is to allow for the immediate determination of that employee's status.

This identification should extend to e-mail accounts as well. Create policies to place the employee status in the signature line in the e-mails. The employee name in the From and To fields should also identify the status. Companies that use caller ID should enter an employee's name and status into the system from the first day of employment.

There is also the concept of employee roles to consider. Whether someone is a regular employee or a contractor or temporary employee, all employees should still have their roles defined within the corporation. Roles are defined job functions, such as data entry, security, system administrator, and janitor. These roles imply levels of information access. These roles should be embedded within computer and facilities accesses.

These kinds of differentiation techniques are even more important in large organizations in which all the employees don't know each other on sight. These relatively simple steps can remove some of the most commonly exploited organizational vulnerabilities.

Coordinating Terminations

I previously discussed that HR should coordinate personnel actions with the IS and security departments. However, when people are formally terminated, there are several other issues to consider and groups that need to be informed. I previously described how I had significant problems getting computers back from people within my own company. That is just one example. You also have to recover cell phones and other company property. Although it sounds obvious, unless there is a clearly defined exit process, you will likely not recover all your property.

You must also consider the cancellation of company credit cards, calling cards, and access to purchasing accounts. Additionally, project teams should be formally informed that people are leaving and instructed to remove the departees from mailing lists and any other venues that give people access to project data. If possible, a short but formal message should be sent to as much of the organization as possible to wish the departee well in his or her new endeavors. This gets out the point that the employee is leaving, and does so in an amicable forum.

Imposing Your Requirements on Contracted Services

Companies often hire other firms to provide security guard and janitorial services. These people, whom you have neither screened nor interviewed, have nearly full access to your facilities at times when everyone else is gone from the premises. Some companies outsource some or all of their secretarial and technical staffs, putting relative strangers into critical positions.

All the personnel countermeasures I have described in this section are utterly useless if you open your doors to companies with lower hiring standards than your own. You must contractually specify that any companies from whom you hire on-site services use the same personnel screening measures that you employ. The *very* same. Anything less, and you might as well scrap your own program.

CHECKING THE CREDENTIALS OF SECURITY PROFESSIONALS

The case study of Alexey Ivanov in Chapter 10 had a very upsetting effect on me personally. As a security professional, I find it abysmal that several companies hired security consultants to come in and stop Ivanov, and they failed miserably. Ivanov used only widely known and preventable attacks. The consultants used were incompetent for not preventing the attacks.

Apparently many companies asked around for advice on whom they should bring in. The people whom they were led to were not very good and created more damage in the process. It is likely that the victims did not want to pay for a more qualified consultant and would have thought that any rate charged was excessive.

At the very least, we should learn from these people, and learn to ask not just for advice from people to find a consultant. We should learn to ask the consultant for references and previous engagements they had on similar work. At the very least, they should provide three references that you verify, even in a crisis. Why not be forward thinking, line up a few people for contingencies now, when you have the time to check the references?

These contracted service positions constitute a major vulnerability. Recall the article published in *2600: The Hacker's Quarterly* describing how to get a job as a janitor (Chapter 4). The target mentioned in the article was a very large company and would probably not have hired the person as a regular employee.

If hackers know how to use this vulnerability to avoid your security measures, you can bet that more profit-motivated individuals know it, too. Don't allow careless contract service providers to become security back doors into your organization.

Physical Countermeasures

All the cases cited in Part II that involved on-site thefts of information were successful primarily because of poor use of physical countermeasures. Physical countermeasures deal with the security of information that exists in a physical form, such as documents, computer disks, or product prototypes, and with facility security. Usually, these two categories are tightly coupled.

Physical countermeasures may seem to be the most obvious steps people could take to secure company data, but in my experience, they are the most frequently overlooked. I suppose these strategies seem too simple and obvious to be very important, but the fact is, time and time again, attackers exploit lapses in physical security to make off with priceless information. Perhaps most surprising to many is that most of these countermeasures are already available.

Lock Up All Controlled Information

Sensitive information must be protected. Although operational procedures control its distribution, the disks, files, and documents on which it is stored must be physically protected from theft or compromise. To that end, your organization must require your people to lock up their papers and other material while they are unattended.

This seems so obvious, so simple, but without a clear message from management, people just won't do it. In the cases discussed in Chapters 6 and 7, much of the compromises of information involved collecting physically unprotected data. Exploitation of this vulnerability is part and parcel of almost all cases of industrial espionage.

Use Available Locks

In the cases cited in Chapters 6, 7, 8, and 9, the thieves came upon many locks that could have thwarted their activities, but the locks were simply not used. Almost all desks, doors, and file cabinets have locks. They provide readily available, cost-free physical security for information of all types. If people would actually use them, many incidents of espionage would be significantly reduced in scope. Remember, too, that Chapter 8 describes a very life-threatening situation.

Although a very determined attacker might try to pick a lock or track down the keys, locks prevent a significant amount of casual theft and force an attacker to take more easily detectable steps. If there are places that need locks within your facility, get them installed and see that they are used. It's a small inconvenience that could save you a bundle.

Using Password-Protected Screen Savers

Another countermeasure that is readily available to nearly everyone is the screen saver. These computer utilities were originally developed to prevent burn-in problems with computer screens left on the same page for too long (after a certain number of minutes of inactivity, the screen saver comes on and sends patterns across the screen, which stops the burn-in). Many people don't realize that these programs almost always include a password-protection feature. When this feature is activated, users must enter a password to "unlock" the screen saver image and gain access to their computers. This means that when people leave their desks for any significant period of time, their computers are automatically locked, preventing others from taking advantage of their absence. The consoles with administrator logons left unlocked in the case in Chapter 6 provide an excellent example of what can happen when this feature is not utilized. Although this initially appears to be a technical countermeasure, it directly affects physical access to the computers.

People should remember that they usually leave their mail logged in all day. This means that anyone who goes by their desk could read their mail and everything else they are working on. That is in addition to having unfettered access to all files on the computer, as well as providing access to all files and privileges that the user has throughout the network. Password-protected screen savers are standard on most major PC operating systems, including all Microsoft Windows operating systems available during the last five years.

Clean Desk Policies

Whenever I'm performing a penetration test, I get very excited at the sight of a messy desk. It's an unvarying sign that sensitive information will be all over the office. Corporate-wide clean-desk policies can help to discourage people from allowing their desks to become too messy to be safe. This is an absolutely essential, no-cost countermeasure that every company should implement. It might even help your business be more efficient. If there are still inboxes on your desks, the materials should be locked up at the end of every day, or be otherwise secured. All these policies would certainly have hindered my penetration efforts at the companies I describe in Chapters 6 and 7.

Conduct Facility Walk-Throughs

To ensure that the preceding countermeasures are being implemented, managers should check the desks and areas of their employees. They should walk around periodically and try the locks and see whether anyone is leaving sensitive information out in the open. They should make sure that keys are not readily available to anyone who walks by the desk, file cabinet, or office door (sometimes keys are left in drawers or in small containers on the desk). Managers should also make sure that passwords are not written on scraps of paper taped to monitors or under keyboards. During a recent vulnerability assessment, I found a cipher lock combination written on the side of a picture frame near the locked door. The walk-through should focus on what a hostile adversary could get if he or she were to walk through the facility.

People on corporate security staffs should also check for messy desks and unused locks. If managers or security people find isolated cases of this, they should lock up the materials and request that the offender be more careful in the future. If it happens repeatedly, more drastic actions should be taken. If this is a company-wide problem, managers should be required to do regular walk-throughs until the problem is cleared up.

Watch for Strange Postings

Creative attackers have posted misleading bulletins throughout targeted organizations. Recall the incident described in Chapter 5, in which a hacker infiltrated a company and posted a fake announcement of a new help desk telephone number. The attacker's own telephone number was listed as the new help desk line. Although this was a rare attack, corporate security personnel should periodically check bulletin boards, just in case.

Locking Cables

Almost *all* companies experience the theft of computers from time to time. For the most part, the thieves are stupid burglars who are after only the hardware. However, you can still lose access to the information on the stolen machine. Many companies sell cables and other mechanisms that lock a computer to a desk. These devices are far from perfect, but they do make the theft of equipment much more difficult.

Place Controls on Copy Machines

Although the theft of intellectual property has moved primarily to being carried out by copying electronic data, there is still a lot to be gained through copying physical documents. Although this problem wasn't specifically described in Chapters 6, 7 and 9, because it was so rampant, all attackers were able to gain an immense amount of documents and make copies of them. Copy machines allow thieves to tromp through your resources, make off with vital information without actually stealing it, and leave nary a footprint.

The monitoring can be done in several ways. You can put video cameras near the machines. This would certainly work, but it might seem intrusive to some people, and it might be expensive. Another countermeasure that is both cheaper and more readily available utilizes an existing feature of most modern commercial copy machines: the accounting feature. Employees using machines equipped with this feature must enter authorization numbers before they can make any copies. The machines then record the number of copies that the employee makes. Organizations using this countermeasure typically review the copy logs on a monthly basis for the purposes of charging the copy costs back to specific projects or departments. The procedure also provides a ready means for detecting an employee making excessive copies.

Even if the thief uses another person's authorization code, someone is eventually going to notice that an unusual number of copies are being made, prompting an investigation. Even if the procedure doesn't prevent all illegal copying, it will be a probable deterrent and definitely helps in detecting thefts.

Library Control

Most large companies maintain some kind of in-house library facilities—places where sensitive information is stored. These company libraries provide one-stop shopping for astute spies. Afshin Bavand and his accomplices made great use of the physical libraries as well as the electronic ones.

To prevent the abuse of company libraries by on-site attackers, organizations should restrict access and lock the doors. When the library is opened, a librarian should be on duty at all times. People wanting access to information should be required to sign and date a log and list the specific documents they borrow. Library logs discourage people from abusing these rooms and taking out documents for nefarious purposes. The logs create tracks, which investigators can follow.

Security Reminders

The Department of Defense posts reminders on every telephone in every office—right on the telephones themselves—reminding its people that their conversations can be monitored by outside entities. In commercial organizations, you can also remind people that competitors can monitor your telephones. Some companies use awareness posters in the break rooms. Other companies remind people not to talk business outside the company in newsletters, articles, or e-mail bulletins. One company placed reminders in elevators.

Whichever method you use, the countermeasure is a simple but effective one: Constantly remind your people about basic security issues. They need to know about information value, the threats, the vulnerabilities, and the countermeasures, and they need to be told over and over again. There are dozens of services that provide awareness posters, newsletters, online training, awareness seminars, and so on for a reasonable fee. Organizations should make use of these services.

Make Shredders Widely Available

Almost all documents produced by your organization, even the most seemingly innocuous notes and memos, could contain something sensitive or something that an attacker could use against you. Allowing your people to dispose of papers by simply tossing them in the trash is a very dangerous policy.

The solution here is relatively simple: Make shredders widely available throughout your organization's facilities. Ideally, there should be one beside every desk or for every person or group of three, but you can get away with providing one for every work group. At a very bare minimum, you should have one next to every copy machine in your company. Remember: The further away the machine is from the individual, the less likely it will be used.

Many shredders cost less than $30 and may be significantly cheaper when purchased in bulk. The cheapest ones shred the paper into ribbons, which may be pieced back together, although this is extremely difficult. For slightly more money you can buy a cross-cutting type of shredder, which cuts paper into ribbons and then cuts the ribbons into smaller pieces, which are nearly impossible to piece back together. If a shredder is centrally located, it should be a high-capacity machine.

Some companies hire an outside service to shred their documents. The company provides bins in which people are to place their sensitive materials. The service then collects the materials and brings them to a central facility for shredding. The efficacy of this type of service depends on how liberally the collection bins are distributed in your organization. It's also a good idea to send someone out to follow the shredder's trucks once in awhile, to make sure that the company is properly disposing of the papers.

I've noticed that people naturally tend to put papers in the company recycle bins and not the shred bins, which are not secure in any way. It's up to you to let your employees know that they should use the shredders.

Lock Dumpsters

No matter how widely shredders are distributed, people will place sensitive materials in the regular trash. Although you can minimize this problem, it is still cause for concern. "Dumpster diving" is a tried-and-true corporate espionage technique. As I mention in Chapter 5, the Masters of Deception hacker group used this technique to secure superuser passwords to the national telephone system—which shows how much damage can result from a little diligent trash shifting. To counter this vulnerability, simply put a good lock on your dumpsters.

Perimeter Lock

Unattended, unmonitored, and unlocked doors provide opportunities for thieves to sneak out equipment and to let accomplices into the buildings. All entrances to your facilities should be locked or manned. When doors must be unattended, they should be not only locked but also wired with alarms that sound whenever they're opened. If it is not practical in your organization to guard all entrances, then consider monitoring them with closed-circuit cameras. Also, don't neglect the gates to storage yards.

Log Unusual Accesses and Removal of Equipment

These days, very few of us can get away with working a 40-hour week. Consequently, it's not unusual to find honest, hardworking employees staying late at the office and taking work home. Unfortunately, this behavior is also a warning sign of potential espionage activity.

As you saw in Chapters 6 and 7, attackers will enter your facilities late at night when their actions may go unnoticed. To counter this vulnerability, require your people to sign in and out of your buildings after normal work hours. The hard workers won't mind and the spies will leave tracks. When you do notice that an employee is frequently putting in late hours, don't hesitate to investigate.

You should also require your people to sign for equipment they carry out of the building, even during the day. Chapter 6 demonstrates how a company at least intended to implement this procedure. Loading dock areas should be closely monitored because people can drive right up to the door and drive away with truckloads of equipment. Using logs is an excellent deterrent, but bold thieves may simply sign a different name and number. Your guards should verify the identity of every person signing the log.

Access Badges

Most companies with security interests use access badges. Unfortunately, many fail to use them correctly. An access badge should indicate employee status—regular, contract, or temporary—as well as to which facilities the person has access. Most important, the badges should be worn at all times. During my penetration in Chapters 6 and 7, I simply hid my temp badge and told people what I wanted them to believe.

No one challenged me, and many people gave me very sensitive information. Organizations should encourage employees not only to wear their badges but also to challenge others who don't.

Card Access Lock

One of the most effective physical countermeasures available today is the electronic door lock. Electronic locks are opened with access cards fitted with magnetic strips or RFID mechanisms (the chips that are read when you wave them over a reader). The card readers in the locks identify the cardholder and record the date and time he or she entered the building. The access cards can be programmed for specific entrances at specific facilities at specific times, effectively restricting access. Perhaps the most valuable feature of this technology is that the cards can be deactivated. This means that terminated or suspect employees can be denied access to particular facilities instantly. The card readers also record attempts at access using deactivated cards, leaving records of the number of times a person has tried to enter restricted buildings during restricted time periods. Companies can use these records to identify employees who try to get into restricted areas.

Properly Trained Guards

Most modern companies of any size employ security guards, and they can serve as very important deterrents to illegal activities on the premises. In my experience, however, the guards in most organizations rarely do the job they should. It's not usually their fault; often they're poorly trained, either by the contract service provider or the company itself. Either way, it's up to you to make sure that your guards are providing the physical countermeasures your company needs.

Chapters 6, 7, 8, and 9 demonstrate what happens when guards do little to actually implement security. People were waved into sensitive facilities by guards without being challenged. Equipment was carried past them. They completely ignored people who were in the process of performing grave acts against their organizations. This is consistent among most organizations.

Guards should look closely at access badges. They should also search unusual packages and bags. They should patrol facilities, looking for things that are out of place. They should notice people in the buildings at odd hours, and they should question them and ascertain whether they are in the "right" areas. They should keep track of unusual incidents, late-night visitors, and odd details in logs. (The purpose of the log is not to compile data on people but to make it possible to see patterns of behavior.)

Most important, guards should be trained to know which items are of value, and to use their common sense. Sadly guards are typically given general guidelines and you are lucky if they actually adhere to them, let alone exercise any independent thought when necessary. Your guards must be trained to recognize the things they should really be looking for.

I find it regrettable that I actually have to mention these things, which should be standard for any security guard. Unfortunately, there is apathy on all sides that results in a deteriorating situation.

Security Patrols

Companies should also have their guards patrol outside their facilities to search for unusual cars and especially vans. This is clearly terrorism-related vulnerability that you would assume that companies would care about. Besides safety concerns for employees, the vans can be loaded with TEMPEST receivers, which can pick up the data on a variety of electrical devices and receivers that pick up the signals from bugs planted inside your facilities. One forward-thinking company actually follows its trucks carrying sensitive documents. Security patrols might also pick up investigators who are trailing your salespeople.

Choose Locations Wisely

Security must be involved with the choice of corporate locations. Along with considerations of space and comfort, you must think about such factors as the location of your competitors and the physical aspects of the area. You don't want to set up shop in a place that allows your competition easy access. Neither do you want to put your head-quarters on a flood plane or an earthquake fault line. You will want to locate in an area with a reliable power supply and a low crime rate. All these considerations should be second nature to your security department. Use their safety consciousness to avoid built-in problems.

Watch Where You Conduct Business Outside Your Facilities

When you are conducting business outside your facilities, you must consider the vulnerabilities around you. Expect that people will overhear your conversations. Count on the person next to you on the airplane to look at your notes and computer screen while you are working. Be aware of your surroundings and the likelihood that all your actions can be seen by others. Basically, you have no privacy outside your facilities, and you must act accordingly. Most important, make sure that the people in your organization, especially those who travel on a regular basis, are well aware of this policy and the reasons why.

Fire Suppression

Fire protection is very important around computers, but the most common fire suppression systems tend to destroy the data that the computers contain. Companies usually rely on standard sprinkler systems to suppress fires. In an office environment, sprinklers are probably the best solution. However, in computer rooms they can be disastrous.

Computer rooms should be equipped with gas fire suppression systems. These systems use inert gases to smother fires. These gases also smother people, so they are only used in certain situations, but they are very effective. I strongly recommend considering this type of system for your computer rooms.

If you've chosen, as so many companies have, to locate your computer facilities in the basement, your equipment might be even more vulnerable to the damage of a sprinkler system. If there is a fire in any of the upper floors, the sprinkler systems will activate, flooding the area with hundreds of gallons of water. The problem is, all that water will eventually seep down into the basement and your computer room. This could lead to millions of dollars in losses. Therefore, you might want to consider moving your computer facilities to an upper floor.

Uninterruptible Power Supplies

Uninterruptible power supplies (UPS) provide backup power when your primary power source goes offline. The sudden loss of power can damage computers and result in a loss of service and vital data. Depending on the industry, this loss can cost billions of dollars.

Computers and peripherals plug into the UPS, which is plugged into an electrical outlet. Some UPSes also connect to computers through computer cable ports and instruct the computer to shut down gracefully when there is a power outage, saving all your work in the process. Other systems simply keep things going for varying lengths of time to allow you to save your data and shut down your machine. Depending on the type of UPS, they can keep your computers running for hours.

UPSes also act as surge protectors. The strength of electrical currents varies as they travel through power lines. Occasionally, there are power spikes that can literally fry your computer. These spikes occur naturally and can be amplified by lightning strikes. To prevent these power spikes from ruining your machines when you don't use UPSes, you can use power strips that have surge-protection capability.

Technical Countermeasures

Although I previously stated that technical security failures are failures of an operational process, this does not mean that technical countermeasures are unnecessary. A good operational security process involves the implementation of technical countermeasures. These are the underlying technologies that a security program implements.

Technical countermeasures can also be effective for stopping nontechnical attacks. When implemented properly, they can actually provide a fail-safe mechanism for catching the spies when all else fails. As a matter of fact, a strong technical security foundation not only repels attacks but also forms the best detection mechanism. Technical countermeasures, when properly implemented, can more than pay for themselves, and they provide the final and most difficult hurdle for an attacker to overcome.

I have not discussed every possible technical countermeasure in this section. You can find many books on this subject; also, technology by its very nature is ever changing. I have included the most commonly available and readily applicable countermeasures, all of which will serve you well. It's a good idea to continue your study of technical countermeasures with other books and possibly a consultant.

Anti-Virus Software

I previously discussed anti-virus software as a fundamental part of any personal security program. It must also be a basic part of any organizational security program. Viruses and worms are growing in frequency and severity. This malware has crippled even reasonably well-prepared airlines, banks, and other organizations, and it is likely to happen in the future. However, these events can be significantly reduced or completely eliminated with properly maintained anti-virus software.

In organizations, there should be anti-virus software on the e-mail servers. Because viruses can enter an organization via methods beyond e-mail, such as web browsers and instant messaging, you should look into installing anti-virus software, as available, on the appropriate servers as well. As always, anti-virus software should be installed on each and every system in the organization as well.

More important than having the software is keeping it updated. This means that you must subscribe to automatic update services. Depending on the vendor, such services can push out updated signature files as they become available. This is extremely important because the speed of malware proliferation seems to be near instantaneous. The auto-updates are critical to preventing infections. Although there is no guarantee that you can completely prevent every infection, you are as protected as you possibly can be. The automatic update feature should be implemented for both the end user systems and the servers.

When you combine anti-virus software with the other tools mentioned in this section, you can have near bulletproof malware prevention.

Firewalls

Although I contend that organizations put too much faith in firewalls, they are critical for preventing a wide variety of problems that originate from the Internet. Firewalls are devices that secure one network segment from another; the device can be either a single-purpose computer or a computer with application software loaded. Good firewalls can prevent many attacks from outside an organization, as long as they are properly configured. Before choosing a firewall, you must determine your specific needs. You should also make certain that any firewall you install is ICSA certified. This ensures that it is a reasonably versatile, secure, and established product.

I cannot emphasize enough that you should use an established firewall product. I was once asked to have my company evaluate a new firewall product. My client wanted to start using the product because it was less expensive than most others. One engineer did a quick code review and found that the firewall company took freeware off the Internet and incorporated it into its product. The vendor did not apparently properly license the freeware, and, even worse, did not fix known problems with that software.

Organizations should also consider acquiring firewalls for internal use. There are many parts of your internal networks that do not need to be generally accessible. The HR department and research departments almost always will not be accessed from outside those departments. Internal firewalls can prevent a variety of technical attacks that originate inside of your organization. Although they will not prevent all types of attacks, they could aid in detection of attacks and will give your organization a warning that they should look for other attacks.

Just as constant updates are more important than the anti-virus software itself, ensuring that firewalls are properly configured and updated is as important as the firewall itself. A firewall must limit inbound and outbound communications to only what is necessary. Many successful attacks could have been prevented if the firewalls in place were configured to allow only what was minimally necessary.

Personal firewalls are available for PCs and should be considered a standard tool. Whenever I travel and hook my computer up to a network through a hotel broadband service or standard dial-up connection, I find that within minutes the firewall reports attempted attacks of my system.

Intrusion Detection Systems/Intrusion Prevention Systems

Despite all your efforts to prevent intrusions and other security incidents, attackers will breach your perimeter security mechanisms from time to time. On top of that, there will be more internally created incidents. If you can detect these breaches early, you can respond, stop them, and maybe even catch the attacker. The case studies in Chapters 6, 7, 9, and 10 illustrate what can happen when there is no intrusion- and abuse-detection software. The software could have alerted the security departments and prevented the intrusions from continuing, stopping incredibly serious losses with national security and terrorist implications.

Intrusion-detection systems look for attacks in progress. They can be host-based or network-based systems. Host-based systems means that the software sits on a single computer and looks for attacks against that computer. A network-based system sits passively on the network and watches network communications go by, looking for signs of security-related incidents. In most organizations, it is best to plan to use both network- and host-based systems.

I do not go into a technical discussion of the difference between an intrusion-detection system and intrusion prevention system, but it suffices to say that an intrusion-prevention system detects attacks and then takes some basic action to prevent the attack from continuing. An intrusion-detection system only alerts you to the fact that an incident is occurring or has occurred. In an ideal world, you would have an intrusion-prevention system, but the fact is that the technology has not fully matured as of this writing. Intrusion-detection systems will be valuable and around for some time to come. It is more likely that intrusion-detection systems will eventually evolve to be intrusion-prevention systems.

Although it can be time-consuming to put host-based intrusion- and abuse-detection software on all your systems, you should at least install it on the systems inside your organization that contain very sensitive information. (Remember the countermeasure of categorizing your data.) Start with those systems and then work on securing others. It might take some time to identify all relevant systems, but you should know where all your sensitive information is kept. Also, most personal firewall software for PCs comes bundled with intrusion-detection software.

Backups

Earlier in the chapter, I mention the importance of backups. Backups are more important for corporations than they are for individuals, and they are clearly a critical part of any security program. I cannot emphasize this enough.

Backups can be automated so that no manual intervention is required. You can buy tools that assist with the backups, or you can create backup tools for yourself. Ideally, every system should be incrementally backed up once a day. Incremental backups save only the files that were changed since the last backup. Full backups should be performed weekly.

On a regular basis, organizations should make extra copies of their backups that can be used as evidence if criminal incidents arise. When you do detect problems, you have the old backups on hand to study, to determine how far back the problem goes.

SECURITY VS. BUSINESS CONTINUITY VS. DISASTER RECOVERY

There is frequently a great deal of confusion and internal infighting with regard to the responsibilities of security, business continuity, and disaster-recovery programs. Although the following statement may anger the purists in the field, business continuity and disaster recovery are essentially the same thing. Both programs essentially ensure that an organization can continue to function when the worst happens. Although businesses must be prepared for September 11–type disasters, they also must make sure that the little and frequent outages don't have a major effect on the organization.

Security programs are tasked to mitigate risk, as I describe in Chapter 2. Although business continuity and disaster recovery should by definition be a part of a security program, the reality of the business world is more convoluted. The mission of the security department in many organizations appears to be to protect the organization from malicious parties.

There is nothing wrong with a separation of duties, as long as both programs coordinate their efforts. Business continuity is clearly a very demanding and critical discipline. The rest of the security effort is clearly demanding and critical as well. In many mature organizations, the top security and business continuity managers report to a vice president of risk management or similar position.

I would like to propose that the security department is responsible for minimizing the likelihood that incidents will happen, while the business continuity department is responsible for ensuring that incidents have as little impact on the business as possible. However you choose to implement these functions in your own home or organization, you must make sure that both efforts receive adequate support.

This really is an essential countermeasure. No matter what problems you have with budgets or staffing, you must assign people to ensure that backups are performed.

Vulnerability Scanners

Hackers seek out vulnerable systems. There is no reason that you shouldn't do the same. Hackers have no special skills or talents that lets them find the holes in your system; they have vulnerability-scanning tools to do the work for them. There are freeware tools, such as Nessus and Netcat, that allow would-be attackers to scan for vulnerable systems. People can use these tools legally against their own systems as well.

Besides Nessus and Netcat, commercial vulnerability scanners are available that are well supported by their vendors. These scanners allow administrators and security personnel to find the vulnerabilities before the hackers do. This way, they can fix the holes before the holes can be exploited. If vulnerability scanners had been in place in any of the organizations described in Chapters 7 and 10, major compromises would not have occurred and tens of millions of dollars would not be extorted, even to this day.

Concerning freeware scanners versus commercial scanners: You tend to get what you pay for. However, that is not a guarantee; it depends on the vendor. Clearly, the more established vendors have large development and support efforts. Smaller vendors could be more passionate about their product but they must also have the ability to support the product. Remember, you must also be able to have a trained staff to use the tool without creating damage, and to know how to use the findings to make necessary fixes. Part of the difficulty is knowing what fixes are necessary, because there may be false findings. Qualys (www.qualys.com) has a vulnerability-scanning service that is well automated and appropriate for most organizations.

War Dialing

Although the proliferation of high-speed networks has decreased the use of dial-up modems, they still exist and are hacked on a regular basis. As Chapter 5 describes, a war dialer searches ranges of telephone numbers to find those telephone numbers specifically connected to a computer. These connections present back doors into your organization. Organizations should periodically use a war dialer to search their telephone exchanges for computer connections to see exactly what potential attackers would find. Think of this as a vulnerability scan for your telephone network.

If you find an unauthorized connection, you should investigate how easy it is to exploit. Does it require a password or a call-back mechanism? After you find it, you should also check telephone records to see who has been trying to access it. Modem connections should be kept to a minimum because of the vulnerabilities they present. Any unnecessary modem lines should be disconnected.

Wireless Security

The benefits of wireless security are immense, and in response, wireless technologies are becoming easier to use. However, the easier something is to use, the more likely it is to be abused, especially when you are talking about network technologies. Poorly secured wireless networks allow anyone to access a network, which is ironically what they were designed to do.

Wireless devices do not have to be so insecure. The devices tend to be insecure out of the box on purpose so that they are easy for the average user to install. To secure the networks, you basically have to look at the instructions to figure out how to change the default settings.

Settings to change include basically anything that you can change. This includes SSID numbers, administrator passwords, and so on. If you don't know what an SSID number is, don't worry about that fact. Just follow the instructions for changing it. If your wireless device broadcasts its presence, turn that feature off. Clearly, you must enable whatever wireless encryption is packaged with your wireless devices.

Anyone who ever does wardriving is familiar with the default settings, and tries them. If the wardrive is unsuccessful, he just moves on to the next device. I remember when Verizon and other broadband providers started giving away wireless routers to all new customers. I could just feel the script kiddies bursting with excitement. None of the companies offered advice for securing those routers. If you take even minimal precautions with a wireless network, there are more than enough low-hanging networks just waiting for the hackers, so the hackers move on quickly.

There is a great deal of discussion about the use of WEP (Wireless Encryption Protocol). Although the encryption protocol is supposedly easy to compromise, it is clearly better than nothing. As a matter of fact, it takes an exponential increase in skill to go from hacking a network with no encryption to hacking one with any encryption. Although you should probably use another encryption standard if available, WEP is more than adequate for the basic use of individuals.

Companies and other organizations must also implement wireless security. Organizations of all types have been extremely quick to jump on the wireless bandwagon. Also, because wireless routers are relatively inexpensive, it is not uncommon for an organization's employees to go out and buy the routers themselves. This leads to a security nightmare. For this reason, organizations must not only actively secure the wireless routers that they know about but also perform their own wardriving assessments to find any rogue wireless hubs, which will likely be extremely insecure.

Clearly, any system connected to a wireless network should be loaded with firewall and intrusion-detection software. This is the minimum precaution you must take on top of changing default settings.

Automated Patching

As I mentioned in Chapter 4, there are really only two basic ways to hack a computer. The first way is to take advantage of vulnerabilities built into the software. To prevent this, and as discussed previously in this chapter, you need a process to regularly update your software. There are now many tools available to assist in implementing this process.

Microsoft implemented Windows Update Service, which is built directly into the operating system. When properly enabled, your system automatically searches for software fixes. The system then updates itself. Although there can be problems with this model, for 99 percent of the general public this is acceptable. Many other software products also have their own update checks.

Large organizations have unique concerns that make automated patching impractical for critical systems. I generally recommend that large organizations acquire patch-management tools for critical systems. I do not want to mention specific products because this market space is extremely new and most of the vendors in existence now will not be in existence later. Organizations can possibly enable the Windows Update tool on end-user workstations; however, that approach is unacceptable for servers that likely have more complicated software installations. On these systems, it is much more likely that making a change to the operating system can break one of the other software programs running on the system, such as the database management system. Before rolling out software updates, administrators must test the updates on a controlled system to ensure that the updates will not create more problems than they fix.

Adequate Software Testing

In the previous section, I refer to updating commercial software due to vulnerabilities and other bugs built into the software. You must also consider that because all software has bugs that could create vulnerabilities, software developed in-house must be thoroughly tested. As described in Chapter 10, Alexey Ivanov offered to do that after he demonstrated the errors in the tools created by the systems administrators. The compromise of custom-designed web sites has led to hacks against all types of organizations, including many banks. This is a very real and costly problem.

Any software that is not "off the shelf" software must be developed as securely as possible. This means that your programmers should be properly trained in secure coding techniques. SPI Dynamics, a security software company, created a set of secure programming utilities that developers can incorporate into custom-designed application code. Additionally, you should have a separate group of individuals perform security testing on the software to attempt to proactively locate vulnerabilities before the system is allowed to go live. If you do not have such people, you should hire a capable consulting firm to perform that testing.

Secure Configuration Baselines

The second way to hack a computer system is to take advantage of the way an administrator or user configures and maintains the computer. Although a computer can be very complex, there are relatively few things to focus on when securing a computer's settings. To initially configure and install a computer system properly, find a configuration baseline that is appropriate for the particular system. You can go to the Center for Internet Security's web site (www.cisecurity.org) to download configuration baselines for many of the most common operating systems in use. There are also similar documents at the National Institute of Standards and Technology's web site (www.nist.gov). These documents are free and well tested. Follow the configuration guidelines in the documents, and I strongly suggest that you do not make any significant changes to the recommendations unless you are aware of vulnerabilities that you may be introducing and agree that accepting the extra risk is necessary.

General issues that these configuration baselines address include:

- Access controls: Setting system, file, and program permissions to be as minimal as possible for each user.

- Account management: Ensuring that built-in account management capabilities are enabled to lock out expired accounts, disabling accounts after three failed login attempts, and limiting account privileges as appropriate.

- Password management: Ensure that passwords are strong and expire on a regular basis by default.

- Turning off unnecessary system services: Because computers are designed to be robust, they typically provide more capabilities than are used. Unnecessary capabilities should be deactivated.

All these features are present on just about all available operating systems. The problem is that many administrators and users do not know they are there, and do not use them.

To support the maintenance of strong configurations, you should run host-based vulnerability scanners. Although most vulnerability scanners focus on finding network-based vulnerabilities, they do not do thorough checks for system configurations. Host-based scanners do perform such checks and can be used to determine whether the system is modified and left in an insecure state. Password-cracking programs can also be used to determine whether users have been able to bypass password controls and use poor passwords.

Multifactor Authentication

Multifactor authentication is a fancy term for saying that a user will use more than just a password to log onto a computer system. There are generally three ways for individuals to authenticate themselves: what they know, what they have, and what they are. Multifactor authentication means that you are using more than one of those authentication mechanisms. It protects against just about all typical password problems, as well as password sniffing, which is a common attack after a malicious party has established access to a network.

"What a person knows" is typically a password or PIN. By this point in the book, you should well know the problems with relying on just a password. "What a person has" can vary greatly by the technology. It can be a USB token, a software program that runs on the computer, a smart card, or other item. "What a person is" involves biometric authentication such as a fingerprint reader, iris scan, or hand geometry measurement. Multifactor authentication can be extremely expensive; however, there are some less expensive and highly effective solutions available, such as TCI by Encentuate (www.encentuate.com).

The more critical the circumstances are, the more a person or organization should consider implementing more than just a password or PIN scheme.

Single Sign-On Software

Although multifaction authentication can help with eliminating problems with passwords, it is an incomplete solution for many organizations. The average employee may need access to three or more systems. From a security perspective, employees should have different passwords for each system. That leads to the problem of having to remember each password. Single sign-on software helps to eliminate most of the problem.

Basically, when a person logs on to a system with single sign-on software installed, the person can access other systems throughout the network without having to enter additional user ids and passwords. This eliminates the vulnerability created by people who write down al their passwords. Although some multifactor authentication tools integrate single sign-on capabilities, it might not. Single sign-on software also enables the single sign-on capability without requiring multifaction authentication tools.

I should note, though, that single sign-on software does also create a vulnerability in that if a person leaves his or her computer unattended, and not locked, someone can walk over and access even more data than would be possible without single-sign on software. For that reason, it is best to make sure that the software expires a logon session after a reasonable period of time.

Audit Logs

The one essential feature all server systems must have is an auditing program. Auditing programs record the activities of each system user. At a minimum, all systems in your organization should record the dates and times of each logon and logoff. But they should also record any security-related events, such as failed logons and attempts to access restricted files. Most systems can also keep track of the files and functions each user accesses. This information can be critical to any investigation of both compromised accounts and insider abuse. You will want to know whenever an employee seems to be accessing an excessive number of files or database records. With that information, you can circumvent an incredible amount of illicit activity. It also helps you investigate incidents after they've occurred.

In a case involving the Social Security Administration (SSA) employees who stole the personal information of tens of thousands of people, the SSA and Citibank (the perpetrators used Citibank as a conduit for their activities) investigators were able to study the extent of the problem thoroughly after checking the SSA audit logs. They were able to learn exactly who had looked at the compromised accounts and then identify the rogue insider. They were then able to view that person's records to see what other records had been looked at.

Although that case was a security success, it also underscores a failure of sorts. The abuse went on for more than a year before someone noticed it. For this countermeasure to work, you have to review the audit files regularly. For this, you need *audit reduction tools*, which filter out unremarkable log entries.

Audit logs could have helped to detect and thereby minimize some of the incidents in Chapters 6, 7, 9, and 10. In each of those cases, someone logged on to a computer system as someone else and performed many unusual actions. In each case, the actions went undetected for a long enough period to allow very important compromises of information.

Audit logs are not limited to computer systems. Most physical security systems also generate audit logs to record whenever access is granted or denied. These logs should be reviewed for failed physical accesses to see where and when people are attempting to gain unauthorized access. Logs should also be audited for successful accesses at unusual times. Although malicious insiders do have legitimate access, they tend to abuse that access by going to places they do not otherwise

need to go and by entering or leaving the facilities at off hours so that
their activities are not noticed by coworkers.

Mirrored Logs

It is extremely common for the more skilled hackers to modify audit
logs to cover their tracks. After they have gained superuser privileges,
they can generally do what they want to the system. This is a common
practice among the better hackers and criminals, but fortunately, few of
them are quite that good. However, to detect the intrusions of attackers
who *are* that good, I recommend utilizing mirrored logs. When you
enable log mirroring, each time your audit program creates a log entry
an identical entry is created in a separate mirrored log, preferably on a
separate computer. When attackers attempt to erase their tracks, they
will delete the entries in the primary log but the mirrored log remains
unchanged. You'll be able to see virtually every step they took.

Administrators should compare the mirrored logs to the primary
logs on a regular basis. When discrepancies appear, they indicate that
someone has tried to modify the logs, and the security department
should be alerted. Mirrored logs do require a skilled administrator;
however, this is a countermeasure that I believe is well worth the effort.

Bug and Wiretap Sweeps

Bugs and wiretaps are traditional tools of espionage. To counter this,
periodic bug sweeps should be performed. When you see any signs of
espionage activities, such as a competitor's consistently beating you to
the punch or other indications of major leaks, you should consider
performing a bug sweep immediately. Many companies claim to perform this service; however, they vary greatly in quality and scope. The
better services use equipment that picks up greater frequency ranges.
A key part of a bug sweep should be a scan of the telephone lines to
see whether they are tapped. Because many high-quality bugs use the
electrical circuits as a carrier, the power outlets should be examined
for unusual signals. This requires special equipment that many services
do not have. The better services will even use metal detectors to
search behind walls for old bugs.

These services are expensive, so larger companies should consider
developing in-house capabilities. If you do decide to contract with a

service, you want to define your critical areas and have the services check only those areas. These companies charge by the room or the square foot, and costs can add up quickly. You should always consider performing a bug sweep when you are having a sensitive meeting, such as a board meeting, away from your corporate locations.

Encryption

Encryption technology could make it possible to prevent nearly all electronic information compromises. It's relatively easy to encrypt both stored data and sensitive information that you wish to transmit over networks. Many commercial encryption tools are available to secure both voice and computer transmissions. For small-volume data transmission, Pretty Good Privacy (PGP) (www.pgp.com) is a freeware encryption tool available from sites on the Internet (commercial organizations should purchase commercial versions). PGP is relatively simple to use and is the most common tool utilized for e-mail security. Commercial, user-friendly versions are also available.

Thankfully, encryption is built into many common applications and devices, such as web browsers. Commercial tools for encryption can be integrated into your communications devices, such as your routers and firewalls. You can also buy special-purpose devices, such as Virtual Private Network devices. These devices allow you to connect securely to other parts of your company over the Internet. These encryption programs are invisible to your users and provide a tremendous amount of security.

To encrypt user files, you'll need one of a number of readily available commercial tools (PGP also does this). In some cases, the encryption function can be made invisible to the user. In other cases, the user may be asked to enter a password when accessing files. I strongly recommend encrypting all your highly valuable information.

Encryption of telephone communications is now possible, and some hardware is commercially available. For those who regularly call specific people, you can acquire and distribute telephones with encryption built right into them. You can also buy encrypting devices that plug into a telephone jack.

Companies that discuss sensitive issues with other parties over the telephone should very seriously consider acquiring some form of telephone encryption. This is especially true if you are calling or doing business in foreign countries. It's no coincidence that when Motorola was testing its new telephone encryption system in one of its Japanese offices, Nippon Telephone and Telegraph (the Japanese equivalent of AT&T) sent a repair person over to its facility within two hours, claiming a problem with the telephone lines. The telephone and fax calls of all large American companies are extremely likely to be monitored at their international locations by the host countries and foreign competitors.

One of the most annoying arguments I hear against encryption is that the code can be cracked. These naysayers also claim that the U.S. government lets people use only encryption that the NSA can break. Whether or not there is any truth to those arguments, they are profoundly short-sighted. The use of any encryption—even relatively weak encryption—makes the situation much more difficult for eavesdroppers and intruders. Sure, someone will eventually be able to break any encryption, but for now, only the most sophisticated attackers can do this efficiently. More often than not, an attacker will simply move on to an easier target. By using an encryption program, you are probably cutting out more than 99 percent of the technical threats to your electronically stored data and transmissions.

As to the argument about "Big Brother" reading your encrypted information, I say he'd be reading anyway. Most of those cynical people out there are using nothing while they're waiting for Big Brother–proof encryption. Assuming that for some bizarre reason the U.S. government does want to read your files, I am much less worried about one Big Brother than 100,000 little brothers who are already out there reading your unencrypted information while you are waiting for an encryption that Big Brother cannot read.

Off-Line Data Storage

If you have any information that is extremely valuable, used rarely, and not shared, it should be stored offline. Sensitive data that does not have to be shared should never be stored on your system. Save it to a CD or tape, take it offline, and lock it up when it's not in use. This countermeasure is simple, cheap, and very effective, yet it is surprisingly seldom utilized, even by the experts.

Conclusion

There is no cookie-cutter approach to security. It would be great if I could just write, "Do these three things and you will be perfectly secure." As I advised at the beginning of this chapter, you should have at least made a mental note as to what countermeasures described are right for you.

The four golden rules (see the sidebar "Ira's Four Golden Rules," earlier in this chapter) are critical, of course. However, I would also make awareness training a very high priority, whether you are an individual or represent an organization. This book goes a long way to increasing your personal awareness, but you need to make sure that you actually maintain and exercise that awareness on a regular basis.

When it comes to espionage and high-tech countermeasures, your goal, as always, should be to optimize your risk. To do this, you must understand the threat to your organization and know your vulnerabilities. You should select your protective strategies according to your specific needs.

Remember, of course, to look around for those countermeasures that are just sitting there unused. To activate them requires no financial cost, just knowledge. Look at every lock, every guard, every computer, and so on and figure out what is not being done. Then do it.

The next chapter provides a framework for putting this all together. It is a major undertaking, but remember to keep everything in perspective and work it through one task at a time.

13

Taking Action

My intention in writing this book is to give you common knowledge so that you can exercise common sense when it comes to security. Common sense is knowing that your information and other resources have value to you and to people who would do you harm or just want money. Common sense is realizing that there are many spies, great and small, and natural events that could cause you harm if you leave yourself vulnerable. These spies are not geniuses but rather opportunists looking for an opening. Common sense is being aware that you have vulnerabilities that spies can exploit if provided the opportunity. Most important, common sense means that you make a conscious choice as to how vulnerable you leave yourself and that you spend the *optimum* amount of resources on your countermeasures.

The amount of risk you accept should be a conscious choice. If it's not, I guarantee that you have more risk than you can imagine. The goal is for you to treat your information security as you would treat your personal physical safety. You wouldn't go into a dangerous area at night unless you had a compelling reason to do so. You don't leave your home and windows unlocked unnecessarily (but if someone entered your home, you wouldn't consider him a criminal mastermind). A small countermeasure in the physical world, such as locking your door or choosing safe travel routes, returns exponential security. Your goal in creating your own security program is to choose information security countermeasures that return exponential security in the information world.

Where to Begin Developing a Security Program

Corporate security managers generally have a formal process for risk assessments, and I don't intend to tell them how to do their job. Frankly, I respect and learn from these people who are constantly in the trenches. However, there is no reason that small and medium businesses, and individuals, can't learn from what I learned from them. There's also no reason that corporate security managers can't pick up a few tips.

Here, I outline the steps for analyzing your security risks and vulnerabilities and then choosing countermeasures. The following process may not be appropriate for all organizations. However, if you have never performed a risk assessment before, this is a good way to start.

Although the information that follows is straightforward, the process itself is complicated and involved. Figuring out a security program is not simple. But don't be discouraged. By working through the process one step at a time, you will figure out what your security program needs to do.

List Vulnerabilities

As you read through Chapter 5, you should have identified the vulnerabilities that affect you. Make a list of these vulnerabilities, large and small—especially the small. Chapter 5 provides a good foundation of vulnerabilities; however, it is not all inclusive (there aren't enough trees for that). Make sure to consider other vulnerabilities and include them on your list if they are relevant to your organization.

Determine Value

At this point, start recording what the exploitation of each of the vulnerabilities could cost you. If possible, try to come up with an actual monetary value. At the very least, describe the value in words, such as no loss, minimal, significant, major, or catastrophic loss. There is nothing wrong with saying that something will create no loss, but remember to consider all types of values (see Chapter 3).

Choose Countermeasures

Now you can start choosing some countermeasures. Write down some of the obvious countermeasures. For example, if you are in a business, you obviously need awareness training. After reading Chapter 12, you may have decided that token-based authentication is a necessity as well. Maybe you want to perform background checks on all your incoming employees. Better training of your technical personnel is also a must. Whether you are an individual or a business, anti-virus software is a necessity, as are the rest of my "four golden rules." (See Chapter 12 for more about backups, updated anti-virus software, and updated personal firewalls.)

The next step is to cross out the vulnerabilities that you truly believe will result in no loss. You can ignore them.

Then start placing the vulnerabilities that you listed under the countermeasures that you listed. Make sure that you identify whether the vulnerability is sufficiently countered or only partially countered. Remember that each countermeasure you list can address many vulnerabilities. Likewise, each vulnerability can be addressed by multiple countermeasures.

At this point, you likely still have some vulnerabilities that need to be countered. Now go down the list of remaining vulnerabilities and determine the countermeasure(s) that address each. List the countermeasure, if it is not already listed, and put the vulnerability under the countermeasure. As you do this, consider whether the vulnerability has been satisfactorily countered with all the countermeasures currently listed or still needs to be addressed. Do this until you have all the vulnerabilities countered.

Finalize Countermeasure Choices

Next, assign an approximate cost to the countermeasures. Some countermeasures are free; others may be very expensive. You can use monetary estimates or estimate categories, such as no cost, low cost, medium cost, and high cost.

It is then critical to look at the costs of the countermeasures and the vulnerabilities they address. It is reasonable to eliminate a countermeasure that costs more than it protects. However, you must then decide whether there is another way to counter the vulnerability that has just reappeared.

Here are some considerations in finalizing your countermeasures:

- **Likelihood of vulnerability being exploited.** Although some vulnerabilities could create catastrophic loss, if the exploitation is extremely rare, it may not be feasible to spend excessive money on a countermeasure. But keep in mind that many countermeasures counter more than a single type of vulnerability, so consider the potential savings across multiple vulnerabilities.

- **Threats.** If you live by yourself, you don't need to consider other people in your house using your computer. If you have a mom-and-pop store, insider theft and abuse are less of a threat. However, if you are a large company, your employees can be your worst enemy. Will you be the target of small-time criminals, or do you have something of value that attracts the attention of bigger players? Remember the example of pizza-delivery services to military bases (Chapter 1). Spies could target the delivery people, or they could target the people who supply cheese to the companies that make the pizza. Spies look to the weakest link to get their targeted information, and there is no weaker link than one that doesn't think it's targeted.

- **Other benefits of countermeasures.** Consider that some security countermeasures create savings beyond preventing loss. For example, administrator training should result in better performance of the computer system and network as a whole. This means that you can delay costly equipment updates and make better use of what you already have. Similarly, good awareness training should instruct employees not to visit malicious web sites or bring in software from home. This reduces not only problems with malicious software but also wasted time.

- **Insurance.** Insurance is not a countermeasure that prevents a loss from occurring, but it does reimburse you for the loss. So if the likelihood of a particular vulnerability is small, and insurance would cover the loss if it ever did occur, there is little reason to implement additional countermeasures. However, remember that loss can go well beyond money, as demonstrated in Chapter 3. Lost productivity or reputation can be much more devastating than the actual loss itself. Insurance cannot mitigate these and other types of what are referred to as "uncontrolled risks." Also be warned that insurance policies can be very complicated, and if you know about potential problems and fail to mitigate them, you may not be covered for the resulting losses. Don't let insurance give you a false sense of security.

After you've assessed the costs of your countermeasures and the vulnerabilities they address, you will know what the cost of your security program should be, as well as what potential losses remain, or your remaining risk. If you see that you cannot afford the countermeasures chosen, you must then make hard choices as to which of those countermeasures you will eliminate. You then consciously decide on the increased risk.

The Culture Factor

The steps I've just described represent the ivory tower approach to creating a security program. If you are in a very strict environment, such as the military, it will work beautifully. However, if you are in an open environment and you decide to lock a storage closet, people will act as though you implemented martial law. (Unfortunately, if you work in an open, trusting environment in which people help one another without question, you've got a problem.)

In developing your security program, you need to be realistic about which countermeasures will work in your environment. Remember that most people will go through more work to avoid doing a simple thing if they don't want to do it than to just do it.

Before you implement any countermeasures, try to get a sense of how people will react to them in your particular organization. In some corporations, the security people are the bad guys; openness is paramount. In others, naïveté reigns: "We're safe. No one's looking at us." Try to describe your corporate culture. Is management weak? Are its edicts usually ignored? Are coworkers more security-conscious than in other organizations? Is secrecy an integral part of your industry? Do the people working in your company know that? You must know the answers to these and similar questions, so you'll know how to approach your organization with your plan. Whether you are the CEO, the head of security, or just a well-meaning employee, your plan must fit your corporate culture.

Management Buy-In and Support

If you're a senior manager, you may be able to give the go-ahead and approve the funding to implement your security program. However, the reality is that most of the people reading this are not senior managers, and many senior managers still need a buy-in from other managers. For that reason, you need to consider how to solicit that buy-in.

Make Your Case

In the ideal world, I would say that you should give the people you need to persuade a copy of this book. That could help you, and it would definitely help me. However, in most cases, you will have a very short period to make your case, and managers will not take hours out of their day to read a book to understand your position.

You might consider having someone perform a penetration test that targets key information. However, you should be aware that a typical penetration test does not usually achieve the results you have in mind. Few people perform the types of penetration tests I present in Part II of this book.

For example, the security manager of a Fortune 10 company had four different, self-proclaimed leading vendors come in and perform penetration tests. Two weeks and $320,000 later, all four companies reported that they had full control of the entire network. The security manager reported this to the CEO. After careful thought, the CEO's reaction was, "Who cares?" The security manager then called me in to perform a penetration test. Three days and much less money later, the security manager handed the CEO his mergers and acquisitions schedule, critical documents in a multibillion-dollar lawsuit, a multimillion-dollar technology still in the final stages of development, and his personal travel plans. The next week, the security budget was bumped up by $10 million.

It's best to begin talking in monetary terms. You must tell them how much money you will save the organization and how much risk you will mitigate. Then you can go on to address the threats. Although I discourage the use of fear, uncertainty, and doubt in selling security products, if that is what it takes to sell a security program, do it. Tell your CEO that the countermeasures identified will make your organization less vulnerable to cyberterrorism. Tell him or her that it will stop brilliant computer hackers. Use the hype in current events to your advantage. There is no problem with this approach, as long as you personally realize that your primary goal is protection against employees, not terrorists. And you're not misrepresenting the security plan, because the proper countermeasures stop *any* threat from exploiting your vulnerabilities.

Management might talk about something called "due diligence." The concept is a somewhat murky standard used to legally justify all manner of losses. When companies take the position that they have satisfied due-diligence requirements, they are saying, "We did everything that similar organizations have done to prevent the loss." In other words, they did as little as possible while satisfying legal requirements. They are, in essence, admitting that they are safe only from claims of negligence by shareholders.

I've seen guards making rounds through buildings, not to satisfy true security requirements but to satisfy insurance requirements. They're there to look for physical hazards—wet floors, broken electrical outlets, or cracked glass—not to protect your company's valuable information.

So be prepared, because the process of getting your plan approved can be quite discouraging. When you seek support for your security plan, keep in mind something that I've stressed throughout this book: You can never have perfect security, and you shouldn't try to sell it as such.

What effective countermeasures will do is minimize the risk to your organization. You can, in effect, make attacking your organization too difficult and too expensive for many likely attackers, and you can improve your company's ability to detect attacks in progress. To do that, you'll need to invest some resources: money, time, and personnel. A phased implementation approach can spread out the costs so that you feel the impact less. You might want to develop a timeline for your plan.

Gain First- and Second-Line Management Support

I performed a penetration test on a company and theoretically stole billions of dollars. This horrified the CEO, and he took some actions, including distributing a letter to the whole company stressing the importance of security. I didn't think I could hope for any better results. The CEO had me come back six months later to see how much things improved over that period of time. Although some things did get better, I soon realized that as a whole, things were the same, if not worse.

One of the network administrators asked to have me debrief him in detail so that he could understand what I did to his systems six months earlier and what holes he had missed. I told him what he wanted to know. Then I asked him what his impressions were as to why things had not improved since I was last there.

His reply seemed obvious, but like many aspects of security, it was too obvious. He stated that people glance through letters from the CEO and then toss them in the trash. There is no specific guidance in the letters; just statements of the obvious.

He then showed me a notice from the head of the physical security department concerning some computer thefts. The letter said that there were too many computer thefts and listed eight actions that everyone must take. The eight actions were extremely basic, including things such as, "Lock your office door when you leave at the end of the day." The letter also said that the guards would verify that those actions were taken each day during their evening rounds. If the guards found any problems, the employees and their managers would be held responsible. Computer thefts were virtually eliminated. This program was effective because the responsibilities of each employee were clear and so were the penalties, as well as having executive support.

Gaining the support of first- and second-tier management is critical. The managers who see the employees every day are the ones who will actually be there to notice when people are following security practices and when they are not. These are the folks who can influence security the most. When they start checking everybody's doors and file cabinets to make sure that they're locked, that is when you will start seeing the rank and file following procedures. Senior management support is useful only when it produces the required funding and gets the lower-level managers to enforce policies.

Your best hope is to get the managers' voluntary support and cooperation, but sometimes force is your only option. Although you might not like to need to intimidate people into being security conscious, it frequently works if senior management supports your methods. Until managers start to consider security to be part of their responsibility, you'll get a lot of lip service and very little follow-up.

Security-Awareness Programs

Security-awareness programs have the highest payback compared with almost all other countermeasures. When the people in your organization become truly security conscious, they will come up with countermeasures that never occurred to you.

Security should always be a bottom-up program, with every employee performing security functions throughout the company. You want your entire organization to be aware of the problems. When that happens, your organization is much more secure than most attackers expect. Most important, you have thousands of people detecting security problems, not just the two people in a typical security department.

Telling everyone to be "security conscious" is pointless. As in the example presented in the previous section, you must let people know specifically what you want them to do. They need to hear "lock your doors" or "log out of the computer," and they need to hear it *frequently.* If an awareness program does not specify exactly what employees should do when they notice a security breach, it is assuming a common knowledge that just doesn't exist (remember, *there is no common sense without common knowledge*).

You should distribute materials that list exactly what procedures people should follow. You should include brief reasons why these procedures are necessary. You should emphasize that managers will be held responsible for enforcing the specific procedures.

Lessons Learned from Homeland Security Efforts

Billions of dollars have been spent improving homeland security since the September 11 attacks. Some of the money and effort is going to good use. But the fact is that good security efforts are a lot like good spies: You never know about them. However, from public information, the most lessons learned are examples of what *not* to do.

We learned that knee-jerk responses waste time, money, and effort and make people cynical. For example, because the September 11 hijackers used box cutters to hijack the airplanes, box cutters were banned. Then government security experts theorized that nail clippers and butter knives could also be used as weapons, so they banned those and similar objects as well. That is a classic knee-jerk response.

Although it is probably a good idea to ban box cutters, the fact is that the key enabler of the hijackings was not the weapon used but that people were previously instructed to cooperate with potential hijackers. Sheer numbers of noncompliant passengers make butter knives and nail clippers moot. If I allow a plane I am on to be hijacked with nail clippers, I deserve to die.

Airport security checkers also started performing random searches of everyone, including toddlers, wheelchair-bound 80-year-old women, and even Al Gore. Although he could still be bitter about losing the election, is it likely that a former vice president (who actually won the popular vote for president) would attempt to hijack a plane? This misdirected and misapplied effort actually makes people more vulnerable. For example, while security checkers spent their efforts searching Al Gore and 3-year-olds, dozens of other more likely hijackers boarded the planes without being checked. It also makes people cynical of all security efforts.

As of this writing, there have been at least three occasions when the Department of Homeland Security stated that we face an imminent risk of an attack on the scale of or greater than the September 11 attacks. On all occasions, the news media later reported that the sources for those warnings were unreliable.

All security people should avoid the "crying wolf" syndrome that homeland security efforts have made a regular habit. Just as the general public has become numb to frequent warnings of imminent terrorist attacks, you can make your organization numb to information security warnings. Although I did suggest earlier in this chapter that you could use some hype to your advantage, if you use things such as cyberterrorism as your only rallying cry, people will eventually see through it. They will become cynical and bypass as many security countermeasures as they can because those measures are perceived to be wasted effort.

There is a homeland security threat. Unfortunately, by the time it is realized, we will be more vulnerable than we should be because there have been too many false alarms in the past and we won't be taking the proper precautions.

One positive result of homeland security efforts is an understanding of the need for good communications. People must understand the real problems they face. Law enforcement must let companies know when they are being targeted. Organizations need to let their employees know about problems they face. Individuals must know when their information has been compromised so that they can quickly minimize their damages. Communication is critical at all levels of awareness, operations, and response.

The Success of Your Countermeasures

After your countermeasures have been in place for a while, you'll want to begin assessing their effectiveness on a number of levels. Are people using the countermeasures? Do they seem to be accomplishing what you want?

People are one of your best resources for assessing the effectiveness of your countermeasures. Talk informally with "typical" workers. During ad hoc conversations, see whether you can find out which security procedures seem to be working and which are turning out to be bad ideas. Make the interview a little longer than necessary, to give the person time to relax and think about your questions.

You should seriously consider performing a vulnerability assessment and penetration test. When your plan has been in place for several months, test it with a professional. Even if the news is bad, it's better to find out before an attacker does. At the very least, you will discover how to fine-tune your security program. Remember that one of the most critical aspects of a security program is not just to prevent attacks, but to detect them, both while they are occurring and afterward.

When things don't seem to be working, don't be afraid to make changes and modify your strategy. You'll need to do this whether your plan is working or not; after you've taken care of what you can do to mitigate your current set of problems, other problems are sure to rear their ugly heads. A security program is actually a continual process that adjusts itself to changing circumstances.

Defense in Depth

As you decide on how you will counter your vulnerabilities, try to never have a single point of failure. Countermeasures can prevent a vulnerability from being exploited. However, no countermeasure is perfect, because it can fail or be circumvented. To account for this, you can use another countermeasure to back it up, even if the other countermeasure is there for other purposes. Then another countermeasure can be there to detect a successful exploitation. This is the concept of *defense in depth*.

Layered defense could go something like this:

- You install a token-based authentication system so that poor passwords are not a problem.
- An attacker calls a user, says that she wants to check whether the token is working, and asks for the current password. However, the user is aware that he should not give out the current password and contacts security about the incident.
- Another user falls for the ploy. However, security personnel were aware that someone was targeting access to the network, so they watched the audit logs and prevented the break-in from causing significant damage.
- The attacker did manage to delete some data before she was cut off. However, there were recent backups, so all the data was recovered.

In this scenario, security wasn't perfect, but it was prepared. There were some small and some significant countermeasures in place that stopped a situation from getting out of hand. This is defense in depth.

Again, security will never be perfect, but we don't need it to be. Acceptance of reasonable risk from the spies among us means that we can cope with whatever comes our way.

Conclusion

Why is Sydney Bristow from the TV show *Alias* the worst spy in history? She always gets caught. Why does she get caught? Because she runs into good countermeasures. She runs into guards. Video cameras pick her up. She sets off motion detectors. Intrusion-detection systems pick her up whenever she tries to break into computer networks. She is reckless at what she does, just like most of the other spies among us in everyday life.

You don't want to be Sydney Bristow. You want to be the supposed bad guys who always seem to catch her. This part of the TV show is close to reality. Good countermeasures can stop even the superspies.

Security concerns are now paramount in our lives. The 2004 Presidential election was influenced largely by homeland security concerns, or the lack thereof. Although those are important issues for government to address forever more, there are more significant issues that individuals and organizations face. Every day, we confront threats that can do us physical or fiscal harm. Although they are not related to terrorism, they have more of a direct impact on our lives.

When it comes to homeland security, we need it to be ubiquitous to our daily lives. We want the government to take steps that we have no clue exist to secure the nation. In our personal and business lives, we also need to make security ubiquitous to how we act. Most of what you need is already available to you at no cost. You just have to recognize and use it.

For the large part, this means taking responsibility for yourself and your organization. I hear too many people and companies trying to deflect blame for something like computer hacking by saying that the hacker must be a computer genius. When you look into those types of cases, you quickly learn that victims did not take even minimal precautions. To protect yourself, you must acknowledge your strengths and weaknesses. I personally don't like to hear excuses. Yes, there may be thousands of reasons that problems occurred; however, they don't matter. I don't really want to hear excuses from government leaders as to why a tree limb caused 50,000,000 people to be thrown into darkness or why we cannot adequately screen ship and airplane cargo. I want to hear an acknowledgment that there is a problem so that the appropriate countermeasures can be implemented.

The trick is to keep security in perspective. Use defense in depth that ignores the hype and is based on the conscious acceptance of potential loss. This way, you and your organization can keep your information reasonably secure for a reasonable cost. There is no hype, just common sense based on common knowledge.

Index

307